To Bill

May you enjoy the journey you were part of.

Cleo D. Robertson
5/1/08

WHIM OF IRON

A Story About a Startup Business...and Going From Rags to Riches in Thirteen Years.

by

Cleo B. Robertson

authorHOUSE

1663 LIBERTY DRIVE, SUITE 200
BLOOMINGTON, INDIANA 47403
(800) 839-8640
WWW.AUTHORHOUSE.COM

© 2004 Cleo B. Robertson
All Rights Reserved.

No part of this book may be reproduced, stored in a retrieval system, or transmitted by any means without the written permission of the author.

First published by AuthorHouse 11/03/04

ISBN: 1-4184-7485-1 (e)
ISBN: 1-4184-7484-3 (sc)

Printed in the United States of America
Bloomington, Indiana

This book is printed on acid-free paper.

To Mom,

who told me I could do anything I wanted;

To my son, Randy Laco,
who helped me create what I wanted;

To David Beyer
who taught me how to get what I wanted;

and

to my family and friends who encouraged me along the way.

A special dedication goes to Jane E. Elchlepp and Robert G. Winfree of Duke University Medical Center. Through their unswerving faith and trust in what I was creating, I was able to complete my work with their blessing.

Table of Contents

Introduction xi

1938 — My Beginning 1

1963 — Cleveland, Ohio to Princeton, New Jersey 17

1980 — A Business is Born 31

1981 — Finding Work Wherever I Could 41

1982 — A Computer Enthusiast is Born 63

1983 — A Wonderful Lady Appears 87

1984 — The Duke Project Begins in Ernest 133

1985 — Money Comes and Money Goes 161

1986 — Many, Many Road Trips; No Cigars 195

1987 — To Sell , or Not to Sell; That is the Question 215

1988 — One Step Forward, Two Back 281

1989 — Mr. Beyer Arrives 313

1990 — Separation of Church and State 387

1991 — Walking the Walk 427

1992 — More Changes are a 'Comin! 465

1993 — The Handwriting on the Wall 505

Epilogue 515

Introduction

When Thomas Allen Robertson met Sara Elizabeth Zahnizer, it was love at first sight. At least for my father. According to his sister, my Aunt Cleo, Dad thought Mom was everything he ever wanted. Aunt Cleo hinted that Mom may not have been as thrilled. In any case, Dad persevered and they were married in Aunt Cleo's New York penthouse apartment on November 26, 1928. They set up household in Washington, Pennsylvania, (next door to Pittsburgh) and in November, 1929, my brother, Tommy, was born followed in 1931 by my sister, Betsy.

At some point they moved to Oshkosh, Wisconsin, and Dad went to work for the Oshkosh Trunk Company selling trunks all over the whole western seaboard. While Dad traveled and had wonderful dinners with political friends of his family (two uncles were governors of North Carolina), Mom was back in Oshkosh taking care of their two children. In 1936 Mom gave birth to my sister, Nancy, followed by my birth in 1938. If she had felt overwhelmed with two children, four wore her plum out. And with Dad on the road three months at a time, she suffered from being alone so much.

When my parents' marriage failed in 1940, Mom decided to move south to a town they had visited on their honeymoon. Betsy was constantly having earaches, Dad was constantly gone on business and money was always tight. She must have figured that being on her own, in a warm climate, suited her better. As she was busy making plans to move, my father expressed his sentiment regarding my mother.

He said, half in anger, half in admiration, to my brother, "Your mom has a *whim* of iron."

Men had "wills of iron;" women had "whims of iron." Many years later I looked up the word whim and here is what the dictionary said: "Whim—a sudden passing, and often fanciful idea; impulsive or irrational thought." Absolutely. That was mom. Impulsive with an iron will.

From that description, I realize I have lived most of my life on whims.

This book tells how I used this trait to start a business and then succeeded in that business, against all odds.

It all began in 1980 when I was 42 years old, unemployed, broke, uninsured and living with my 17-year old son in the middle of the black district of Princeton, New Jersey.

Thirteen years later, in 1993, I retired from my very successful quality management software development business. I was financially secure, single, 55 years of age, and able to do anything I wanted. I returned to Florida to happily wallow in my success and renew old ties. I had worked hard, it had paid off, and now my time was my own.

But lots of people work hard and it doesn't always pay off. People asked me a lot of questions. The most common question, "Was it the realization of a dream?" was easy to answer. No, I can honestly say, I never had such a dream. As a kid, I had no dreams, no goals, and no fantasies of what I wanted to be in the future. For me, each day was successful if I managed to eat, see my mom, keep my clothes clean and keep up with my studies. When I was in my senior year in high school, someone asked me what I wanted to be. I said, "A mom with six kids." Wasn't that what all girls wanted to be in the '50s?

In 1997 while I was in London sharing the care of my new twin granddaughters, I turned on the TV and Donald Trump was being interviewed. He made a statement that spurred me to move forward with writing this book. He said something to the effect that starting your own business took all of one's energy at the expense of all relationships—lovers, wives, children and friends.

When I heard him say that, I realized that I, too, had put my family second just as my youngest was finishing high school, Lisa was in college and Gary was off traveling... I had to do that in order to succeed in my business. My children suffered along with me and supported me many times when I was down. Unfortunately, in the end, they got less than what they wanted from me. I hope after reading this book that my children better understand some of the choices I made.

I love the story about a person walking out into a field and finding a turtle sitting on top of a fence post. The person says to the turtle, "Well, I know you didn't get there all by yourself."

I didn't "get there" all by myself either, and this book is about the people along the way who helped make it happen.

It's also about my many whims, and the will of iron I had to follow through.

1938 — My Beginning

I was born September 22, 1938, in Oshkosh, Wisconsin. I was the third Cleo Robertson in our family. When I was two, Mom packed up everything she could into two Oshkosh trunks that my father sold for his living. She then took me, my sister Nancy, who was 4; my sister Betsy, who was 10; and my brother, Tommy, who was 12, on a train to St. Petersburg, Florida. A realtor, Mac Granger, whom Mom had met when she and Dad had visited years ago, met us all and drove us to Pass-a-Grille. Pass-a-Grille was a little fishing and tourist community at the southern tip of 22 miles of barrier islands, west of St. Petersburg and Tampa, on the Gulf of Mexico in Florida. Mom had fallen in love with Pass-a-Grille during a vacation there with Dad.

We arrived on January 1, 1941. Mom had little money, no skills other than typing, and no job prospects, but she didn't let any of those obstacles stop her. She simply acted on a whim.

Cleo B. Robertson

She went to work at the Don Ce Sar Rehabilitation Hospital for shell-shocked air force pilots sometime in 1941 as a secretary. Even though she made very little money, somehow she kept a roof over our heads, paid the utility bills, and raised us up in a wonderful paradise.

Betsy and Tommy were in school all day so Mom assumed that Nancy, who was four, would take care of both of us. Years later, local people said that in those early years they never saw Nancy without me in tow. Shirley, who ran the local drugstore, recalled changing my diapers on many an occasion, and others pitched in to take care of us. An old resident said that everyone on the island was shocked we were alone all day, but since we didn't get into trouble, they left us alone.

Pass-a-Grille is one mile long and one block wide, bordered by the Gulf of Mexico on the west side and Boca Ciega Bay on the east. We knew everyone, everyone knew us and they all watched out for us. During my early years, Mom told me many times I could do anything I wanted. I never doubted her. I learned from a very early age that if I kept on trying, I *could* do anything I wanted. If I ever needed help, all I had to do was go to the Police Chief or the Fire Chief, the drugstore or the local garage, and someone would listen to me and help me solve my problem.

Although Mom was never home, we always knew where we could find her. We could see the Don Ce Sar, a large pink building, from the beach. She also

WHIM OF IRON

taught us rules like "Don't talk to strangers" and "Stick together."

After work, she could be found in one of the seven bars in Pass-a-Grille, visiting with fishermen, tourists, friends, and bartenders. People loved her because she was gracious, well-informed, funny, and a great listener. Though she spent very little time at home when I was growing up, she was always nearby. Mom never learned to drive a car, so, as my sister Nancy said years later, "She was never any further than our bare feet could take us."

My brother said that Mom brought us to Pass-a-Grille and said, "Okay, there. I've brought you to a great place. Now grow up." And we did.

The following story will demonstrate just how independent I became.

By the time I was five, Tommy, Betsy and Nancy were in school. Mom enrolled me in the Sunny Hours Beach School, about three miles from my home, to solve the problem of what to do with Cleo during the day. The school masters (a married couple by the name of Mr. and Mrs. Kauhfold) had built the school on the principle of providing lots of fresh air, beach time, good food and activities for their students. My first day started out great. We went to the beach, played ball, and best of all, sat down and ate lunch together.

Then Mr. Kauhfold made an announcement that changed everything for me.

Cleo B. Robertson

"All right, children," he said. "Get your mats, lie down and take your nap."

I blurted out in front of all the other children, "But I don't take naps! Only babies take naps," I added fiercely.

He was most patient, and said, "Now Cleo, everyone here needs to take a nap. So, just be a good girl and lay down on your mat."

I could see there was no way out of it. He was insisting I take a nap. I lay down on my mat, turned my head towards where he was standing, and pretended to close my eyes. When I saw the two teachers turn and head out the door, I waited a few minutes, hoping the other children would fall asleep quickly. After what seemed like an hour, but was probably more like five minutes, I got up quietly and walked out the opposite door.

I walked past the airplane Mr. Kauhfold had built for us for playtime. I walked past the playground, and the toys, and finally out to the main road, Gulf Boulevard. It was about a mile to the limits of Pass-a-Grille, and as soon as I could, I headed directly for the alley. Something must have told me someone would be out looking for me, and I definitely didn't want to get caught. The miles went by quickly. When I finally came up to my house, Mom was waiting on the top of the steps. Mr. Kauhfold had called her at work, and a friend drove her home.

"What's the matter, Cleo," she said patiently. "Didn't you like school?"

"No," I replied emphatically. "They wanted me to take a nap, Mom. You know I don't take naps."

She sat down with me on the steps, and tried to explain to me that if I didn't go to school, I would have to be home alone, all day during the week, for nine months. Didn't bother me any. I figured it would be great with so many places to go and so many people to see.

In the end, she let me stay home, alone. A close friend of hers told me years later that mom didn't really have the money to send me and she was relieved I didn't want to go. She arranged for a neighbor to feed me lunch, but I seldom went there. I usually was too busy elsewhere, to go all the way back home just for lunch. I spent my time visiting the fishermen at 21st Street. They would all be sitting under a big, old sea grape tree, mending the places in their nets cut by the sharks. Everyone knew me, because everyone knew my mom. They taught me to mend nets too, and I would sit by the hour, listening to their stories about horrendous storms, fish lost, as well as loves, hopes and dreams lost. Some days I would head to the beach, particularly after a storm. I could look for shells, make sand castles, or swim, as long as I didn't swim alone; that was one of the rules.

Since no other little kids were staying home from school, I spent a lot of my time alone. I invented a boat that was also a submarine, and I would pull the trim, long piece of 2x4 wood with a nail smashed in it and a string attached, all over the island after a rain. I had many adventures that were exciting, and I was free to invent anything, about anything, for as long as I wanted. I felt sorry for the kids who had to go home at five for dinner.

In the early years, Mom cooked us dinner at night, but we were free to eat when we got home, whenever that was. After Betsy and Tommy left home, she figured we could manage on our own, and we did. I was 11 and Nancy was 13. Nancy and I became devoted to peanut butter and banana sandwiches, and saltines with cream cheese and guava jelly. We got fruit from trees like mulberry, mango and sea grape which were all around the town, and every now and then Mom would come home with a fresh piece of fish someone had given her. Nancy and I thought we had a pretty sweet life.

We shrimped, stone crabbed, and fished for our food. Nancy and I learned at a very early age to be responsible for feeding ourselves. We thought nothing of getting a free, gutted fish like sheepshead or yellow tail, undesirable by customer standards, but lovely by ours, from Bell's Fish House. We would trot off to the beach, stick a palm frond through it, and turn it over an open fire we would build. When it was done (we could tell by the smell), we would lay it in the sand, skin down, and pick away at the succulent meat with our sandy fingers. For years, I thought sand was salt.

This carefree lifestyle came to an end, however, when I started first grade.

WHIM OF IRON

People today, when I tell them my story, always say, "Oh, it was safer back in those days."

Not true. Prisoners from the chain gangs that cleaned Florida's highways would escape and come to Pass-a-Grille, not knowing it was a dead end. Once, they even found a chain and ball on the seawall, but no one was ever found. Another time, I remember hearing a loud announcement being made from a megaphone on top of a passing car. It told us to get in our houses and stay until we were given the all clear. A prisoner had escaped and had been seen in Pass-a-Grille. The police finally found him hiding in the bathroom of the Seahorse Restaurant on 8th Street.

When my sister and I were under 10, a man on 8th Street opened his raincoat and flashed us. We ran as fast as we could to the police station, and he was soon sent on his way. That was another rule: when in trouble, run to the police. We knew they were our friends.

No, it was not safer. The difference was that we had been taught the rules of the road:

- Don't talk to strangers or, if you do, make sure others you know are around (as when on 8th Street, in the grocery store or in church).
- Don't swim by yourself.
- Don't swim over your head.
- Always be aware of who is around you.
- Don't take candy from anyone.

- If you need help, and can get there, go to the police station. If you can't, go knock on any door.

These rules were my beacon. Even today I follow most of these rules. However, I will admit I have taken candy from a few people!

There's no question I was raised differently from most people. I was taught responsibility at an early age, and I was expected to handle it - so I did. In fact, I think I thrived *because* my mom showed so much trust in me and I didn't want to let her down. I was taught to mend my own clothes, hand wash my school clothes on a scrub board in the tub, and then iron them, stiff, using starch. I polished my shoes every day and would never have thought to not do my homework. Mom taught me good standards and then left me to figure them out.

After growing up in such an original way, it's not surprising, that the way I left home, at the age of 17, was original too. The following story about my leaving home, tells a lot about me, and suggests a reason for me zeroing in on quality management in health care later on in life.

During my last year of high school, I dated a young man who was two years older than I and repeating twelfth grade for the second time. I didn't care. He was handsome, popular, and he liked me. I helped him with his homework - he made me feel important just to be his girl. During the school year we often visited an orthopedic surgeon who took care of the football team players. He had become very attached to Mark and wanted to see him "make it," meaning graduate, go to college, and become a great football star.

On the last night of school, Mark and I went to the prom, followed by a night in a Tampa motel like so many of our friends. The next day he didn't come to see me. I learned he was done with me and had moved on to other interests. I was so disappointed he didn't even say goodbye. Within a month I knew I was carrying his child. My mom had no solution to offer me, so I didn't know what to do. A friend suggested I get an abortion. I would not.

When word of my pregnancy got out, I got a call from the surgeon, Mark's mentor. He said he had heard I was pregnant, and he also recalled that I had a lot of pain in my shoulders – at the time we thought it was the result of a bout of pneumonia. He convinced my mother and me that he could eliminate the cracking and pain in my shoulders, suggesting that I would have a hard time going through pregnancy and labor without doing something.

His first treatment - numerous shots of Novocain into my back - was administered rather brutally in his otherwise empty office one evening. The pain was still there. A week later he suggested x-ray treatments. This, too, was unsuccessful, so he suggested that I have surgery. He reasoned that the cracking in my shoulders was from the bilateral scapula rubbing against my rib cage, and that by trimming off some of this bone, I would be pain free. What did we know? He was a well-known orthopedic specialist in St. Petersburg.

I was admitted to the American Legion Children's Hospital in September 1956. All I remember is being rolled to the surgery suite, and then waking up hours later, in excruciating pain. It was the middle of the night, my arms were crossed on my chest and secured by bandages, and I was lying on my side. I cried. I hurt so much, but I had no way to get a nurse. I finally rolled out of the bed, feet first, and went to the nursing station, where a nurse barked at me, "What are you doing out of bed?" The staff had been belligerent to me ever since I had come in. One even said to me, "It's a shame, you taking up a bed when others need it more." I had no idea what she was talking about.

I told the head nurse about the pain. She said, "Sorry, the doctor wrote no orders for pain killers so you'll have to wait until morning," then went curtly back to her work. Considering that he had cut every nerve and muscle in my back where they attached to my shoulder blades, the lack of pain killers made no sense. I begged again, but she refused, so I spent the rest of the night walking the floor, crying. At some point, another nurse came in and brought me some aspirin. The next morning, the doctor apologized for forgetting about the painkillers and he promptly ordered them.

The wire coil that held my surgical wounds together was to stay in until the wounds healed, and then would be removed. Essentially, the doctor had taken a piece of wire, threaded it into a needle, and did a circular stitch all the way to the bottom of the 6" incisions. When the time came to remove it, he cut the coil at the top, and using pliers, gave one mighty yank from the bottom. I passed out onto the floor. By the time I came to, he had gotten me onto the stretcher and cut the coil out slowly—the skin had healed over the coil, and so, of course, it would not come out in one yank. My only thought was, if I had a father, he would not have let this happen to me.

Did all these unexplainable and brutal treatments cure my back pain? No. Why didn't I question him? He was a doctor. He knew best, as my mother said. Did he have a personal agenda because I was pregnant with his protégé's baby? A baby he did not want Mark to have to father? It was 1956 and many things were done in the name of medicine without knowing the full ramifications.

Years later, I thought about this event in my life and wondered if from it grew my burning desire to implement quality management in hospitals. I can't be sure. But, I am sure that my desire to help others be protected from physician and hospital errors drove me with such a passion, that I accomplished what others thought was impossible.

At the end of September 1956, when my back was pretty well healed, outwardly, a nurse who was a friend of the doctor's suggested I go to her parent's home in Ohio to rest and have my baby. Her parents had agreed to help me. Two days later, I packed up my few belongings—the Singer sewing machine Mom had bought me, some clothes, and all my photographs—and I was ready to leave. I didn't want to be in a home for unwed mothers in my own hometown, and I had no place else to go.

As I left, I walked past my mom sitting on the porch, drinking her coffee laced with alcohol. I told her I was going away. She just nodded her head, I gave her a kiss on her cheek and I was gone. I didn't see her again for three years. My friend drove me to the Greyhound bus station, and I left for Cleveland—pregnant, 17 years old, with $28 in my pocket.

As the bus pulled out of the station, I started to cry, quietly. I knew I was leaving home, and I didn't know when I would ever come back. For quite awhile my tears could not be contained, but as we pulled farther and farther away from familiar sights, I stopped and tried to think of the future. At the moment my future was just getting to Cleveland.

I got off the bus on October 1, 1956 in 40-degree weather. I wore a bright yellow cotton dress, which I had made for the trip, not realizing it would be cold in Cleveland. A man with pure white hair and a gruff-looking face walked up to me and immediately gave me his jacket to wear until we got to his house. His name was Sam and over the next few weeks, Sam and his wife, Faye, and I came to know each other.

They learned that I had few, if any, "housekeeping" skills—I couldn't cook or garden, and didn't know how to dust or vacuum. It was quite a change…from living with Mom in Pass-a-Grille, where I could do nothing wrong, to being in Cleveland, where I never seemed to do anything right. To make matters worse, every night when I went to bed, I missed the sound of the Gulf lulling me to sleep. In every sense, I felt like a fish out of water. Sam was a high school teacher and I remember that he was shocked when he saw that I wrote my F's backwards. Faye was appalled at just about everything I did.

She sent me to cut roses and I came back with one lovely one on a stem with 6 buds!

She told me to iron but wanted me to use a mangle machine, which I had never seen before.

She tried to teach me to cook, and I blew the first eggs I boiled right up on the ceiling of the kitchen. Saltine crackers were more my style.

I learned a lot from these two wonderful people, and they took good care of me, but I never felt like I could please them. Within a month, Faye had helped me get a temporary job at Otis Elevator Company, a manufacturing plant in downtown Cleveland. I started to adjust to life in the north. It was November and I was numbly going to work every day, riding the bus an hour each way, thinking about the child growing inside of me and what on earth I would do after it was born.

On February 1, 1957, I went into a home for girls run by the Catholic Church. For one month I mended clothes from the attic which were given to girls as they left the home, I cared for babies in the nursery and I resized a very intricate set of clothes for a statue of Jesus that the Mother Superior owned.

Cleo B. Robertson

When my water broke during the night of February 28th, I was quickly put in a taxi, alone, and sent off to a local hospital. There I was left in a hallway, in labor, for over eight hours. The hospital was used to taking care of girls from the home, but they had very little sympathy for us. I remember in the surgical suite hearing the doctor make jokes about "us girls" as he delivered my baby.

On March 1, 1957, I gave birth to Gregory Robertson. He was beautiful. I was allowed to see him for three days, and each time he was brought to me I would look in wonder at this little boy who had grown in my belly. And then, as I had agreed with Sam and Faye, the baby was taken away for adoption on the third day. I still cannot begin to describe how I felt that last visit, looking at him through the nursery window, knowing that I would never see him again. I kept running through my head how I could keep him. I didn't have a job, a car, or any money. It was hopeless. Finally, I ran off towards the woods, crying and crying. One of the girls, who had already given up her baby, came after me and helped me pull myself together.

I went home to live with Sam and Faye again. We never talked about my experience, not even one sentence. After two months of recuperating from hemorrhoids and trying to mend my heart, I got a job as a secretary at Fenn College. Within two more months, Sam and Faye left to teach in Pakistan, and I rented a room in a house close to the college.

Every day I had to keep focused on feeding myself, paying the bills, and getting my work done. It was a lonely life. Men were always flirting with me, particularly when they heard I was living alone. I didn't always handle their attention well, and would end up feeling used and even lonelier. I learned to knit, worked on putting my photographs into an album, and prayed to get through each day. Life wasn't as easy as it had been in Pass-a-Grille.

1963 — Cleveland, Ohio to Princeton, New Jersey

In 1959, I married a student from Fenn College, and between 1960 and 1963 we had three children, Lisa, Gary and Randy.

My mom died seventeen days after my third child, Randy, was born in March of 1963. At 61, her body simply stopped functioning after years of alcohol abuse. I could not go to her funeral, first of all, because I had a terrible urinary infection, and secondly, we just couldn't afford it. I've learned since why funerals are so important...I never felt that I told her goodbye. As time passed, I continued to miss my mom. She was always so supportive of me. Knowing when I went back to Pass-a-Grille that I wouldn't see her sitting at the bar, talking with friends, and being the center of attention, was very saddening.

My dad died two years later of throat cancer. He was 72. I hadn't known him very well, having seen him only eight or so times since I was a toddler. I cried at his passing, but it was an existential crying, instead of one based on experience. Besides, by the time Betsy called to tell me, he was already buried.

In 1963, we moved to Princeton, New Jersey, to a better job for my husband. He went ahead of us and found a house in the country. I had no car so my days were spent caring for the children, the house, and a huge yard. I kept busy moving trees, building rose beds, and playing with the children. By 1968, the distance between my husband and me was too great. Repeating my mother's pattern, I packed up the children and moved...about six miles away.

By 1969, I married a second time, and with this marriage I became the stepmother of three boys, who lived with their mother ten miles away, but were with us often. Our six children ranged in age from 6 to 11, and for the next nine years we did our best to raise them well and keep ourselves financially afloat. In 1973, I got a good position as a secretary for a hospital-consulting firm, located in downtown Princeton. After five years and advancement to the position of statistician (I put together the data for 15 hospital long-range plans), something started to stir within me. I wanted to do more, to make a difference in the world rather than be "just a mother" or "just a secretary," accomplishments which didn't seem to count much in society at large, or to me for that matter.

By 1978, however, this marriage, too, was coming apart at the seams. At the same time, my work was becoming less and less satisfying. Deciding to leave my second marriage was one thing—that decision was mutual. But, at what point did I decide to leave my job that was paying me $21,000 per year? And how did I make such a big decision, when I had no savings, no investments, no insurance and no assurance? I wish I could give answers that would sound logical, but the truth of the matter was, I did it on a whim.

One day while still on the job, I had a meeting with the president of the hospital-consulting firm. I asked him if I could go out to the hospitals and gather the hospital operating and medical staff data firsthand, rather than relying on inaccurate computer information.

I remember his words clearly…"Frankly, Cleo, there is no way you will ever represent this company in the field as a woman with no degrees."

He was right. I didn't have any degrees, and I was a woman in a man's field, but hearing him say that to me jelled up whatever had been soft inside, and within two months I had left my well-paying job to take a huge risk. In today's terms, I was ready to be an entrepreneur. I agreed to take a purchase option on an old bookbindery. The owner was 70 years old and wanted to retire, and I had gotten to know the business a little through my stepson Dan, who worked there and loved the old books.

The bookbindery was located on Witherspoon Street in Princeton and had been in business for many years. It was originally Princeton University's bindery, but at some point the administration decided they didn't want to be responsible for it any longer, and an employee was asked if he'd like to take it off campus, and run it. He agreed, and that's how it got started.

He took with him all the 1900's equipment, from large sewing machines to even larger cutting machines that could take a man's arm off in a second. There was typesetting equipment, gold stamping tools, leather cutters and huge presses to flatten even the most stubborn book. The sewing machine that kept the books together required precision and watchfulness, as well as lots of patience—sewing hundreds of books took a great deal of time. All of this equipment was housed in an old run-down building located in Princeton's black district. The building had housed a bar in previous years but had run into hard times. There were two apartments upstairs, one occupied by Hazel, the other by "Big Butt." Hazel was the town bootlegger (but more about her later), and Big Butt was a local entrepreneur who rented chairs out in his apartment for $5 a night, to anyone who didn't have a place to put their head. And yes, they slept sitting up.

The bindery had operated out of this old building for 16 years. The owner and employees kept sewing and gluing, as boxes of student theses, long forgotten, piled up in the front reception room. Dust made itself at home in every nook and cranny, and the old wooden floors had softened and settled into grooves and ruts. The back rooms, where the work was done, were decayed and falling apart. The landlord, knowing that the bindery owner couldn't pay any more rent than he was already paying, just let everything continue to rot, and didn't raise the rent.

The bindery's main business was binding the university students' theses, a custom carried over from the old days. Every year, for one hectic month, students would bring from two to ten copies of their papers in to be bound in blue buckram for undergraduates and black for graduate students. This was the main business. During this hectic season, everyone worked long hours because the cash made in that month would have to last for most of the rest of the year. There was other work—repairing old bibles, old books, and other cherished items that only a bookbinder could do—but by and large, thesis season was the bread and butter of the business. Little wonder that the owner was tired and wanted to retire.

Dan and I approached the owner and asked for an option to purchase. We didn't have any money to put down, but we figured if he let us take it over, we could make it a success and pay him a reasonable monthly sum. He agreed I could take it over and pay him $400 a month towards the purchase price. Since Dan worked there already, it seemed like a good idea, if for no other reason than it got me out of my current job. The thought of running a business appealed to me and it never entered my head that I needed any expertise beyond hard work. I didn't know what a market survey was. I didn't know how to run a business, and I had no collateral to back me up. However, by September 1978 I was behind the counter at the bookbindery, up to my ears in debt, scared to death, and still flashing a great smile of hello to every customer who walked through the door. Another whim come true.

A few incidents took place that certainly were memorable. One late afternoon I was in the reception area of the bindery talking to a white, slightly-built professor from Princeton University, when Big Butt pushed open the door and staggered in, bull-roaring mad and drunk as a skunk.

He came right up to the counter and yelled, "Bitch, you kick my dog again, and you'll find out who can get things done around here."

I knew the only way to handle this was Hazel's way. I let him rant and yell, keeping a watch on my very nervous professor out of the corner of my eye, until Big Butt seemed spent.

At that point, I leaned across the counter and put my pointing finger onto his chest, and said in a slow, steady, yet angry voice, "Big Butt, I have a right to walk on the sidewalk, and if your dog snaps at me again while I am walking, I will kick him in the ass again. And, I'll do it every time he attacks me, do *you* understand?"

Big Butt said something under his breath, backed out the door and was gone. You can guess who was right behind him within a few seconds! That's one professor who never came back. It took a few minutes for me to push my heart back into my chest. I went upstairs and told Hazel the story. She laughed till she cried. Big Butt and I had respect for each other after that. I kept out of his way; he kept out of mine.

WHIM OF IRON

Another evening when I was cleaning out cupboards, I heard a big commotion outside. When I looked through the window I could see two Jamaican women yelling at two police officers, who seemed to be trying to quiet them down. Curious, I went quietly out the back door, walked down the little alley, straining my ears to hear what was being said. I was just about to cross the street, when Big Butt's long, blue '57 Lincoln came gliding up under the trees right in front of my house, just feet from the police. Big Butt rolled out of the driver's side, walked towards the back of the car, very casually passed by me, and shoved a gun in my hand!

I knew two things instantly. I needed to not react, so the police wouldn't figure out what he had done. And, I needed to do this for Big Butt so I could stay in the neighborhood, unharmed. I pushed the gun into my pants and went on over to the Pizza Parlor to get a Coke.

I heard Big Butt saying very innocently, as he walked up to the police with his hands up in the air, "No, sir, I don't have no gun. These bitches are just lying. I don't have no gun. Search me."

My legs were shaking while I waited for the clerk to get my Coke, and I could hear yelling between the women and Big Butt. I walked back very casually, heart in throat, up the alley and in to my back door. I was never so glad to be home. I wrapped the gun up in a towel and shoved it under the couch. I figured he'd come get it sometime. Dan was off somewhere, Randy was in Durham, Gary was off to his father's, and Tom and Dave were at school. Knowing there was a gun under the couch, and that I had been involved in it getting there, didn't help me sleep that night.

The next morning before 7 a.m., I heard a hard knock on my back door. When I went to it and pulled the curtain back, there was a smiling Big Butt.

"Okay, I'll take my gun back now," he said as I opened the door.

I said, "Gladly," as I went and got it and handed it very gingerly to him.

He smiled, said, "Thanks," and was gone. Nothing like a little excitement to spice up the day.

For nine months Dan and Bob, a skilled bookmaker, and I worked up to 20-hour days, trying to save a dying business. There was no volume in our work. Each book we repaired had to be hand sewn, hand bound, hand cut and hand stamped. From old bibles to family albums, we labored with love to give the customers something they were proud of...but we couldn't charge enough to cover our costs. It didn't help that in the last two days, before signing the purchase option, the owner's son stepped in and raised our payments to $400 per *week*. That sum was more than the bindery had ever earned. I knew it was a good deal gone bad, but I forged ahead anyway. Once I chose to do something on a whim, I put my will of iron behind it to make it work.

I now understood the joke, which goes, "Do you know the difference between being involved and being committed?" "When you eat eggs and bacon for breakfast, the chicken is involved, but the pig, he's committed!" There was no question I was committed; I had already quit my job, and I wouldn't have gone back if they had invited me anyway.

We did our best. The first room we cleaned up was the reception room, which only had a path through the trash and boxes going towards the workroom where the owner ran his business. We cleaned out corners that hadn't seen light in sixteen years and we painted wherever we could. Dan washed the floors, which must have been shocked by the feel of water. We washed and then painted the old walls, and placed a lovely antique rug, bought at an auction, on the floor. Bob cleaned the equipment for the first time in his memory. He also made a new sign for outside, retaining the original name because it was known.

One day, as I sat on the toilet, wondering what to do to earn more money, I heard scratching on the baseboard near my feet. As I watched in shock and horror, the biggest rat I had ever seen climbed through the hole in the wall and ran into the bindery. I jumped up and ran into the bindery yelling, "There's a rat in the shop!" I heard Dan in one room and Bob in another, yelling at the same time, "Cleo, there are rats *everywhere!*" And they were everywhere. Dan was standing in the gold-stamping area, which was small and cramped, but a rat went right in and scared him out of his wits. We struck at them with brooms, sticks and our feet, but there were so many, we finally had to retreat to our house next door. That night, we threw rat poison all over the bindery, including the cellar. The next day we picked up 28 dead rats, and slowly the siege was over. We learned that day that the rat siege started when an old house behind us was torn down, and the fulltime residents had come looking for a new home.

While trying to put out rat infestations, I also tried to bring in more business year round. I looked for business in every conceivable place, but in the end, there was just not enough business for hand binding anymore. Dan invented new thesis bindings with ribs and gold leaf, while Bob created hand-covered leather boxes lined with hand-dipped end sheets that I ordered from Michigan. No matter that our gold stamping was lovely, we used the best of leathers, or we invented new products. In the end, it was just too labor intensive and the market too small and I was too inexperienced in marketing and sales.

Towards the end of one very long day, Dan found me standing in front of the large paper cutter, frozen. My hand was on the handle that would bring the large 3-foot cutting blade down swiftly and surely. My mind refused to work. I couldn't have told anyone what I was doing there or what I was supposed to do next. My mind had shut down…from exhaustion, lack of security, and working too many hours. I think the rats had been the last straw. Dan took me home and I slept for 24 hours before returning to the grind. I didn't want to give up, and I didn't know what I would do without the bindery. Finding a job seemed less viable now after I had run a business on my own. I didn't want to be a quitter, and I didn't want to die at the cutting board...I knew a choice had to be made and I just didn't want to make it.

During all my adult life, I kept a diary. It has the following entry for June 1, 1980, which sheds some light on the final days of my proprietorship at the bindery:

> *I'm waiting for the owner to call the option; not knowing what I'm going to do. Recession deepening. Am I making a mistake giving up? I can't help it under present terms.*
>
> *Too tired to even resolve what to do. Sad thinking of taking everything out—rug, sofa, lamps, plants. The end of an era, short as it may have been.*

On June 27th, on the advice of a lawyer, I walked out of the bindery for the last time. I told the owner I could not pay him more than even he was able to earn, and I was going to look for a job. My lawyer advised me to sign up for unemployment. I balked, feeling that doing so was a terrible thing, but he insisted, and as it turned out, it was good he did.

I sent out 300 resumes immediately, and waited. I never got one nibble. Years later I could see that my resume showed I had no degrees and had held many jobs for short periods of time, not a good combination to have as an employee in an academic community. This was a most difficult time for me. My daughter, Lisa, was away at college. My middle son, Gary, was trying to figure out what he wanted to do.

And, my youngest son, Randy, had just finished high school, and didn't know what he wanted to do.

Randy was the only one living with me by this time. For six months we struggled, bartering baked cornbread for fried fish with our black neighbors, and receiving free beer from "Miss Hazel," the town bootlegger who lived above the bindery. It was a unique time and place to be at this time of my life. If you're going to be broke, it sure is nice to do it with people who understand and still know how to share, and have fun. For all the worry and fear, I had a lot of fun with local blacks who hung around the area and still knew how to laugh and make a joke.

In an attempt to exhibit some control over my life, on June 11, 1980, I took back my maiden name. I had had two other names, but now I wanted to be Cleo Belle Robertson again, and so it was. As an added indignity of divorce, I had to get my soon-to-be-ex-husband to *give me written permission* to take back my own name. That was the law in those days, and though it galled me, I did it! My diary is full of my signature as I practiced writing my given name once again.

By the end of June 1979, my diary showed I was moving forward, even if with fear. I was unemployed, had no car, no health insurance, no collateral. I owed a bank $8,000 (money my second husband and I had borrowed) and no job in sight.

I feel my legs are separated, each foot firmly clinging for life on a log as I bounce down *a churning riverbed studded with enormous, protruding rocks and boulders. My life is at stake. I've <u>vowed</u> to come through strong. No cop-outs. I'm tough. Am I willing to be tough enough?*

I had no idea what was ahead—no goals, and certainly no answers! How would I earn money? What did I *want* to do? Towards the end of 1980, my 17-year-old son, Randy, was the surprising bearer of the answer!

1980 — A Business is Born

It's late November, and Randy and I are sitting in my bedroom in Princeton. The house is quiet and cold—we're both bundled up—and the feel of poverty is all around us. We had just spent an hour trying to find 56 cents to buy a Coke, but after searching all our pockets, behind the couch cushions, and many drawers, we gave up. Randy and I had been living off welfare since July, when I walked out of the bindery. My daughter was off to college, my older son was busy traveling and discovering who he was, and my three stepsons were all pursuing their careers. It had to be hard for my children to watch as their mother floundered, trying to catch my step, but not knowing where to put my foot. It was Randy who finally provided the foothold. As he sat in a chair watching me go back and forth in my rocker, I said to him, "I can't stand another poor Christmas, Randy. I don't want to go through another Christmas with no money and no prospects."

"Mom," Randy responded, "You know how to do so many things, why don't you start your own business?"

Two weeks later, I picked up my first letterhead from the printer. As I looked at what my ex-husband had designed out of the name I had chosen, CBR Associates, I wondered how I had gotten to this point, and where I was going to take it. I had thought about having my own business over the past few years, but I'm not sure I would have actually started a business on my own. But once Randy gave me the encouragement, I ran with it. Nothing in my past told me I couldn't! I chose CBR because they were my initials—Cleo Belle Robertson—and the Associates indicated that other professionals worked with me. A business was born, without collateral, credit, experience or much of a plan. None of which fazed me one iota since I didn't know anything about profit and loss, debits and credits, or marketing and sales, anyway. What I did know was that I needed to make a living, computers gave me a tool and I knew how hospitals ran. Seemed like enough to begin a business with to me.

At 42, I did have a lot of skills. After being a secretary for most of the past 24 years (with a 6-year hiatus to raise children), I was good with the English language and I could type 100 words per minute. That gave me the skill of being able to type faster than I could think, which meant I could type and write at the same time. Valuable if you're writing a lot. I was also good talking with people and creating new ideas.

WHIM OF IRON

My real skill, however, came from working for the hospital consulting firm (from 1973 to 1978). Those years taught me a lot about how hospitals work. The company created long-range plans for health care facilities, from large community hospitals to rehabilitation facilities to long-term care homes. My task had been to collect data from every department and service that reflected the current activity of the hospital. It was my job to answer the questions: how many admissions and surgeries had there been? How many x-rays, meals served, pounds of laundry and emergency room visits had there been? Forty to fifty departments would be analyzed for activity and then, after cleaning this data to make it consistent, I would utilize this data from the past five years to show trends.

My favorite analysis always had to do with the medical staff of any health care facility we were studying. I would gather the number of admissions, discharges, surgeries, average length of patient stays, and charges billed, and then display this data by department and specialty. This kind of analysis done for a five-year period would show trends in practice patterns such as which doctors had increasing admissions and which had decreasing admissions, and whether this was due to their age or because they were admitting elsewhere.

My next task was to collect all the demographic data for the area served by the hospital (age distribution, number of births, unemployment rates, etc.). In most cases, the service area would be a specific town or county. In the case of a long-term care facility, the service area might be statewide. For children or specialty centers, it could even be worldwide. I would display trends in population, such as increases or decreases by age group to answer the question, "Do we need more pediatric services or long-term care? "Would a clinic be useful?" and, depending on the trends in births, "Do we need to expand or decrease our obstetrics department?"

Once all this data was cleaned, arranged in charts and presented, the principals of the firm would "read" it and draw conclusions. These conclusions would then become the long-range plan (usually covering the next five to ten years). They would write the text. I would display the data in tables, charts and graphs. I would then type it into a report and it would be presented as a <u>Plan for Development</u>. A plan most usually suggested more space was needed, because populations were always expanding (except in rural areas). A planning company, such as the one I worked for, would oversee the construction of new space and receive a fee of "x" percent of the construction price for their services. It was a sweet business.

As I contemplated what my new company would do, I thought a lot about what I knew. I had gathered data for and completed 15 long-range plans. My mind could see each department, their data and their interdependencies. It took me all of one day to decide on a whim that I would offer my services to hospitals to do medical staff analyses. After all, I reasoned, the doctors bring in the money and the doctors authorize the spending of money. Wouldn't hospitals like to know which doctors were doing the hospital the most good financially, and which ones were costing the hospital money? The two ex-administrators I had worked for had each taught me an enormous amount in developing and interpreting statistics and learning the political side of hospitals and their medical staffs. I got a copy of the New Jersey Hospital Guide and started targeting hospitals that were close to Princeton to which I could market my analyses.

This was just like me. Decide on a whim to offer medical staff analyses to hospitals without ever checking out whether hospitals *wanted* to manage their medical staffs. I didn't care about the answer actually. I thought they should, so I decided to help them do so. That's the iron in me.

My old Opel was on its last leg, so I didn't want to have to drive too far. It never occurred to me that being a woman, or that having no degrees or any other experience, would be a handicap. My mother had said I could do anything I wanted, and I *wanted* to do medical staff analyses—they were fun and challenging. As I was busy getting ready to launch my new business, I was also busy trying to pay the bills. I continued to collect food stamps and unemployment checks.

It was about this time that I also decided to start some Gestalt groups again. Back in the early 1970's, I had become interested in and later studied Gestalt therapy. I had gone to my first workshop in Philadelphia with a well-known therapist, Neil Lamper, in 1973. It was the first time I had felt that I had a way to deal with my emotions. This discipline, developed by Fritz Perls, assumed that if you acted out your feelings, dreams, fantasies, or thoughts, you could understand your behavior and then change it. After years of acting out, I must admit I didn't really change any of my basic behavior that I went into therapy to change, but I had a wonderful time with a great group of people and grew up in ways I never expected.

After two years of weekend workshops that I organized for Neil in and around the Princeton area, I finally went for seven weekend training workshops to be a facilitator. After this training I put together two Gestalt workshops—one titled <u>Self-Image and Hunger—A Seesaw</u> on body image, and the other on dream interpretation. They had both been very successful at the Women's Center in Princeton, so I decided to make some spare money that way again. The Women's Center was now closed, so I placed an ad in the <u>Town Topics</u> and other area newspapers, and slowly a few clients appeared. I saw them in my home, and the extra cash of $30 per hour was most welcome.

In December my old car died, but I kept right on calling hospitals and trying to set up interviews. Friends offered me their cars or I would take a bus to Trenton, where there were five hospitals I wanted to investigate. During this time, Randy continued to give me emotional support to make the business successful. He was the real entrepreneur. During his last year in high school, he spent all his spare time and money writing a book on how to start a mail order business. He taught himself from reading at the library and ordering books on the subject, and he then typed his own book. I read it at one point and thought it was

WHIM OF IRON

terrific! As so often happens in life, he got busy and never finished the book for publication.

Christmas was right around the corner, which added pressure. When the children were growing up, and we had little cash, I had made a policy that all gifts to and from everyone had to be handmade. I still have some of the gifts the children made for me. Now, with money so tight, I decided to make as many as I could in my spare time. Randy bought a kit for a winter jacket for $10, which he intended to sew himself, but it was quite complicated with corduroy shoulder inserts, three linings, zipper and cuffs. I took the project over, and it turned out terrific. I had sold my diamond engagement ring to send Lisa tuition money, which I had agreed to pay, but I had nothing left to send her a gift. She swore it didn't matter, but it did to me. For the children, I made small gifts, wrote poems, and generally tried to keep the spirit, without spending any money.

It was about this time that, on a whim, I decided to paint the house Randy and I were living in, partly because it looked so badly and partly to barter for free rent. My landlord agreed to give me three free months of rent for painting the two-story stucco house.

One day, as I was up on a ladder scrubbing paint onto the stucco on the outside of the house, a group of black men approached and started saying with slightly angry voices, "Hey, girl, don't you know you're taking work away from us men?"

I turned and looked down at them, climbed down the ladder and said, "Wow, that's too bad. Here, you can paint the house for the same amount of money I am getting."

As I held the brush and paint can out to them, one asked, "How much are you getting?"

"Nothing," I said.

After that, they left me alone. Or at least that group did. I had many unusual experiences during the five years I lived there, all of them good and many funny.

As a gift to me, my sister Betsy and nieces sent me a ticket to come home for my 25th high school reunion that was to be held right after Christmas. It was held at the Don Ce Sar—the large, majestic hotel built in 1928 where my mother worked for 23 years. Twenty-five years had passed since I'd seen my friends, and it was great fun. It was interesting to talk with them about their perceptions of me in high school, which certainly didn't match with my own. My memory was of being slow, needing lots of extra help studying, and always being an outsider. Classmate after classmate told me they saw me as confident, smart, an organizer, and someone with lots of friends. It was fun hearing such good stuff! I told everyone excitedly about my new business dream, which I felt could come true. Their reactions ranged from surprise to outright skepticism. While home, I made appointments with three hospital administrators in St. Petersburg, but no one could see my vision of how to manage their medical staffs. One told me flat out that it wasn't any of his business.

WHIM OF IRON

When I inquired about jobs through personnel, I was always told the same thing—I had to have a degree for the jobs that interested me. I got discouraged at times, but not for long. When I returned to Princeton two things happened, one good and one very bad. The good was that Rahway Hospital was willing to talk to me about the medical staff analyses. The bad was that I had no unemployment check waiting for me.

Today panic rose in my throat until I almost lost control. Unemployment would not pay me for the two weeks I missed while I was in Florida, even though I looked for jobs there; car got flat and oil smoking in 0 degree weather; no job in sight; electric bill $187!

I lodged a complaint against unemployment, and got proof of my visits to administrators in Florida. The wheels of progress, however, moved very slowly.

Dan, my stepson, had gotten the Opel running again, but it kept having one problem after the other. I have no idea how I paid the electric bill, but I never did have it or the phone or water turned off, so somehow I came up with the money. If Christmas or New Years happened that year, I made no note of it.

1981 — Finding Work Wherever I Could

In January of 1981, I was introduced to Jim Butler, a consultant from Washington, D.C. He was working with a Princeton firm putting together a complicated special report for the Robert Wood Johnson Foundation on how physicians spend their time, by specialty, across the United States. He had gotten my name from a mutual friend and interviewed me to see if I was capable of editing the charts, data, and text of the report. When he understood that I knew how hospitals were organized and how they worked, he hired me, and I had my first really big project. I was ecstatic. Not only did I have a project, but also they would pay me $40 per hour. But my ecstasy was short lived—I found out they wouldn't need me for months.

Concurrently, I met with people from the New Jersey State Department of Planning to describe what I was doing in medical staff analysis. I had met these people while working at the hospital consulting firm so it was easy to get a meeting. It was not as easy to get them to understand what I was doing. No one analyzed doctors' practice patterns in the 1980's, and hearing a young upstart, and a female at that, suggest such an idea, went over like a lead balloon. I thought they would want to *know* where there were problems in the system so they could be corrected, but I never did get any work from them.

My private life consisted mostly of my family, since I had little time or energy for friends. Dan was around a lot giving support and encouragement, as were Gary, Randy and Lisa, when she was home. When I wasn't working on a project or on the road trying to sell my concepts, I wrote. At the time I was working on a book called, <u>Sisters in Madness</u>, about my sister and I and living with her schizophrenia. Nancy and I had gone through many a trial during her illness and yet I could always feel her unique spirit, even when I would encounter her on Nassau Street, the main street in town, with turban and all, and not deigning to say hello to *me*! But that's another story.

Writing gave me a sense of doing something when little was happening in my life. It filled in the long evenings. When I wasn't writing, I was usually over at Hazel's place listening to stories about growing up black in the South. She had some funny stories to tell, mixed with others that were very sad. Hazel was the town bootlegger, and she was less than thrilled when I moved in next door.

She told me later that when she first saw me moving in, she remarked to a friend, "Well look at that white bitch moving into the neighborhood!"

WHIM OF IRON

I need to say more about Hazel, because she was a friend of mine for over twenty years. Here's a story that will help you understand this remarkable woman.

One night when we had been out drinking and had had a few too many, we walked home together, and as I fixed us some grilled cheese sandwiches, she told me this story. Hazel grew up in Snow Hill, Maryland, the daughter of a sharecropper and his wife. Her mother had four children that lived. She said life was quite good for them—her dad got money for his share of the work on the farm, and they raised all their own food and made everything they could. She remembered when she was about four or five, having to watch a mark on the porch—a mark that her mother would make each day, and when the sun hit that mark, Hazel would put the bread in the oven. That way, when her parents got home from the fields, the bread would be baked, and the family could eat. Sometime in her mid-teens, her dad gave her a shaving knife that was like a switchblade that he put around her neck. He told her not to ever let anyone mess with her.

One night she went to the outhouse at dusk to go to the bathroom. As she sat on the seat, the door suddenly was pulled opened, and there was a large, black man with his penis hanging out. He was clearly intent on getting himself some "pussy," as Hazel put it. The man was drunk, and without a second thought, Hazel whipped out the knife, and slashed at the man, cutting his penis off, or at least damaging it badly. He staggered backwards, screaming in agony and disbelief. Now, Hazel was no dummy. She knew that the black man and the community would be allowed to do anything they wanted with her for what she had done. In her culture, females, especially young girls, were on the bottom of the heap.

So she pulled her pants up, carefully looked out the door of the outhouse, and feeling sure all was clear for the moment, she started walking. She walked across the field. She walked across the road into the woods, and she just kept on walking. She walked mostly by night and slept in bushes or wherever she could by day. She walked all the way to Philadelphia. When she got there she didn't have any soles left in her shoes. She went around to the black bars until she found someone who knew her cousin. A phone call was made, and pretty soon Hazel was eating food and was taken in to live with her relatives.

From there, Hazel slowly drifted towards Princeton, where there were lots of jobs cleaning houses and taking care of children for the well-to-do of the community. She spent the next 60 years doing just that. She also, at one point, ran a bar in the same building that the bookbindery was in. When that bar closed, she just moved business upstairs, and that's how she became a bootlegger. And cook! Anyone who bought a drink could also buy a dinner. Fried chicken, collard greens, black-eyed peas...she was great at good old home cooking. She ran a good establishment, and the police had never been called to settle a dispute. If you saw Hazel, you'd know why. Built to stop a battleship (a description I don't think she would feel is unflattering), she took care of any disputes or unruly behavior, personally.

WHIM OF IRON

Having Hazel as a friend was wonderful for me because she laid down the rules...Cleo only has two beers a night, anyone want to dance with Cleo better talk to Hazel first, and Cleo only goes home with Hazel. We were friends for twenty years before she died, and as I tell my story, you'll understand why. Hazel passed on at the age of 89 while I was in Europe taking care of my twin granddaughters. I still sorely miss her.

So there I was, living in the black district, unemployed, and full of energy. After sending out 300 resumes, I just waited for a call. I spent my restless days swimming at the YWCA, reading at the public library, walking the Princeton campus, and writing. I often felt lost at the bottom of humanity. I was on unemployment and still trying to market myself to local hospital CEO's. Walking into the unemployment line each week was degrading. The staff there seemed to do everything they could to re-enforce that feeling.

Sometime during the spring, a friend offered to pay me under the table to do secretarial work. The extra money helped Randy and I survive because, as frugal as I was, the unemployment money just wouldn't take care of us. I came to respect how hard it is for poor people who do try, sometimes working two and three jobs, and still they can't make ends meet. Because of discrimination, lack of skills, low pay, different cultural backgrounds, and expectations, some just have a very difficult time in the world.

My ads for Gestalt work finally paid off. By May 1981, I had a group of six people in my dream workshop. Each paid $50 for a six-week course at night for one hour, so this was good money for me. I was still working as a secretary, and I continued to market myself. I was learning to network. Ken, a manager with the State Planning Department agreed to have lunch with me. From him, I learned that I'd always have to go through consultants to do work for the State because I was too small a business and I had no degrees.

Allow me to digress for a moment because the dream workshop turned up some surprising insights. One in particular sticks in my mind.

My first group of six people consisted of all women, mostly working mothers. One night I had everyone tell a dream they had had the week before (they had learned to write them down during the night). One young woman told of feeling helpless and out of control in her dream. After each had told her dream, I would have them sit in two groups of three and explore the possible messages in their dreams.

One heavily overweight mom said to me, "I have no control in my home."

"What do you mean?" I asked.

"Well," she started very heavily, "in the morning my daughter is always late for the school bus. No matter what I do, she is still late. Which means I have to drive her to school, which means I'm late to work. From there on my day just gets worse. I have taken her spending money away, I have given her more chores, and I have threatened to take her movie money away. Nothing works," she ended despairingly.

After listening for a while and hearing what other ideas the women in her group offered, I suddenly came upon an idea. I said, "Why don't you tell her that if she is late, she may call a cab and she can pay for it out of her allowance!"

The woman's eyes popped open and she said, "That could work. Then I wouldn't be late to work!"

Everyone was happy and the meeting broke up. I never saw that woman again in that workshop.

About two years later I'm standing on the corner of Witherspoon and Nassau Streets in Princeton and a woman walks up to me and says, "You don't remember me, do you?"

I looked at her and knew that I didn't have a clue.

She said, "Two years ago I took a workshop from you. In it I learned that I had choices. I went home, made a bunch of choices, lost 50 pounds, lost a husband, moved down here and got a great job at the hospital…all because of one little dream."

I gave her a hug and wished her well on her journey. I only did that one series of workshops but it certainly had been productive!

Cleo B. Robertson

About the same time I was putting on the dream workshops, I appeared before the Unemployment Appeals Board. When I had gone to Florida over Christmas I had told them I was going to look for work, and I did. They refused to pay me when I came back, however, because they said Florida was a vacation spot at Christmas. I told them that I was from Florida, and was thinking of moving back, but no one seemed to believe me. It took me two months to finally get the $246 due me, which at that time was a fortune, and essential. For two months I was on pins and needles trying to make ends meet.

One day I got up the nerve to call one of my old bosses from the hospital-consulting firm, who was now president of the New Jersey Hospital Association. He agreed to meet with me, and we talked, but in the end nothing came of the contact. It was becoming clear to me that I was not going to have an easy time convincing people I knew anything of value in the hospital field, due to the fact that I had no credentials. I also didn't know how to get my message across.

Lisa came home whenever she could. Her visit in June of 1981 was a happy one. A large accounting firm had hired her. I was so proud of my daughter. In addition to doing well in her studies at Penn State, she had worked as a waitress to pay most of her way through college. Getting such a good job was just reward! Her dad helped her financially, too, but she did a lot on her own. Her 15 years of French lessons would turn out to be a major asset, and it was Lisa who had stuck to it.

WHIM OF IRON

Randy turned 18, and we celebrated quietly at home. He had no idea what he wanted to do, but college didn't seem to be on his list.

Between food stamps, unemployment checks, Gestalt classes, and secretarial work, I was just making ends meet. The bonus of working for my friend was that I had access to good equipment, and could use the copier. My first thirty promotional letters for CBR Associates were done at his office at no cost. I just couldn't afford to pay for these types of expenses. All my free time was spent trying to make money, and market myself. About this time, all my networking started to pay off. Communications Media in Princeton Junction hired me to edit a medical book. During this time, I kept up my delusional thinking that at some point in time, I would get work and all the worry would be over, forever.

My first meeting with the director of MASSC, the Middle Atlantic Shared Services Corporation, took place due to contacts I had. The director liked that I was interested in computers, and he was a natural teacher. We got along great. My background in hospitals and data was useful to him for a project he wanted to do on Emergency Room Information Systems. The fact that I had no college education didn't bother him, because he knew he could teach me whatever I didn't know. Besides, that made me cheaper ($25 per hour to start and $40 in 3 months, which wasn't bad for either of us).

In March, the project with the Robert Wood Johnson Foundation (RWJ) finally started, and I began editing medical text and data in a Special Report they were producing. It was a very exciting time for me. The one wool, tailored suit I owned made me feel like a real professional, and the RWJ staff always treated me like one. I learned a great deal about editing and also about marketing my services. Soon, money started to come in. First, from my editing, and then from the RWJ project. It was a heady time for me. I stopped taking unemployment because I was sure I was on a roll. Because I was being paid hourly, between $20 and $35, I thought I was making a lot of money. Of course I wasn't. I only worked three or four hours a week. I had no experience handling money, so seeing checks for hundreds of dollars made me feel rich. I treated money in keeping with my personality—last cash in, was the first cash out. Savings? What savings? It didn't occur to me to save money. I needed every penny that came in just to survive.

One day, as I was leaving the YWCA, I saw a brochure from the Small Business Administration (SBA). I knew I was a small business, so on a whim I picked it up and started reading. President Carter, the brochure explained, was giving $20,000 to women entrepreneurs who had no collateral! Boy, that was me, for sure! I eagerly read on. What it came down to was a loan that I could apply for—there were a limited number—so I immediately sent the forms off, and prayed.

By May, I was working a lot on the Emergency Room System for hospitals. That meant steady money coming in. I went to a health conference in Atlantic City as a vendor but it turned out to be a bust—such a waste of money promoting to people who didn't know what I was talking about. What I was trying to do by studying the medical staff was so clear to me. But, I didn't know how to convey my message to others.

In June, I went to Freehold Hospital and sold the first Emergency Room system for MASSC, which I had helped develop. It was great fun and exciting to be in on the development of something so new. I was now working four days per week at $35 per hour, so I was making enough to survive. In addition, I was writing a Certificate of Need application for a hospital that wanted more beds, and that was good money.

Randy finally decided to find his own place. He was angry with me, perhaps because I had pulled him out of his high school in West Windsor at the beginning of his senior year and moved him to Princeton. The fact that we had no money, and we were living in the black area, didn't help either. I went to see his new place and it was fine for him. I had little energy for anything but the business (for which, I again say "I'm sorry" to all my children).

My house seemed empty after Randy left, so I bought a K9 dog that had failed police school—he couldn't seem to learn whom he was supposed to bite, and who he wasn't. He was a BIG 95-pound German shepherd, and his name was Max. He was my very first dog. Though he gave me lots of headaches because he was not well behaved, he became my friend and I depended on him. His size alone ensured I was safe. In my neighborhood, people would move to the other side of the street when they saw us coming.

Cleo B. Robertson

By July, I was broke again. I recorded in my diary that I was down to $200 with no money billed out to clients. That's the life of a consultant. Money rolls in sometimes and at other times, there's not even a drizzle. I hadn't learned to put money away for a rainy day. An all-day Gestalt workshop I put together brought in $200. I was saved again for a short time! I bought a used IBM Selectric typewriter with the money so I could get work editing. It scared me to spend the $80, but I felt I had to do it. Everyday I carried apprehension around in my belly, fearing the next disaster that would come.

Toward the end of August, I got a call from the Small Business Association and they told me to come to Newark to get forms for a loan. That was just like them—ask a person struggling to survive to find the money and time to get on a train and go to Newark, *just to get forms*. This was just the first of many insane encounters I had with this government group.

Work was not coming in for CBR Associates. It was mostly because I didn't know how to market myself. What I could seem to get was editing work, so I decided to start a second company—Princeton Editorial Associates. I placed an ad for editors (in retrospect that seems crazy because I didn't have any work yet, but I can honestly say I always thought big). A friend asked if she could do an article on my new business for the local paper. I was delighted, it was a great article, but I never got any business from it.

Randy joined me for lunch one day. After hearing about all my ups and downs, he said he thought

WHIM OF IRON

I was just afraid of success. That sounded right to me! I had not a clue what success would look like, except to know that I would be able to pay some bills and not be afraid to hear the phone ring.

Spent the day cleaning and getting things filed. I have no money to pay the monthly bills. All my energy is going in to making enough money to live on. Life is tough and life is wonderful—I wouldn't do my living any other way than "on the edge."

By October, things were drastic:

I have no rent money, food money—I can't even buy milk! Another autumn broke!

Randy was struggling, too. He had ended high school with good grades, and with a record of 22-0 in wrestling for the year. He didn't want to go to college though he had sailed through high school without studying very much and did well. He didn't know what he wanted to do. He finally decided to go live with his dad in Virginia and I spent the next few days crying a lot.

So broke I am. Down to last stick of butter with no money coming in till Oct. 13th Gestalt group. Life is a challenge every minute and I'm up to it!

As I look back, I have no idea where my enthusiasm came from. I guess I just had to keep pretending things were going to be all right, or I couldn't have gone on. About this time I read a book about women who had started and succeeded at their own businesses. I remember reading that they never had a doubt they'd make it. I envied them. I had doubts often.

Two different diary entries show two different pictures, both in the same month:

Princeton Editorial Associates and Gestalt brochures done—thank God! Walked around aimlessly for a while. I'm hanging by my fingertips financially—I have $6 in savings and $300 in billables and the bank wants my ass! They'll have to wait—I'm going to pay that damn loan off soon. I'm healthy and strong and excited. WOW!

Hospital consulting at standstill. Freehold Hospital hasn't started Emergency Room system.

In October I went to my first expo for women in business and I learned a lot. Mostly, I learned I wasn't as experienced as I thought I was, especially in marketing! In retrospect it was good I didn't know that, but at the time I really thought I knew everything I needed to know to succeed. I still thought that if you had a great product, it would sell itself. It would be many years before I learned that without marketing and sales, product doesn't mean a thing.

The 52 hostages in Iran for 444 days are flying home; Ronald Reagan became our 40th president; and I am almost finished with another book manuscript—<u>Choices, Energy</u>

<u>and Action</u>. Danced my legs off on empty floor at Hudibras to wonderful Jones Brothers' band.

The book I was working on was going to reflect my belief that it was an art to make a new choice for oneself. Once you do make a new choice you have to find the energy, and put it into action. I truly believed and still do, that anyone can learn the art of making good choices and then practice making them. It is not always easy, but it is always worthwhile. I assumed success would follow.

I felt I knew something about making new choices and then finding the energy to make them come true. What was strange was that I also thought I knew something about success. I guess I just thought having any work made me successful. My Gestalt group was going well. I had finally negotiated my $8,000 loan with the bank, and that seemed to be off my list for the moment, but I was still not making any money.

Success, in the business world, is measured by income. Based on general norms, I was not doing very well and would certainly not be called successful. My lack of a college education kept me from realizing the truth. Thank goodness!

A woman from the SBA came to visit me in October. She wanted to interview me regarding my business plan for CBR Associates and Princeton Editorial Associates, which I had added to the loan request. I figured they'd be impressed that I could do two businesses. Of course, they weren't. They knew I had no money and no collateral. They were wondering how I could do one. But, I kept my hopes up as always.

The next day I was up at 4 a.m. to work on some marketing letters. Then at 6 a.m. I went out in the dark to jog with my dog, Max. I had to be at Freehold Hospital by 8 a.m. In my rush, I fell and sprained my ankle. A doctor put it in an air cast, and I kept right on going.

Dan bought my dirt bike for $200, which helped pay the rent. Early in November I got a project with Dow Jones proofing symbols on some sheet they had. They were testing my skills, and I worked hard to show them I could do it. In the end, this was the only job I got from them. They decided to do all the work in-house. I contacted Ethicon, a large company, to see about editing. But I was too small a company for them. I also went to the Hillier Group, an architectural firm, but they, too, were doing all their work in-house. By this time my body was starting to hurt just from being overtired all the time.

Early in November, the bank closed my account because I had not made my payments. Now I was without a checking account, which hurt my new business a lot. By this time I was behind in my rent, my electric, telephone and water bills, and I had no money for gas. What I thought the solution would be turned out to be a total failure, but I gave myself credit for trying.

WHIM OF IRON

I had to get cash. Many times I had passed a Go-Go Dancing Club in Bordentown, New Jersey. My daughter had given me a bodysuit she didn't wear anymore, and it almost fit my 30-pound overweight body. Combined with some blue leotards and visions of dollar bills sticking out of them, I decided I was ready to go. I drove out to the club one Wednesday night when they said they tried out new dancers. The manager was able to keep a straight face when I told him I was there to audition. He allowed me to go on stage, and I danced with all the good energy I always feel when I dance. At first the bright lights kept me from seeing the audience. When I finally could, I saw there were four very drunk men leaning on chairs or the stage. One yelled at me to bump and grind. Another told me to come closer so he could touch. I finished the dance, barely, and as soon as I walked off, I told the manager that I may be broke, but I wasn't *that* broke. The next night I applied at a conference center outside Princeton for a waitress job.

Spent an hour interviewing at Scanticon for cocktail waitress job—I'm hired (I think any warm body would have been) at $2.25 per hour plus tips. Forty hours per week 4-12 PM.

Unfortunately there were more waitresses than customers, and the customers were more interested in getting laid than leaving tips. The first night I made $18 for 8 hours of work. During the day I met with a hospital in south New Jersey and presented a proposal to study their Same Day Surgery for $5,500. They would pay me $2,000 to begin. My spirits were up for about a week until they told me they were going to do it themselves. I began to realize that these places were using my very detailed proposals to do the work themselves. I swore I would get smarter, but I didn't know how.

A doctor from the Hartford HMO in Connecticut called and asked if I'd come up to assess their admissions. It didn't occur to me to ask for travel money. I scraped it together, went up, told them too much, and came home with nothing to show for my efforts. I learned later they did it themselves. On the way home from the airport my car died—water in the gas. What next?

Besides the usual stresses being broke brought, new, interesting stresses would pop up out of nowhere. One day as I was editing in my front room in mid-November. I realized that the house felt awfully warm.

This did not make sense to me because I had little money for heat so I tried to use as little as possible. I checked the thermostat and it was at 60, so I went down to the basement. When I saw the boiler, it was as red as a pin when you hold it in a fire, and I ran as fast as I could upstairs to call the police. They called the gas company, and a man was at my house within ten minutes. He told me to leave, but I said if he was going downstairs, so was I. We went together. He proceeded to disengage the gas line that had become stuck open. He told me that in a few more minutes, it would have exploded and ignited the whole gas line out to the street and God only knew how much more. It felt just like my life—ready to explode at any moment!

WHIM OF IRON

In one day I had learned that two hospitals I had presented to, were doing their own studies. I felt sick to my stomach, scared and desperate. I called a friend and tried to rent out my spare bedroom, but it didn't work out. As if that wasn't enough, the lawyer for the SBA called and said they couldn't give me the loan because Princeton Editorial Associates influenced public opinion and therefore did not qualify. I argued that I edited, he said I could edit text to reflect my opinion. I said, "If I did that, I wouldn't be in business long." We went back and forth for an hour and when we stopped, I had no idea if I had won or lost. He said he had to take it to his committee and that didn't sound good.

On December 2nd, 1981, the lawyer for SBA called me back. My rebuttal had been accepted, and I would receive a check for $20,000 shortly. I felt like I had hit the lottery! When the papers came through, however, interest on the loan was 15 ¾ percent! I had thought it would be eight percent. I called them. They said I was lucky to get the money at all, considering I had no collateral. I suppose they were right. I walked around in a daze for a few days, thinking about all the doors that would open now because I had money. It took years for me to learn that having money isn't what matters; it's what you do with it.

It was exciting deciding how I was going to spend the money. I needed a car. I had to pay back bills of about $5,000 to the bank, landlord, and utility companies. And, for reasons beyond me, the SBA required that I spend $8,000 on equipment. I had an electric typewriter. What other equipment did I need?

Cleo B. Robertson

I asked them if a car would do, but they said no. I talked to my consulting friend on the RWJ project, and he told me to buy a personal computer. He had a Vector Graphics, which he said made him much more efficient at writing, editing, and in every other way. Not being one to miss a chance to do something on a whim, I immediately located a dealer and purchased a Vector Graphics (IBM PCs weren't out until 1983) for $8,000. Boy, I had no idea what I was getting in to! My only concern was that the SBA check arrive before the computer.

For the price, I would get two days of training—that's it. If you know computers at all, you know that isn't much. Back then it was even less, because the manuals were written by programmers, for programmers. In addition to word processing (Memorite), I got a database that was still under development and a spreadsheet that was really good, but complicated. The system was to be delivered in February, so I decided to start learning the word processing software right away. A firm in Cranbury was using it, and they agreed to let me go to their offices and practice. They spent one day showing me what they knew, and suddenly I knew what the first person to discover fire must have felt—power!

The year ended with little in the bank and lots of hopes and plans. Somehow I had managed to stay in business one full year, which seemed like a miracle to me. My personal life was a few one-night stands, and many lonely nights walking around Princeton. If Hazel hadn't been my friend, I wouldn't have had any at all. My life was too full for anyone else to fit into it.

As I looked back on 1981, however, I was proud. I had started two businesses and I was still in business—quite an accomplishment in my book.

1982 — A Computer Enthusiast is Born

This was a time of very big steps. On February 12th my computer arrived. As I watched the female technician uncrate the boxes and take the huge manuals out of their wrappers, I had a feeling I was really stepping into deep water. It all seemed so unreal. It must have seemed unreal to her too. Here she was, delivering a very expensive machine to a woman living in a house that was ready to collapse. Little did she know the sophisticated work I expected to do on the machine. I could hear her talking about how to "sort directories and name files," but my mind couldn't quite get over all the books, cords, cables and plugs! She gave me a two-hour lesson on hooking things up, starting the computer, putting in a floppy disk into a drive that was connected to my main computer by a cable. After she left, I felt like a new mother feels when the nurse leaves her alone with a two-hour-old baby. I leafed through the books, but the terms and language were very foreign to me. Hard disk, boot, DOS, subdirectories...I had to learn "computer-eeze"! I dug in slowly, reading page by page.

The next day I went to Princeton Junction for computer training. There were two days included with the purchase, and after just a few hours I was feeling rather lost. I knew that I was good at learning from scratch, and I had confidence I would catch on soon. That was on the 13th of February. Within days I had gotten scared again.

Worked on learning computer. Stomach wrapped in knots, mind scared, need rest.

I put in hours reading through the manuals, trying something on the screen, watching what it would do, and then reading some more. The manuals were written by techies for techies, but again my habit of reading something three times before I gave up was invaluable. I had always learned things from books, and I was sure I could again.

After a week, I started to get a handle on it all. The words, which I had by now read three times each, were starting to make sense. I was getting a lot done in the word processor, and the database was difficult, but, I enjoyed the challenge. Only the spreadsheet left me feeling stupid and incompetent—feelings that washed over me every few hours as I struggled to understand how to do what I wanted to do. Slowly, I began to see how it worked and could create spreadsheets that were meaningful. Empowered by my new capability, I answered an ad in the Princeton newspaper for someone to write a manual for a telecommunications software program that resided on Princeton University's mainframe. I didn't know what they were talking about, but I knew I could figure it out.

On February 18, just a week after my computer was delivered, I went to New York City to visit with the president of the telecommunications company. After hearing what they wanted, on a whim I bid $8,000 on the spot. Two days later they accepted my bid. I learned from the programmer that I had bid one quarter of the $32,000 that two large New York City firms had bid. I didn't care. It was a fortune to me. As the project proceeded, however, I began to understand why they had bid so much.

The first few weeks of the project I spent trying to understand the Princeton University telecommunications program. I kept feeling like I was swimming in water over my head, but slowly it started to make sense. The company was evidently impressed with my abilities, because they were talking about having me train their new users at $400 per day. Serious money gave me great hope! Much later I realized how easy it was for people to offer carrots like $400 per day for training, without really thinking it through. Most of these kinds of offers evaporated over time. Within the same week I was asked to write two long-range plan proposals and received a project from Educational Technologies to edit a medical book. I was on a roll…again!

By February 25th the schedule was all set with the user manual people, and all I had to do was meet it. My diary shows that I had absolutely no clue what I was in for:

> *Met with user manual people—schedule all set—now all I have to do is produce! Will learn telecommunications software on Princeton University's mainframe and write manual for analysis of WATS and Foreign Exchange lines to lower corporation's telephone costs. No documentation of the software exists—should be quite a challenge.*

Looking back now I wonder how I had the confidence to tackle the job that lay ahead. Ignorance certainly is bliss and in this case it was essential.

The next day I woke at 4 a.m., feet running as soon as they touched the floor. I was so excited to be challenged. The man who wrote the software was to spend time with me using his computer and teaching me how the program worked. Telco, the company that had hired me, had a good product, but without a user manual, it was difficult for them to support or sell it. I soon learned there were 124 prompts on the screen, usually questions like "Do you have more than 50 phone calls per day?" How a person responded to each prompt determined where you branched off. It was a maze, with statistical calculations lying at the end of each path, depending on the answers entered. The customer's telephone bill would have been downloaded to the software prior to analysis, and the point was to help them identify how to route their phone lines to lower phone costs. Because there was no documentation, I had to follow every path and see where it ended up.

The programmer took me to Princeton University so I could actually see the program running. Then we spent time at the programmer's apartment going through the prompts with him explaining to me the very complicated program. The first time through, I was overwhelmed and lost. I told him so. He went through it again, but it was no help. Without any documentation, I had to listen to a man who knew the program too well try to teach it to someone who didn't have a clue. After three attempts, he finally got a woman who knew the program and used it a lot to sit down and teach me. That helped. By now, of course, the words and logic were starting to make sense. Slowly I started to get the picture.

Towards the end of February, I started going to a nearby town, Cranbury, on a regular basis to learn more about Memorite, the word processor that came with my computer. I spent hours practicing. Within a short time, I had caught up with and passed my teachers in understanding what the software could do. Never was there a more eager student. I knew that with the word processing software, writing the user manual would be much easier. However, because I was writing a manual, I needed to use the more sophisticated features of the software, such as building an index and table of contents, spell check, and extensive formatting.

I had a vision of how professional this manual would look. I knew I had to learn the tools to reach that vision. The fact that my vision was way beyond what Telco had asked for or expected never occurred to me. The iron in me made me always strive for the best. My days were long, exhausting, and very exciting!

One day as I opened my mail, an envelope with Small Business Administration on it suddenly appeared in my hand. The check. I had the check. I could hardly believe it.

I'm working 18-20 hour days with great excitement. I still can't imagine a 43-year-old, single, penniless woman can be given that much money to start her own business! Thank you President Jimmy Carter!!

Long day finishing edit of a J&J article, worked on the Emergency Room Assessment for MASSC, and made calls for the user manual. I'm exhausted and taking extra vitamins. I'll be all right. God is very good to me. I asked him to help the SBA check come and he did!

I had never handled much money. During my marriages I would have a small budget, but generally money came to me and I spent it on essentials. There was never any extra to think about. Here was a lot of money at one time and for the most part, I spent it wisely. I was enjoying the challenges and enjoying using my brain. I was learning that I could create, digest and reason. That was a really great feeling!

After paying $8,000 for the computer, I decided I needed a car. My Opel was not reliable, and hadn't been for some time. If I was going to drive all over New

Jersey doing work for my new business, I needed a car. I found a lovely 1978 Celica lift-back for $4,000 and it turned out to be a gem. Not only was it reliable for many years, but the back opened up easily for transporting my computer to wherever work took me. My motto was, "Have computer, will travel." The fact that after buying a computer for $8,000, a car for $4,000 and paying my bills, I would only have $3000 left, didn't phase me at all! I had learned growing up as a beach kid that I could survive on very little cash.

My personal life consisted of my dog, Max, my stepson, Dan, my three children and my friend, Hazel. Somehow they all believed in me, and their belief gave me strength to go on. In the past, I always had plenty of energy. Now, however, I was exhausted from trying to learn too much too soon, but I felt time was of the essence. The SBA loan required repayment starting the first month I got the money. So, I started paying $344 per month *out of the loan*! Panic was back as my constant companion.

By mid-March, I was swimming in computer jargon and technology and loving it, but not without cost! My 4 and 5 a.m. sessions on Princeton's mainframe were taxing my strength. I had learned how to use a modem and access the mainframe early in the morning when usage was light. That way I could work at the least cost to my client. But, I was simply trying to do too much.

Worked on computer all day and trying to learn it—so hard. I am so scared most of the time that my stomach is in a constant state of upset.

The next day I recorded:

Up early with Max to run. Had to get up—my stomach is so sick only moving helps. Some of the things I want to do with the software I can't figure out. Finally talked to programmer where I bought my software. He's going to help me. Studied manuals and feeling better.

My contact at MASSC turned out to be a great resource for me. Dick understood how I yearned to learn, and he was a good teacher. His years of mainframe programming gave him a background that helped me with the telecommunications software, but he also could help me understand how the word processing software worked.

I'm finally coming to grips with the manual. Burned myself out creating—who would think that writing a user manual could be so taxing? I make it harder than it is. I won't let me enjoy. Though I'm starting. Spent some time scared, hiding in bed, then took Max for run. Bought 1½ pound live lobster. I had a lovely evening eating lobster, listening to music and dancing and playing with Max.

A call from the Princeton Medical Center gave me a diversion. They wanted me to do a medical staff roster. At that time they didn't have one by specialty with addresses, phone numbers, etc. Even though I hadn't done such a task before on my own, I thought I knew what it would require. This project taught me lessons in computers I'll never forget. The medical staff roster contained approximately 150 physicians with about 50 pieces of data on each…name, department, specialty, office location, etc. I spent a lot of time cleaning the list from the various paper sources at the hospital, none of which correlated with the other.

One night when I was updating the data for the last time, an electrical storm was raging outside. Just as I went to save to the floppy drive, which was external to my computer, a lightning bolt searched out the electrical energy, and wham! It flashed right through the window. It hit the floppy disk, and a flash of light burst in front of my eyes. My heart sank. In panic I tried to access the data, but a message said there was none. Slowly I began to realize it was all gone. I sat looking at the blank computer screen in total shock. Weeks of work were gone, and the project was due in three days. This is when I demonstrated my persistence and learned unequivocally "there are no mistakes!"

After about three minutes of sitting and breathing, I took the reports I had printed along the way, and immediately began re-entering the data. What had taken me three weeks to do initially, now took two days. Soon I was printing really impressive reports. This incident taught me two important lessons. First, when working on a new database, it is always best to practice, and then at some point throw it all away, and start all over again. Why? Because the way I designed the database the first time, in complete ignorance, was incorrect. Since I had to do it over, I did it correctly, based on solid knowledge and experience. The final product went far beyond what I could have ever done with the original. Hard lesson well learned. Second, I learned to back up my data, and now I always do!

Between projects, I was busy running my life.

Up at 4 am, put new pockets in coat, made cover for computer, hemmed slacks, ran Max, wired living room speakers, cleaned tool boxes and caught up on my ironing. Met with programmer on manual.

How did I do it all? Genes were a major part of the answer. I had come from German and Scottish ancestry, and working was what life was for, in my mind. My children and dog were around, which recharged me too. I felt most fortunate.

By April, I had the user manual well under way. I delivered 150 pages to the programmer on the 20th for final edit. It was not without personal cost. The stress of getting the SBA money, learning the computer, starting my businesses and doing the manual had taken a toll on my health. An old ailment resurfaced, and luckily I was able to treat it. But I heard the message—slow down or else. I immediately tried to lighten up my workload and allow more time for walking my dog. I felt confident I was handling the project well and learning the computer. My marketing was paying off too! I could pay my bills with money to spare, or so I thought.

By the 28th of April, reality hit. After paying my bills, I was down to $200. That's all that was left of the

$20,000. I had spent it wisely, it just wasn't enough to jump start a new business, particularly when $344 had to go back to the SBA every month from the first month. I hadn't even gotten my business going. To make matters worse, my daughter and I had planned a trip to St. John to celebrate her graduating from Penn State. Clearly I didn't have the money. Once again she showed her true colors. We were going to St. John... on the money she made from waiting tables!

The project on the user manual for the telecommunications program at Princeton University was progressing well, but I knew by this time why it was so hard for clients to use the program. The prompts that they had to answer on the computer screen had been written by a programmer and made no logical sense. I finally realized that if we redid the prompts in easy-to-read English, the client wouldn't need so much support, and the product would be easier to sell. I shared my thoughts with the programmer, who talked with the president in New York. They heartily agreed that I should go ahead and rewrite the prompts. I submitted my nomenclature for the prompts, and waited to hear what they thought. My plan had been to draw a map from the original prompt to the new prompt, once they approved them, so I could follow the work I had done to date. To my shock, when I went online to work one morning, all the prompts had been changed to my wording. It was a disaster. All my work to that point used the old prompts. Now I had no idea what prompt led where. I was both furious and scared.

I woke up at 1 a.m. sick because I have no money again. Got up and worked until 6 a.m.

Cleo B. Robertson

Stopped, took bath and figured out that I'm working 90-hour weeks and have no money. Something's wrong. I finally realized I bid on an $8,000 project and I'm giving them a $20,000 book! Because they changed all the prompts without discussing it with me first, I have to redo all my work! I have to renegotiate!

After a call to the programmer, who was livid with my demand, and then a talk with New York, it was agreed I should go in to the city and talk things over. I went and told them that they could have the work I had done to date for the $8,000 or they could agree to $8,000 more, and I'd finish the full manual and incorporate the new prompts. After some tough talk, they agreed to think it over and let me know when I returned from my trip to St John.

Lisa and I left to spend nine days in St. John. It took a lot of control, but I did not let my panic over lack of money ruin my trip. Lisa and I had some wonderful times, and we had some awful times. The short version of the trip is that we were visiting the Virgin Islands in their rainy season and were almost carried off by mosquitoes that make Florida's look like midgets. To make things worse, a friend Lisa met asked me to sail his boat around to another beach. We were both almost carried out to sea in a sailboat that I had no business sailing. And finally, everything was so expensive, we had to eat at the canteen every day and spend our time taking lots of walks on the beach. Despite all that, we had a good time.

When I returned home, the people in New York had not yet come to a decision. I had some free time, and that was scary. It hadn't made sense to get work when I was already working so much, but now all of a sudden I was idle and on edge. That first morning after we got back from our trip, I awoke to a barking dog in my neighborhood. This had been a problem for months. I had finally had enough. I got up at 6:30 a.m. and walked around the block until I found the offending dog. He was barking his head off in the dark while his master was inside, sleeping. I knocked hard on the door several times and finally an older black woman stuck her head out and said, "What?"

"What?" I said angrily. "You let your dog out each morning to bark and wake up an entire neighborhood and you ask me, What? Lady, I am going to come to your door, and wake you up *every time your dog wakes me up*, that's what."

With that I left, and I never heard the dog again. Peace reigned. Letting off steam helped!

In July I heard from New York. They gave me the go ahead to finish the manual, so I immersed myself in work again, happy to do so. By August, I was broke again, because they had only given me a small part of the second $8,000. An unexpected solution appeared:

I had made an error in my checkbook and have $420 more than nothing! God is helping me out.

During my busy days, I still found time to make marketing calls, and they began to pay off. In August my Washington friend asked me to help on a Commonwealth Fund project. I was elated, mentally. Physically, my lower abdomen hurt a lot, and an old stomach ulcer started kicking up. By mid-August I had to go see a doctor, an expense that was certainly not planned in my budget. He told me I had an infection in the lining of my uterus. I started medication and kept right on working too hard. Luckily, the stomach ulcer responded well to a home remedy I was given: ¼ cup of orange juice, ¼ cup of milk and 1 packet of plain gelatin taken three times per day. Within days the ulcer pain was gone.

It was Hazel along with Dan and Randy who most often kept me sane during this time. Hazel was constantly providing lunch or dinner, knowing I had little money. She also was always encouraging me. I knew I could always go over, sit in her kitchen, and watch her serve her customers as I told her my story of woe or success, whichever it happened to be at the time. We had become friends and she trusted me.

On one of the first nights I had gone with Hazel to the American Legion bar, quite a party ensued. I wasn't much of a drinker, so she made it clear to one and all that they could buy me two beers, and that was it. Everyone gathered around Hazel to pay her homage, a custom in the black community I envy. They also were eager to tell me stories about Hazel, and one by one they would come up and share an event.

WHIM OF IRON

One man rolled up his sleeve and showed me a knife mark a good 8" long, and said, "Yup, Hazel done that. She didn't like how I was behaving, and she put a stop to a fight right quick."

Another man told of being thrown down her steep stairwell, a good 30 steps, because he tried to get a drink without paying! Others told stories, and it was amazing to me that all I heard in their voices was admiration and respect. I guess they couldn't afford to do otherwise. We made many visits to that bar together.

By September, things were going well. I was getting up by 4 to 5 a.m. to work on the user manual, which was ahead of schedule. My work with the Commonwealth was going nicely, and it was now just a matter of getting the bills out and waiting until the money came in. On September 3rd I recorded that I had $27 and was two months behind in my rent and bank loan. But, I also had $5,800 billed out and payable within the next two weeks. On September 9th, I worked 17 hours straight and printed out 278 pages of the manual that was due on that Monday. I also drove to Howard Hospital and got $1,300 for the medical staff analysis I had done in the midst of everything else. My meeting with the administrator was very interesting.

He told me that what he had learned from my analysis was that his heaviest admitting physician was taking his patients elsewhere. He recalled an incident they had had in the hallway one day when the physician had gotten angry with a decision the administrator had made. By the reports I had provided, he could see that

Cleo B. Robertson

soon after, the doctor had started admitting patients to a competing hospital. This event confirmed to me the importance of knowing what the medical staff was doing. It just fueled my passion!

Over the weekend, as I looked through the finished manual, I suddenly got a brilliant idea. Clients who were buying the telecommunications software were paying a statistical analyst big money to answer the prompts, study the analyses of phone line usage, and make recommendations. After writing the manual, I realized that if I reduced it to two pages of just prompts with branches to other prompts based on how the analyst filled out the form, a secretary could get online to Princeton University, enter the analyst's answers, and give him/her the reports. These reports would then be analyzed. This innovative solution would reduce the cost of running the program for the client by a large amount - and would make it easier to sell. I worked almost non-stop all weekend and finished the final two pages by Monday morning. I pushed the computer and software to great limits, and they did an impossible task in two days!

As I rode on the train to New York, I couldn't have been more proud of the large, black manual sitting in my lap, than if it was a new baby. A lot of hard work had paid off, and I would now receive a check for $5,000—I patted myself on the back, mentally. My client was very pleased with the manual and especially the two-page form. The check weighed heavily in my pocket as I rode the train back to Princeton. I also knew that writing user manuals was very hard work with little pay. I still hadn't found my niche.

WHIM OF IRON

My return trip yielded one other bonus that has helped me through the years. The man in the seat next to me turned out to be an electrical engineer. We started talking about computers, and I told him I had just bought one. I also confided that I didn't have a clue as to how they worked.

He smiled and said, "Well, let me tell you very simply how these electrical gadgets work. Picture a large corral with lots of cows inside and a closed gate. What happens when the gate opens? The cows go out the gate, don't they? But when the gate is closed, the cows can't go out, right?"

I nodded yes, but clearly did not get his point.

"Well," he continued, "a computer runs on electricity. When the gate is open, and electricity can go out, the computer reads the number 1. And, when the gate is closed, the computer reads the number 0. So if we say that the letter A is 00011000, then when the gate closes and opens in that pattern, the computer puts an A up on your screen. This is called Assembly language, and it is the basis for ALL program language. It's just the opening and closing of circuits that allows the computer to put things that mean something to us on the screen." [I've made up the numbers because I really don't remember what an A is in Assembly language and don't care!]

A smile crossed my face, he knew I got it, and from that point forward I felt I understood how my new friend, the computer, worked. It all boiled down to: don't pull the plug!

Cleo B. Robertson

On October 4th, Lisa and I loaded up the Celica for a long drive to San Diego. She had gotten a job in Los Angeles with an accounting firm, but she wanted to visit with her boyfriend before starting. I decided it would be a good opportunity for me to market my work in California and spend some time with my daughter, too. The fact that I couldn't afford to do business in California because of the distance and time difference never occurred to me. It was a long, flat drive across the United States primarily on Highway 10, and it was the first time I had seen that part of the country. We had fun sleeping in the car and changing off driving, so that within two and a half days, we were close. She decided that the night before arriving we would stay at a nice motel, which we did. She treated me to my first hot tub experience, which I thoroughly enjoyed!

During our long drive we had one experience that was a little mystical. We were driving on a long, flat road without any signs of life anywhere. I had begun to sing "Home, home on the range, where the deer and the antelope play," and just as I said those words, we looked up, and there on a mesa was a herd of antelope, the first I had ever seen! I thought it was a good omen. When we got to San Diego, Lisa's boyfriend showed us around and we enjoyed ourselves, even though the maze of highways left me numb. I enjoyed the beaches for walking, but they were nothing compared to my Florida beach.

I stayed with Lisa for over a month, all the while making visits to hospitals, private companies, and even a university, but no one understood what I could do for them. I never thought to pre-qualify potential clients or even seek out the right person within a company to talk with, before wasting time and energy. My company was too small, the technology too new, and I had no experience in how to sell myself. The experience however, was good for me. Toward the end of my time in L. A., I was getting pretty depressed and discouraged. I remember one afternoon walking to the strand in Manhattan Beach and wondering what to do. Should I give up and get a job? Should I try some other line of work? Should I? Should I? Should I? Should I…I felt like I was floundering. I was down to less than $2,000, and the insecurity of never knowing where the next dollar was coming from was getting to me. [I know I've said that before, but each time it was a surprise to me—what, no money?]

As usual, an angel led me to an answer. I walked into a drugstore by the pier, and looked through the paperbacks. I decided to buy a book, go lie on the sand and read all afternoon. I needed the beach and the sun. As I looked through the book titles, I noticed one that said something like, "Who become Millionaires and Who Stay Millionaires?" Being a millionaire had never been one of my goals, but the title intrigued me. I bought the book, went down to the beach, dug a little nest beside a sand dune and started reading. That book gave me direction for the rest of my business life—unfortunately, I have lost the title of the book, but here's what it taught me.

The book's author had conducted a twenty year study of high school students to see which ones would become millionaires, which ones would stay millionaires, and which ones would lose their millions.

The conclusion was that those who started out just to make millions often did, but they often lost it. Those who did what they loved, often made millions and kept it. The book cemented my mind—I would stick with health care, because I loved it, and the money would follow. Or so I hoped!

On November 3rd Lisa drove me to the airport. I had a mid-morning flight back to New Jersey. Because she had to go to work, she dropped me off several hours ahead of my flight time. I checked in then carried my portable computer (more luggable than portable) downstairs to a coffee shop to have breakfast. A businessman saw my computer and sat down at my table. We proceeded to have a delightful conversation about using the new technology to get our work done.

Suddenly, I heard my flight announced and I jumped up, grabbed my computer, and ran upstairs. He came with me, since he was leaving on a flight right after mine. When I got to the counter to present my ticket, I discovered I didn't have it. Nor did I have my purse. I was panicked. I ran downstairs to the restaurant, where I reasoned I must have left it on the seat next to where I was sitting, but it was gone. People helped me look, and we found my wallet in a garbage can, but no ticket. I ran back upstairs and told them my bags were already on the plane, and I must get on. The ticket agent said, "No problem. Give us your credit card, we'll issue you a new ticket, and if in three months the old one hasn't been used, you'll get a refund."

WHIM OF IRON

I said lamely and with some embarrassment in front of the other passengers, "I don't have a credit card." I added quickly, "I do have a check though."

"Sorry," he said, dismissing me. "We can only use a credit card."

I tried to argue. Finally he said, "Look lady, this flight leaves in three minutes. Either give us a credit card or move out of the way, please."

I started to turn and leave, when the businessman I had been talking with walked up and handed his American Express card to the ticket agent and said, "Give the lady a ticket."

The three agents at the counter all looked at him and said, "Are you crazy?"

He insisted, and I soon had my boarding pass. I quickly wrote a check for $239, and gave it to the man, assuring him it was good. As I got on the plane, I felt a mixture of relief, appreciation and thankfulness that good people do exist in this world.

Two weeks later I got a call from this man. He said, "Thanks. The check cleared and we're squared away. I just want you to know that someone did the same for me two years ago. That person told me that I could repay him by doing the same good deed for someone else, when I got the opportunity. I am very happy to have that obligation off my list, and now it's on yours!" I laughed and assured him I'd honor his request. It took me seven years to do a good deed of the same magnitude.

As soon as I returned home to Princeton, I learned that I had gotten a project with the Commonwealth Fund, thanks to the consultant with whom I had worked with before. That helped ease my financial panic, but my cash flow was simply not flowing. The bank was getting nasty again about my paying them something, so I gave them $1,000. After paying my utilities and rent for the month I'd been gone, I didn't even have the money to buy gas. Luckily, my stepson, Dan, was able to loan me some money. It wasn't until years later that an advisor told me I should have told the bank to go pound salt. What were they going to do? Take my old car? Take my old dog? Take old me? But, my values just wouldn't let me do it. Somehow I thought I should still try to save my credit rating, but in truth that had gone by the wayside long ago. I did finally pay the bank off, but it took several years. I'm very proud that I never did "stick" anyone for money in all my startup years.

In mid-November, I got a call from a man who worked for a hospital data collection service in New York City. He had heard from the administrator, whom I had met in Atlantic City, that I might be able to provide services to his company. Again, I borrowed money to take the train to New York, went to the company and saw their services, and wondered what on earth I could provide such a big corporation. At lunch it became obvious that he had no interest in my professional services. He wanted a date that evening. I was furious, said so and left. I now knew that my name was being passed amongst the men, presumably for them to see who could bed me. That was interesting to me, because as highly sexed as I was, I made a policy of not mixing sex and business. From then on I was much more careful about going "willy-nilly" to appointments until I had thoroughly checked out what the true purpose of the meeting was. I finally was beginning to ask the important question, "Do *I want* to go to this meeting or do this work?"

By December, financial prospects were limited to the Commonwealth job, and I was eating with my friend Hazel more often than not. I kept on marketing by making random calls to hospitals, following up on leads, but nothing came of any of it. I had not learned how to qualify a buyer yet.

During these hungry times, I discovered a new source of food and a life-long passion—wild mushrooms. I don't remember who taught me originally, but my diary notes that on December 1st I went mushroom hunting on Princeton University's soccer field and found a lot of big Puff Balls. There were so many, I took bags of them home and invited friends and family for a feast. We fried, baked, and sautéed them in butter—the latter turned out to be our favorite. An expert who had written a book on Puff Balls said there were no poisonous Puff Balls, so that became a favorite pastime—walking about Princeton looking for these delicious fungi. A friend cautioned me not to pick near highways or golf courses where they spray (they probably sprayed on the soccer field too, but I was too ignorant at that time to know better), and to stick to the woods when I could.

Cleo B. Robertson

The Christmas of '82 was bleak. The saving grace was that the children didn't have much money either, so we gave little things, mostly homemade, and enjoyed just getting together. I always enjoyed cooking and had become an expert at making delicious meals out of grains, vegetables, and fruit—I can honestly say we never ate badly. The blacks in my neighborhood, especially Hazel, also taught me tricks to making a dollar go further. Again, living where I did gave me a good support system and an education at a time when I really needed it. By this time I was spending all my spare time working on the computer. I loved figuring it out. My only hope, as the year ended, was that 1983 would be less stressful and more profitable.

1983 — A Wonderful Lady Appears

In January a wonderful call came from the Robert Wood Johnson Foundation. They wanted to interview me for a staff position. They knew my work because I had done projects for them with a Washington consultant. After a good talk and understanding of the position, we agreed that it wasn't for me. I knew that I would not work well in a large corporation where there were other priorities than "getting the job done." I very much appreciated that they even interviewed me, because I had no degrees and that was one of their requirements. The interview helped my ego but not my pocketbook.

Out of desperation, I started watching the local want ads and found one for a telemarketer. I knew that was simply a telephone job. At this point I didn't care. I needed income. I called, was interviewed, and the next day, hired. Finding people to do that kind of work was tough and only paid $10 per hour, so I knew they were just glad to get a warm body. I went for an orientation to the product—some kind of consulting for manufacturing efficiency—and was totally bored in minutes. I accepted, however, and started that same day. One good thing, I had flexibility in my hours, which meant I could continue to market my services. I still spent several hours every day calling potential clients and trying to market my business. There seemed to be a market for installing and setting up computers. The first company I approached, a car repair shop, could see how useful a database of their inventory would be, but didn't want to pay for one. I also contacted computer supply stores to see if they needed trainers, but I was overqualified for what they wanted, which was another way of saying they didn't want to pay.

I tried to present myself as able to do *anything* and *everything,* as is often the case with people starting their own business and having a hard time getting going. I contacted Mathtech and IBM for writing manuals, ETS for installing and training on computers, as well as every software development firm in the newspaper and yellow pages. I needed to see if I could write documentation. At the same time I was still working with a subsidiary of the New Jersey Hospital Association marketing their emergency room system. I hadn't yet learned to read the "buy" or "no buy" signs of clients. I spent way too much time trying to get data processing people to see how I could help. After a lot of effort, I finally understood why they didn't want my help—they were worried about the security of their own jobs.

Medical staff analysis was not an easy sell either. My contention that physicians brought in the money, oversaw the spending of money, and therefore should be held accountable for their actions, did not sit well with administrators. The fact that such self-scrutiny would protect the physicians in lawsuits, meant little to them. Although they agreed with me in theory, helping physicians manage themselves was not something they were interested in.

On several of my projects I had run into Mitch, a gifted journalist/writer who also became a very good friend. He and I started talking computers. By this time, my knowledge had grown considerably. He was intrigued with the thought of using a computer, but he was also hesitant for a zillion reasons, just like so many others. We spent several afternoons going to stores and looking at computers, but it would take him several years to actually buy one. The benefit of computer shopping with Mitch was that it taught me what I *didn't* want to do for a living! As much as I enjoyed trying to teach people, there simply was too much resistance in 1983. The friendship, however, was to last for years and have a significant impact on my business later in the '80's.

My personal life was an interesting blend of family, a few loyal friends who didn't get bored to death over my constant talk about business, and my uptown friends in bars, stores, and restaurants whom I frequently visited. There was a bar/dance place on Nassau Street I would frequent often. I would go in, have a beer, dance alone for thirty minutes, and then go home.

Cleo B. Robertson

By mid-March I was desperate for money again. I went to the Red Cross to explain to the manager how I could set up a computer so they could track who gave blood, their blood type, etc. He said it sounded good, but they simply had no money for that kind of information. Two hospitals were on my marketing list for over a year—Princeton Medical Center and Hunterdon Medical Center—but nothing ever came from either one. Both had their own strong in-house information systems people, and they simply didn't think I could be useful.

By this time I had learned about product shows, computer shows and trade shows all over New Jersey and Pennsylvania. Each one had an entrance fee, and I would stand all day on the floor demonstrating databases of medical staffs, employees, inventory—you name it—but there was no interest. I thought the Chamber of Commerce would be a good source of contacts, but there, too, I was a strange sight in the midst of traditional service providers. It would pain me sorely to add up how much money I spent on these product shows and trade shows that didn't go anywhere. Thompson Land Company, whom I had worked for years earlier, was receptive to having me do a sample list of their properties on my computer. They wanted to see purchase price, date of purchase, sale price, date of sale, acreage, etc. by site. I did it, and they paid me a minimal amount for my time, but they didn't feel that it was useful or that they could keep it up to date. Years later they became totally computerized.

A consultant friend again saved my life, this time with a project located in Washington, D.C. The thing I liked most about going to Washington was visiting with my brother, Tommy, and his wife, Sandra. They were both very interesting people and very interested in and supportive of my business. They were the only people at the time with whom I could talk and receive constructive advice. And, for a long time, they didn't find me boring. They had a small apartment, and I slept on the couch. They were easy to be with and gave me a sense of belonging to a family. The Washington project however, lasted just a few days.

As I started back to Princeton after this short project, disaster hit. I had gotten behind in my Shell credit card payments, but they had agreed to a payment plan. Before getting on the highway as I left Washington, I decided to fill my tank and went into a gas station right outside the city limits. Before putting gas in, the attendant took my card and ran it through a machine. He came back and said that he could not give me gas and could not give me my card back because Shell had reported that I had bad credit. I was devastated. I begged with the attendant, but he explained that the owner got a bounty for each such card he could collect. There was no way he would give the card back. I had $15 on me, so I got that much gas and drove the rest of the way home, hungry, and very scared.

Going to marketing appointments was my only way of getting business; without a car, it would be impossible. The daily struggle to find gas money added a lot of stress. I never fail to appreciate these days when I can pull into a station and afford to fill up my tank.

I was literally having a love affair with my computer by this time. Learning how to make it store data on a physician for instance, then designing reports to answer questions, was a big thrill to me. I loved to see 150 physician names neatly printed with their department, specialty, number of admissions by year, and change in admission patterns over time. The spreadsheet (Lotus) that I used was important software because I could keep my checkbook in it. I had spent hours designing a checkbook manager to run quickly and efficiently and give me the reports I needed to understand my cash flow. Never mind that I had little or no cash flow, the challenge of figuring out the computer was a constant source of delight (and frustration!).

Finally realizing I couldn't sell myself, I hooked up with a Princeton firm that had developed an accounting package. Weeks of learning to use the software, giving feedback to the company on bugs, and marketing the package turned up nothing. People were just not ready. In addition, the company did not appreciate my finding bugs in the software (a "bug" is when the software is supposed to do something and doesn't or it does something it shouldn't). They simply didn't want to know about the bugs because development seemed to go on forever, and they needed to sell the product. This company in particular resented when I told them that something didn't work right and how to fix it. They felt I was a little nobody who was trying to tell them how to do their work. I was.

Most of the software I used in the early years was full of bugs and poorly designed. I wasn't a techie. I was a businessperson who just wanted to get my work done, efficiently.

The best example of this kind of resistance was the first database software I used that was designed by a Ph.D. in Princeton. I was using it to enter all the data on doctors and then print reports. In the first few weeks of learning it, I found 36 bugs. Each time I would call the company and talk to the programmer. Ed would make the changes and give me back an updated disk to use. One day I got a call from the woman who had sold the software to me, and she informed me that I could no longer expect support on the product because my time had run out. I told her I was finding bugs. She was insulted and hung up the phone. Well, Ed and I worked out an agreement whereby I would call his personal number, give him the bugs; he'd fix them and then deliver me an update from time to time without anyone knowing. I was improving their product, but they didn't see it that way. The only reason I continued to do this was to get what I wanted from the software—reports and graphs, primarily.

About this time, an administrator whom I had met through mutual hospital friends called and wanted to know if I was going to the Middle Eastern Hospital conference in Atlantic City in May. I lied and said I was thinking about it. He said he'd like to get together and talk. He was new at his hospital, and he thought what I was doing might be useful to him in understanding his medical staff. I agreed eagerly, as my mind projected charts and graphs that would give him a valuable view of his staff at all levels. I didn't have the money to go to the conference nor stay overnight in a $90-a-night hotel, but as usual, I saw these as small obstacles. When the day came, I threw an old fake sheepskin blanket and pillow in the back of my car and made the three-hour drive to Atlantic City. When I got there about 5 p.m. I was hungry, so I checked with the administrator's hotel and was told he would not be available until the next day. I was dressed for the conference, so I walked along the boardwalk until I saw a hotel where a conference was being held. I didn't know what kind of conference it was, and I didn't care. I went up the escalator until I found a hospitality suite by following the sound of loud voices. Without any hesitation, I went up to the delicious dinner buffet and helped myself to a little of everything. Someone eventually asked me what kind of hospital beds I sold, and I said I didn't. Period! The man left me alone to eat.

About 6 p.m. when there was still daylight, I decided it was time to find my sleeping quarters for the night. The way I figured it, Atlantic City was a beach town and I had grown up in a beach town. I certainly could find some place to sleep for the night without cost. I got in my car and started driving south on the main road, going strictly by instinct. My odometer said I had gone five miles from the main road when I turned right on a whim. Then I turned right again and sure enough, I came upon a desolate area along an inlet. There were no buildings or regular roads that I could see as I stood on the bank. As if God had known I was coming, some boat had dumped a load of straw in the water, and there it was, drying at the edge of the waterway—a perfect mattress. I walked around and made sure the spot would be comfortable. Then I walked into the woods nearby to see where I could park my car. I didn't want the police or vagrants to know I was sleeping on the bank.

Realizing I would be returning at night, I laid sticks and stones along a path from where I would park my car to where I would set up my bed. Once all that was done, I drove back to the main road, changed my clothes in a gas station, and then went to the conference again to see if I could meet up with the administrator. He wasn't available, so I just walked around to see what was happening. By 10 p.m. I was tired. I bought some take out Chinese food, and I drove back to my "room by the water," parked my car as planned, and followed my trail using the flashlight I had brought. I was soon spreading out my blanket on the straw. It was a lovely night. Stars were out and the water was rippling by. Silence was my only neighbor. I ate my takeout Chinese food happily, thanking God for such a lovely retreat.

In the morning I opened my eyes, and to my surprise, not 6" from my face, were two ducks looking at me with a lot of curiosity! The water had risen. An hour later, my bed would have been very wet. As I looked at these lovely waterfowl and saw the sunlight on the treetops, I knew that I had a better room than I could possibly have gotten for $90 at a hotel. After changing back into my business suit at the gas station, I went off to find another hospitality suite for breakfast.

Cleo B. Robertson

At noon, I finally met with the administrator. We walked and talked, and in about 30 minutes I realized that he had no idea what I could do, nor did he care. He was fishing around about wanting to meet up with me later on. Bummer. I closed the meeting and left soon after, so that I could get home to Princeton before rush-hour traffic. It took a long time for me to have the skill to know how to distinguish between a potential client and a hot crotch.

By June, I was again desperate. Fortunately my consultant friend called again and wanted to do another project in Washington. I drove down and stayed with my brother and his wife again. I was planning to leave for Princeton the next day, and the project was to take only two days. The night before I was to leave, I got a phone call. It was my Aunt Peg, my mother's sister, whom I had not talked to nor seen in many, many years. She very briefly told me that her husband of fifty years (my Uncle Harry) had died, and she wasn't doing well mentally. She had been told by the administrator of her retirement community that she either had to get a family member to come help take care of her or they'd have to put her in a special care unit. She made no bones about the fact that I was the last person on her list. She had always disliked my mother, jealousy being the prime reason, I suspect, and she certainly didn't like having to ask one of her sister's children to help her out. Desperation alone had driven her to find me. Both of her sons were busy elsewhere furthering their careers.

What the heck, I thought. Maybe a few days of support and caring, and she'd be just fine. I had my luggable computer, a serviceable car, and plenty of time. I said I would go down for a few days. I had never been to North Carolina, so I saw it as a mini-vacation. Within two days, I set off and enjoyed every mile of the drive to Chapel Hill. My aunt was living in Carol Woods, an upscale retirement center. When I saw her for the first time, it was quite a shock. She was a distinguished looking woman with soft, wavy, pure white hair and perfectly dressed in every way. Only her eyes gave her away. They were wild and erratic. I could tell that the jolt of Uncle Harry's death had taken the very earth out from under her feet. She was living in a very nice home on the edge of the acreage. I could see that she would definitely be a challenge. She had never made a decision on her own in her life. Harry had not only made all the decisions, he paid all the bills, and he decided where they would go on vacations, etc., etc., etc.

I could see that Aunt Peg was scared to death, but that was no problem to me. I had been trained as a Gestalt facilitator and felt up to the challenge…but it would take some time. I talked with the administrator of the Center. I told him that I would have to stay at least six weeks. He didn't hesitate to agree to bend the rules. Peg and Harry had been charter members of the Center. I went back to Peg and told her I needed time to go home and put my life in order. She agreed to pay me $1,500 for the six weeks I said I could stay with her, which would take care of my immediate problems of rent and utilities. It seemed to me that we would both benefit, so I agreed to return on August 1st.

Cleo B. Robertson

The drive home from Chapel Hill to Princeton was a long one with lots of mixed thoughts. I wasn't sure I was doing the right thing. Leaving at this time would stop marketing completely. The $1,500, though desperately needed right now, was not very much for six weeks' commitment. The thought of living with Peg for that length of time wasn't terribly appealing either. But in the end, none of these considerations made any difference. She was my aunt, she needed me, I would go. It was the least I could do for a member of my family. When I got home, I pulled together all the notes and written pages on the book that I had being writing called <u>Sisters in Madness</u>. If I was going to go away for that long a period of time, I would at least be able to write.

Early in July, I got a call from my brother. He had been hired to put together a study of the natural resources of sixteen South American countries. Did I want to put them in a database and print reports for him for $1,500? Of course I did. So on the 15th I headed back to Washington in my car with my computer, and in a last minute decision, my son Randy. He wasn't doing anything, he'd never been to Washington, and I thought it would be fun for both of us. Taking Randy turned out to be a Godsend. The data for the project was contained in many different books with lots of different assumptions built into the numbers. There were footnotes that had to be taken into account as well as different groupings of resources. For instance, one country might list coal, oil, and gas under one column called "fuel," while another might list them separately, each in their own column.

WHIM OF IRON

Randy volunteered to help. He would sit and question the validity of the data until we felt comfortable we both understood it, and then I would enter it into the computer. All the data had to be consistent or I wouldn't be able to print out any reports of value. We worked for nine days on the project and ended up with clean, usable data and very interesting reports. My brother was very pleased with our work. I was very pleased with how well my son and I worked together. I came to respect his ability to think and read data.

Between hours of work, we managed to squeeze in some sightseeing and had great fun going to all the monuments, enjoying a hot air balloon show, and visiting the Smithsonian. When we got back to Princeton, I got ready to leave for Chapel Hill. I paid bills with the money from the Washington project, but I was so far behind in SBA payments, I decided to call and see what I could do. They were very nice to me, and said that they would move the money I owed to the end of the loan, and I could just start paying again as soon as I had income. That sounded wonderful to me. What they were actually saying was that they would add the payments *as an additional loan* to my present loan, and I would pay interest on it, all over again. I didn't feel I had any choice.

My stepson Dan was going to live in my Princeton house and take care of the mail etc., as well as my dog, Max, for the six weeks I would be in North Carolina. I said goodbye to the few friends I had, and I was on my way. The drive down was lovely, and I could see that North Carolina was a very beautiful state with lots of different topography. My head was full of fantasies of finishing the book, and selling it for big money, meeting someone, and falling in love or getting a big project with the retirement home where Peg lived. The truth turned out to be much better than fantasy.

The first day settling in with Peg was very strained. Peg was not sure she was glad to see me but she knew she had no other options. I moved into the one bedroom in the small house and slept in her dead husband's bed located right beside Peg's. We started living just like Peg and Harry had lived for 50 years. "Honey, don't you think it's a little chilly," meant that I was to turn up the heat. "Honey, aren't you hungry?" meant I was to get us something to eat. Within one day, I knew that I had to break this habit and get her to start making her own decisions, or she would never be able to live alone. She told me of her life with Harry, which consisted mainly of playing bridge or golf, traveling, raising their two sons, and taking care of the home (but not the bills). At lunch on the first day, I knew she had something on her mind.

She started to tell me about her two sons and grandchildren, and then shot to her point—"Cleo, don't expect to inherit anything because of what you're doing for me. Everything I have is going to my children."

I was hurt, of course, because inheriting something had never occurred to me, but I let it go. I assured her that was not why I was helping her. I don't think she ever did understand that I did it because we were family.

On the third night when I was sound asleep, I awoke to a terrified scream. I jumped out of bed. There was Peg, running up and down the hallway, screaming like a banshee. My Gestalt training kicked right in—I understood that she was just expressing her horror and anger at being alone after all these years, and that she needed to be able to let go, to feel her loss, and to feel how alone she was. I decided to do what I was trained to do—help her get her emotions out—so I ran along with her and encouraged her to yell more, "Great, Peg, good, yell more, YELL LOUDER!!!" I started yelling with her, and although she was surprised, she did continue for a few minutes. Soon she was spent, lying down on her bed, and collapsing into a flood of tears. The dam was broken. This was the only episode we ever had. After that, she began to cope a little better each day, and she knew that nothing she did was going to shock or upset me.

Within a week, however, I recommended to the administrator of the complex that Peg be moved into an apartment. She didn't cook, she didn't clean, and she simply couldn't manage alone after I left. He agreed, and they soon located a very nice apartment bordering on the woods, but close to the dining hall so she could walk to breakfast, lunch, and dinner. By this point she was beginning to make a few decisions. One thing she wanted to do was to get some new furniture and lamps. Everything she had, she and Harry had brought with them. Some of it was pretty shabby. She wasn't up to going shopping, so she asked me if I would buy chairs, couch, lamps, paintings, and other amenities that I thought she would enjoy. She gave me a budget for the apartment, and I picked out wallpaper, and had the place redone. She had a bedroom, living room, storage room, and small kitchen with a balcony facing the tall evergreens that lined the facility. I even got her a new telephone that was push button instead of rotary (which took ages for her to adjust to).

On moving day, I supervised the placement of furniture and got everything set up. When she walked in the door for the first time, every picture was hung, the new lamps shone, and the soft wallpaper welcomed her. She was quite surprised and pleased with how lovely the place looked. I don't think in the fifteen years that she lived there, that she ever moved a thing—she lived in it just as I arranged it.

I spent my days taking care of her affairs. There was a large 1957 white Cadillac that had to be sold, legal papers to be reviewed, and estate taxes to be explained. Slowly over the weeks, things got sorted out and she started to calm down. Each morning I would fix breakfast, but for lunch and dinner we would dress up and go to the Dining Hall with all the other residents. Carol Woods is an upscale facility so the dining hall had good food, lovely flowers, and original handmade quilts on the walls—in other words, it was fine dining. In the beginning, Peg loved getting together with friends she and Harry had shared, but over time, she found single women who shared her love of bridge. She adjusted quite well.

For me, living on the campus of a retirement community was quite interesting. Anyone under 55 years of age was an employee. The residents were ex-professors, businesspeople, lawyers, and other higher-ups in society who had done well enough to be able to afford coming to Carol Woods. They accepted me, and I was invited, along with Peg, to cocktail hour from 5 to 6 at another resident's apartment. A cocktail or glass of wine would be served along with simple nuts or little sandwiches. I was very interested in what these older people had done with their lives and what they could teach me. One Duke professor had written the definitive guide to Puff Ball mushrooms, and he shared an evening with me, instructing me in the varieties of Puff Balls and clear identification of the more delicious ones. There were investment people who shared their knowledge of the stock market and botanical professors who shared their knowledge of the gardens around the grounds. I took long walks in the mornings and enjoyed seeing them working in their private gardens — growing huge, healthy plants, because they had all the time in the world to give the lettuce, tomatoes or corn the love they needed to grow.

My evenings, however, were quite a different matter. Once Peg and I had returned from dinner about 8, she would soon go to bed, and I would immediately set up my portable computer on the dining room table and start writing on my book.

On a few occasions, I took the Cadillac and went to town. I had no interest in meeting anyone, no energy to go dancing, and little possibility of meeting friends. Writing filled my private life ... writing and Elton John. He had just put out a tape called "Too Low for Zero." For six weeks I listened to that one tape again and again and again. At times I felt crazy for not getting a job, for not looking for a man, and for having such a passion for computers, data, and writing. While I was feeling crazy, the people of Carol Woods gave me respect and encouragement. They appreciated what I was doing for my aunt, and they respected what I was trying to do with my business. My association with them continued for many years after I left Carol Woods, and I always appreciated the time we shared together.

On September 6th, just days from when I would leave to go back to Princeton, Peg and I went to dinner like every other night. After dinner, she asked me to take her down to the Post Office next to the dining hall so she could check her mail. She was in a wheelchair by this point because her legs and hips were weak. After she had checked her mail she suggested we go sit in the lounge for a little while.

As we sat there, a very bouncy, full-of-life woman walked up and said, "Oh, hello, you must be Peg's niece."

"Yes," I responded, putting out my hand, "I'm Cleo Robertson."

"Well, Cleo Robertson," she said as she held my hand, "and what do you do?"

In one sentence I said "hospitals," "computers," and "management" and she immediately said, "Well, I have someone you must meet, but I'm in a rush now. I'll call you later this week."

Peg explained to me that Jane was head of the Department of Botany at Duke University, and that she was working on a book showing the medical communities' opinion of various herbal remedies. She left almost immediately, so I took Peg back to her house and didn't think anything more of it. The next afternoon about 4 o'clock, Peg's phone rang, and she told me with great surprise in her voice, that it was Jane P. for me. I took the phone.

Jane said, "Cleo, can you come to my house for dinner tonight? I have someone from Duke University Medical Center I would like you to meet."

I said, "Yes", immediately—I was never one to turn down an adventure.

I was excited to be recognized as someone who knew something. Aunt Peg was astounded they thought I knew something. Peg arranged for someone else to take her to dinner, and I dressed very casually with my very limited wardrobe. Off I walked to Jane P's house several blocks away. Her house was lovely, with flowers all around and beautiful plants gracing the entry. She had never married and had moved to Carol Woods for safety and friendship. Inside, I met Jane Elchlepp, a craggy-faced, imposing woman in her 60's. She had a presence that I felt immediately. Jane E. directed the conversation for a few minutes, establishing what I had been doing for the past two years, and then we sat down to a wonderful dinner. We chatted about everything from mushroom hunting, to my three children, and to the bookbindery I had run. I was so flattered to have these two Janes asking me so many questions, I didn't find out much about them. After dinner, we got down to business. Jane E. started asking me details about the work I had done at the hospital consulting firm, about whether microcomputers could be used in hospitals, and what obstacles I saw to implementing them. We talked for four hours. It was one of the most exciting conversations about computers I had ever had, because it was specific to what I knew—hospitals, computers, and management.

How I got my assuredness that what I was developing was right and good and necessary, I don't know. But my passion was there. I had fervor. I had religion! And I let Jane E. know it.

When I left that night, I was very happy. Jane P. had told me that Jane E. worked at Duke University Medical Center, but that didn't mean anything to me. I only knew Northeast hospital names. Her title was Assistant to the Chancellor, but that, too, meant nothing because I had never heard the word Chancellor used in a hospital setting. All I knew was that one person had finally understood the vision I had for microcomputers in hospitals, and that was enough. I slept well that night.

In the morning, I received a call from Jane E. Aunt Peg was quite impressed that Jane E. had called me, but even more impressed when she learned that Jane had asked me to go to Duke, at $50 per hour, for a few hours that very afternoon to talk with her some more. I wondered what more we had to talk about. I also wondered why she was willing to pay this princely sum just to talk to me. I didn't hesitate for one

WHIM OF IRON

moment before saying yes. Dressed in a lime green, old-fashioned knit suit I borrowed from my aunt, and driving Jane P.'s car, I headed off onto the 15-501 highway with very specific directions as to how to get to Duke Hospital South in Durham, North Carolina.

As I saw the signs to Duke, I started to realize this was not just one of your general community hospitals. After driving to towns all over New Jersey, Pennsylvania and New York, I knew the difference between signs to a 200-bed hospital and a 1000-bed research/teaching hospital. As I turned into Duke's tree-lined property, my heart was beating fast. Before me was an enormous complex which continued to sprawl as I turned each corner. When I got to the security information box, I told the woman who I was, and she immediately waved me through. I felt so important. As I pulled into the circular driveway at the front entrance, Jane E. emerged. She had obviously been waiting for me. She was dressed in a white doctor's smock and directed me to park on the side as she put a sticker on my car.

Walking through the hallways of the old South Hospital, I could feel the respect of Jane's colleagues, as she confidently walked through double doors and welcomed me to the Administrative Suite. We went into her office, piled high with books, catalogues, computer gadgets, and paper. She beckoned me to sit next to her. She wasted no time. Since the evening before, she had been doing some thinking, she told me. For the next three hours she questioned me about physician data, hospital operations, departmental interdependencies, and finally about how computers could assist in each of these areas. I had no problem giving her my vision. I could *see* the data arranged neatly that would tell medical staffs how they were doing. I could *see* the reports that would tell administration how the hospital was doing. And, I could *see* the flow of information from one department to another to enhance efficiency and reduce costs. With great willingness and abandon, I gave her my visions.

About 4:30 p.m., Jane said to me, "Hold on, Cleo, there's someone I think you should talk with."

She left the office, and I sat, not knowing what was happening, yet knowing somehow in my gut that it would be good. She walked in a few minutes later and invited me to follow her to meet someone else. As I walked into his office, I remember being impressed. There was a big square tray on his cocktail table with sand in it, and a little rake. The room was casual, but somehow I knew big things went on in here. Bob was gracious, interested in my knowledge, and totally professional. In about two minutes we knew we liked each other. He was quick with a joke, and I loved every one of them. He was Jane's boss and second in command at Duke Medical Center.

Slowly we danced around the subject of hospitals, Jane staying pretty much in the background, with Bob asking me questions. I think Jane took me to that first meeting simply to see if Bob agreed with her choice for a project director. I have no doubt that if Jane said I could do the job, Bob would believe her. He talked about small hospitals and how Duke wanted to help them use the new microcomputer technology to compete. I agreed heartily and added some thoughts of my own.

Within half an hour Bob said, "Cleo, we have a project that needs someone to run it, and it looks like you might be the right person."

Without hesitation I immediately answered, "I am."

Bob looked at Jane, and then said, "Well, you go on back to Princeton, and let us do some homework, and then we'll get back to you within a couple of weeks with a contract." Nothing was said about money, time frame or scope of the project, and I didn't ask any questions. I didn't care. I just thoroughly liked being with two people who had the same interests at heart that I did. If they would hire me, I would work for them, and that was that!

I drove back to Aunt Peg's on cloud nine. When I told Aunt Peg what they had said, she seemed quite impressed—for the third time in one day! She then told me that Duke was the "Harvard of the South," and had a large endowment fund. Having never gone to college, none of that meant much to me. I was just happy to have people who understood me for once. I was anxious to use my skills and knowledge.

This all happened on a Friday, and I was scheduled to leave on Monday to go back to Princeton. Jane E. called and asked if I could stay a few extra days to attend a conference Duke was holding on microcomputers. Of course I agreed. I then decided that

Cleo B. Robertson

I was going to spend my last weekend in North Carolina camping on the Eno River—a wonderful, winding river that one woman had saved from development. Early Saturday morning I went to a local camping store and rented a tent, sleeping bag and lamp. After arranging a dinner partner for Peg, I took off about 8 p.m.

I got to the campsite in a totally deserted State Park just as darkness fell. I never realized how dark "dark" is. I began to set up the unfamiliar tent, which I was in the midst of doing, when I heard a noise that scared the heck out of me. The thought went through my head that if anyone or anything came to hurt me, I couldn't protect myself. I hurriedly looked for my flashlight... my knife... anything that I could use to protect myself... but darkness was all around me. My heart was in my throat. I was full of terror and ready to scream, when I remembered that I had a choice. I could choose to be scared or I could choose to calm myself. I slowed my breathing, searched my camping bag with my hand and found my flashlight. Blessed light, it instantly gave me a feeling of safety. Praying to God did help! My knife tumbled out of my grocery bag along with the three baking potatoes I had brought. By this time I was hungry, so I built a great fire, and in a very short time I was roasting a piece of fish and a potato, both wrapped in foil. I sat in the absolute darkness watching my dinner cook and feeling like I had really accomplished something—both at Duke and here in the woods.

That night, when I decided to go to bed, I heard noises all around me and I still felt scared. I tried to listen and identify the noises. At some point I fell asleep. When I awoke several hours later, I stood up outside my tent in the clearing near the fire, which had gone out. I looked up at the brightest, clearest sky full of stars that I had seen in many years. I went back to sleep and woke feeling like a new person in the morning. I had learned that I could make a choice to be scared or to stay calm, and I had chosen to stay calm.

After a breakfast of goat cheese with parsley on crackers, I went out on the rocks in the river to fish. After a few hours, it was evident that there were no fish or none that wanted my bait. Besides, if there were, I'm sure they knew I didn't really want to catch them. I just wanted an excuse to lie out on the rocks. I tried not to fantasize about the Duke project, but rather just be there in the woods, see the animal life, and rest my mind. In the afternoon, I lay in the cold river water, and then dried in the sun on the riverbank. I saw no one for three days. It was magnificent.

The conference at Duke during the following week was good for two primary reasons. First, Jane was introducing me to important people as though I was someone, and that felt wonderful. Secondly, after hearing professional after professional talk about computers and their application in the hospital setting, I realized that my knowledge was experiential, which was much more valuable than many of the speculative ideas being put forth. It occurred to me later, that Jane probably had taken me to the conference so she could see how I handled myself with the "people in the know" at Duke. I had no doubt I had done well. I attribute to my mother the fact that I have never felt "less than" anyone, even though I didn't have a degree or a penny to my name. Immediately after the conference, I drove home to Princeton and thoroughly enjoyed a great reunion dinner with Randy, Gary, Dan, Dave and friends they brought along. It was good to be back, particularly because I had an opportunity to do some really good work. It made me feel like I was finally starting to "make it."

Just before I had left for Chapel Hill, my first husband had written me a letter and said, "You know, Cleo, if you got a job you could probably make $14,500 a year, and that would give you enough to live on." He was right, but he didn't understand. I wanted to *do something*, not just make a living. As I sat talking to my family about the Duke experience, I was inwardly very glad I had held out for my dream.

On September 22nd I turned 45 and that same week a project from Mediq to do some coding using the ICD9 code list (International Classification of Diseases) came in. Again, cash flowed, though very gently. It was enough to help me pay the bills. I waited anxiously to hear from Duke. Finally I got the call from Jane E.

She said straight away and in a very matter of fact way, "Okay, we want you to do the project."

I tried to be casual. I tried not to let her know how much it meant to me, and yet I knew she knew. She immediately went on with the terms.

"We want you to come down to Durham for six months, and we'll pay you $24,000 for half your time, plus expenses," she said candidly.

Again, using as casual a business voice as I could muster, I said, "That sounds fair. What do you mean by half time, and what do you mean by expenses?"

She went on to detail the contract. Half time meant just that, half a day, five days a week. Expenses meant they'd pay for my hotel room for the six months plus all travel costs. I would pay for my own meals and personal needs. I could hardly believe it; they were being so generous. It wasn't until many years later that I learned they knew they had themselves a deal. Jane knew I wasn't capable of working half time on something if my heart was in it! Both Bob and she knew that $24,000 for six months' work was cheap by their standards. It was a win-win situation and that turned out to be truer for me than Duke ever dreamed.

Now I had to kick into high gear. My Aunt Peg loaned me $1,500 (which I repaid within two months), but there was so much to take care of in order for me to leave for six months. Dan agreed to live in the house again and take care of Max and most of the utility bills. Another project awaited me in Washington, which I eagerly took so I would have the money to buy some clothes. I had gotten by on one suit for two years because I seldom saw anyone twice in one week. Just before I drove to Washington, D.C. to do a quick project there, Jane called. She said they wanted me to attend a conference with the North Carolina

Hospital Association, which would also be involved in our project. She agreed to buy me a ticket from Washington to Raleigh/Durham, and then I'd return to Washington and drive on to North Carolina after my work was done.

The Washington project was easy and only took a few days, but at $50 an hour, it gave me extra money I needed. My brother drove me to the Washington airport, and I can still feel the utter disbelief of what was happening. I didn't question why it was happening to me; I just marveled that it *was* happening. Even my brother was impressed and that's saying something.

My friend Hazel was getting older and needed to slow down. I had mixed feelings about moving to Durham—did I have the right to leave people who needed me? I did leave anyway, but I took my guilt baggage with me.

I'm excited about doing public speaking and learning computers better and meeting people. I'm excited to have a full routine.

The first meeting with the North Carolina Hospital Association (NCHA) went very well. Everyone was exploring exactly what this project was. A foundation had given Duke a great deal of money to implement microcomputers at Duke, but part of the deal was that Duke had to, in turn, help out small hospitals around North and South Carolina with the new technology. The Hospital Association wanted to be part of the project because it would create goodwill amongst its members and make the smaller hospitals more likely to

WHIM OF IRON

join the Association. After hours of talking, it was finally decided to call it the Small Hospital Project, defining a small hospital as one with fewer than 250 beds. A large percentage of the Carolina hospitals fit this description. NCHA also agreed to coordinate meetings between the small hospital project and hospital administrators. We ended up choosing six hospitals, each with a little different need from the others. The plan was that Jane and I would go out to each hospital we thought suited to the project and identify their need for automation. We would then create a software program to meet that need. The truth of the matter was, none of us knew what we were doing, but all of our hearts were in the right place. The small hospitals needed help and had no money. This was a way for everyone to help; it was a project born of good intentions—and it actually succeeded.

The day after this meeting, Jane drove me to an HSA conference in the North Carolina mountains. HSA stood for Health System Agency, a new federal group that was to help implement health care policy change. By the time we arrived, I had a temperature of 102 degrees and was very sick, but I pretended (to myself and others) that I was just fine. I wasn't going to let a little cold take away my pleasure of being introduced as the new director of Duke's Small Hospital Project. It was a thrill that people wanted to know who I was and how Duke had found me. I'm afraid that my ego enjoyed being stroked so much, that I hardly learned who was who at the meeting. No matter. That came later, in great profusion.

Cleo B. Robertson

On October 21st I flew back to Washington and then drove home. I still had no credit card, so I was operating strictly on cash, but I had a little money in my pocket and great hopes were brimming around every dollar. The drive back to Princeton was long and I was still feeling ill. I saw a hitchhiker along the road, but I drove on past. Usually I would have picked up a hitchhiker to keep me company on the long drive. Over the years, I had done my share of hitchhiking when I needed to because my car was broken or I was too broke to take the train or bus. I didn't view hitchhikers as necessarily bad people out to kill me. Growing up on a tourist beach, I was a cautious soul who had learned to assess people pretty well. In all my years of driving, I never regretted picking up anyone. In fact, I learned from and enjoyed every one of them.

This time, however, I had driven on past because I was too tired to interact with anyone, but suddenly I realized that the man had a dog with him. It was raining, and I realized that the reason he had looked downtrodden was because he was dripping wet. I thought for a second about my very nice, clean car, and then I turned around at the next exit, and again at the next. I finally pulled up alongside the man and the dog. I got out and threw an old blanket that I kept in the trunk over the back seat, and told them both to get in. The man did as I said, with disbelief showing on his face. He dried off with a shirt of mine that was in the backseat and the dog munched on the leftovers of a sandwich.

Jim, as the hitchhiker introduced himself, was down on his luck. He had found the dog along his travels, and he hoped they were both going to better times. He told me wonderful stories about living in the mountains and mushroom hunting, his family, and how they had struggled, and about a marriage gone sour. His job in the mines had been discontinued and his unemployment exhausted. He had felt up against a brick wall until he had finally decided to hitchhike to New York and see if he could find a job there. He was going to stay with his brother.

By the time we reached Princeton, I knew I could not put the two of them out into the rain again. I drove to a motel that was low cost but decent and arranged for two nights' keep. I gave the man $20 for food and went off feeling very good about myself. There has never been any question in my mind that God is good to me, so I'm going to share that goodness with others. Besides, the trip home seemed to take half the time it usually does!

Anyone who has ever had hard times, then turned them around, will understand how proud I was to go around Princeton saying goodbye to all those who had watched me struggle and telling them about the project I had been hired to direct. It was validation. It was like proof that I hadn't been talking through my hat all that time. It was like being able to hold my head up high for the first time in a long time. And, it was pure heaven.

In no time at all, I had my Celica lift-back loaded down with everything I thought I'd need for six months. Family and a few friends gathered to say goodbye. As I drove off, my car looked like one of the pictures of the migrant workers as they move around the country finding work. My skill of leaving a place and not looking back helped me drive out of Princeton and get on the highway. Even though I knew it was only for six months, I also knew I would miss my family, my dog, my house, my neighborhood, Hazel and friends. I headed south, crying for sadness and crying for joy.

When I got to Durham, I followed Jane E.'s directions, and went directly to her house. As I drove up her gravel-lined, winding driveway through the woods, I had no idea what to expect. Jane P. had told me that Jane E. had built this house herself, subcontracting the plumbing, electrical, etc., out. The first sight that surprised me as I emerged from the evergreens was that of sixteen tree trunks, each 20' long, lying by the parking area next to a log splitter. The second surprise was a 25' x 4' x 4' swimming pool for doing laps. Already I knew this was not your average woman's house!

Jane's house was as remarkable as she was. She had designed it herself to take advantage of the 20 acres of woodlands bordering on Duke Forest, which she had bought many years ago. Large, 20' windows in the living room gave a breathtaking view in both summer and winter, with the natural wood walls covered with horsehair rugs she had collected in the southwest. This was the main room. All the other rooms—bedrooms, office, and kitchen—were totally in keeping with someone who doesn't care about decorating, cooking or daily amenities. The living room was where she operated, and it was unusual, just like Jane. We decided it made sense for me to stay with her a few days while we sorted out my living arrangements. It was a heady time for me because I was with a real independent woman who did her own thinking and decision-making.

Jane was raised in and around Missouri, but she moved often as a child. Her father was an erratic man who made and lost millions, several times. Her life went from one of opulence to poverty year by year, and she changed schools often. In her final years before graduating from high school, she and her mother lived with Jane's grandmother, and there was no money to speak of. How she worked her way through college, getting two degrees along the way—a Ph.D. and an MD—is not all clear to me, but she did it. Her friend, Jane P. was the one who brought her to Duke, first as a planner. She did such an outstanding job that she was soon working for the chancellor. She worked so long and hard for Duke that sometimes they would find her passed out in the hallways in a diabetic coma. When a new hospital was needed to bring Duke into the new age of medical care, it was Jane who was sent around the world to see what other facilities were doing. There is a bronze plaque in the very lovely main lobby of Duke Hospital North with a dedication to Jane Elchlepp—without her, no one felt that the hospital would have ever become a reality.

Jane never married and didn't seem much inclined towards men except as friends. She had some very good men friends, however, but not many women friends. Jane was a very masculine woman and too bright for most. She and I got along because she knew I totally respected who she was, her values, accomplishments and mostly, her heart. And, it was reciprocal. Over the years, Jane and I never had a falling out. Major differences occurred twice, but in each instance she deferred to me, and I proved myself correct in the long haul, which I think she knew would happen. She had a great ability to let people do what they felt they needed to do, even if she didn't agree.

Each day that I spent with Jane, I learned to question more, to think more clearly from a decision-maker's point of view and to stick to the basics. We saw our differences; we also began to see our similarities—honesty, hard work, caring about outcome, accountability, and professionalism. We were both glad to have a new friend. The second day she took me to the Hilton Hotel near Duke to see about a room for six months. The cost was outrageous and even though the Foundation would have paid the bill, I simply couldn't see spending that kind of money to live in a *hotel*! I suggested Jane check on graduate housing. At Princeton University, I knew that many visiting people were given this type of place to stay and it was very economical. Within a day, Jane had arranged for me to see a place on Alexander Road right near the campus. As soon as I saw the apartment with kitchen, bathroom and living room/dining room combination, I knew it would work for me. Jane made a phone call, and on my third day in Durham, I moved in. I loved working with people who had such power to get things done…now!

My first weekend on my own was occupied with unpacking, nesting, grocery shopping, finding my way around and generally getting settled. I didn't have time to feel lonely. On Monday, Jane met me again at Duke and took me to my office—a very nice room about 50 feet from hers and just as close to Bob's. There was something unreal about all that was happening. Here I was with my own office, working at what I now knew to be one of the most prestigious medical research and teaching schools in the country and working alongside professionals of the highest level. I loved it and I was scared to death. Most of the time, however, I was so busy I didn't allow myself to think about it.

Of course, disaster was bound to happen...I was having so much fun. About the fifth night in my new apartment, I was working on my computer, which I hadn't taken to the office yet, and got up to get a cup of tea. As I was returning to my table, I noticed that the printer plug was almost falling out of the computer socket, and I pushed it in quickly. There was a flash of electricity, and my whole computer went dead! Oh, God, I thought, what have I done? I called friends in Princeton, Washington, and Durham over the next day, and it sounded like I had blown the circuit board. Quite an auspicious beginning for a computer wizard, right? In fact, I had only blown a $2 fuse, but it was months before I found that out, and probably just as well I didn't know, for reasons that would soon be obvious. This was one of those "there are no mistakes" times.

Somewhere in my travels during my Gestalt years I had heard the expression, "There are no mistakes." When I first heard it, I thought back on all the mistakes I had made in my life—not going to college, two divorces—the list went on and on. I wondered how anyone could think there were no mistakes. Of course there were. But slowly over the years, the expression had stayed in my head, and I had begun to see that every choice I had made added a new dimension, perhaps an unexpected or painful one, but nevertheless one that helped me move along my path towards where I was at that very moment. And, there was no question I loved being at Duke and heading up this project! So, on the night that I blew up my computer, and during the ensuing days of frustration and fear, I kept saying, "there are no mistakes," over and over again in my head. Why did this happen? What will the result be?

On Thursday, with great trepidation, I told Jane what I had done to my computer. The smile that spread over her face shocked me. Her words did not. "Well, thank goodness. You're on a CPM-based system and we're going to do this project on a DOS-based system, and I didn't know how I was going to get you to switch. Now I do!" That very afternoon we went looking for a new computer, and by Friday afternoon, I was the proud (albeit a little intimidated) owner of a brand new Compaq portable computer. My first night at home with it, I felt totally overwhelmed and bewildered. I had been hired for a project because of my computer knowledge, and here I was, a beginner. How could they pay me if I didn't have my skills anymore? I still thought my work was my worth. I didn't realize it was my knowledge Duke had bought.

Tuesday was my first real day of work, but I found trying to work on my new computer and to think in the chaos of a busy office, very distracting. Phones were ringing, people were in and out—some to see me, others just to see who was in the new office— and each time that I would start to understand or get organized, there would be another disruption. Jane and I met several times over the week, discussing our project and how to set it up. Mostly, however, she left me alone to get used to my new surroundings. No one was in any rush to begin a project that was still very fuzzy in our minds. The computer came with a manual that was written, if not in good English, at least in readable English. When the weekend came I spent all day and night, both Saturday and Sunday learning the disk operating system, DOS. It was so different from what I was used to. At first, I felt I couldn't learn it. But by Sunday I was sorting files, copying, renaming and viewing files easily. I even taught myself how to write a batch file (a little program) that would sort my directories automatically.

Suddenly I said to myself, "Cleo, what are you doing in this sterile office when you could be comfortably working in your little apartment?"

At about 4 p.m. on Sunday, I walked out the front door of the hospital, portable in hand, and not one security guard stopped to ask me what I was doing. I soon had my small, round dining-room table set up for work, and I continued teaching myself late into the night. Life was starting to get sane.

By Monday morning when I took my new computer to Duke's Micro Information Systems Department, I was ready for my new word processing, spreadsheet and database software. By Thanksgiving time I had learned more about those three packages than most people would ever know. For whole days and nights I practiced, practiced, practiced until I understood the *logic* of the programs. Once I got that, I could make them do anything. Because this small hospital project was to find ways to use microcomputers to help them, I felt I needed to know everything the software could do. For the first time in quite a while, I was feeling totally in control of my new computer and all my new software. There was a lot more to learn, but I was well along the path.

Jane had set up a meeting with the General Services Department and Information Systems Department to discuss the Small Hospital Project and what we were going to try to do. One afternoon we were all seated around a large table, about eight of us. Jane asked Tom, the head guru of microcomputers at Duke, what he thought were the most important qualifications for a good microcomputer user to have. We wanted to identify one at each hospital to manage the computer we were confident they would want to buy.

He said, "Well, first of all, of course, they should have a college degree."

Jane looked at me, and those who knew I didn't have one, looked around the room uncomfortably.

I finally said, "We'll put that one aside for now. What else do you think they need to have?"

After quite a bit of discussion, it was agreed that a user needed communication skills, organizational skills, and hopefully a good working knowledge of whatever application he or she was using. [An

WHIM OF IRON

application is a task—accounting, word processing, personnel, banking, email, etc.]

It turned out that each of the hospital people we worked with knew what they wanted to get done and what they needed from the software. Their experience and their ability to communicate their needs turned out to be the most valuable asset. My not having a degree never proved to be a problem. My lack of political savvy also never proved to be a problem. Jane backed me 100 percent through some pretty tough times. Bob backed me, too, and as Assistant to the Chancellor, his backing was invaluable.

Once we had gotten a team together, consisting mainly of Mike, a very experienced PC user and developer, Jane, and myself, we were ready to further define the project. Bill, another Duke programmer, was very helpful in assisting in the design of the project, as was Tom, the head of PC computing at Duke. Over several weeks we talked daily about what we could do to impact small hospitals positively. We decided to meet with all the top health care people in the state, to see what they felt the hospitals' needs were. We also decided that Jane and I should meet with the administrator at each of the six hospitals we had chosen to see what they felt their needs were. Everyone agreed that we had to have administrators who were on the leading edge or they wouldn't be willing to allocate resources for our project. A very busy time was in full swing!

The first state healthcare official we worked with was Barbara, who was then head of health planning for

Cleo B. Robertson

North Carolina and an innovator if there ever was one. I liked Barbara immediately. We had great conversations about health care needs. Ruth was also very helpful. Ruth had been analyzing numbers to identify trends for the state for many years, so her view of what was needed was most important. We also met with Ed, president of the North Carolina Hospital Association, and one of the more progressive presidents in many ways. It was Ed who paved the way into the hospitals for us. Ed assigned Bill to our project. Bill had been around for a long time and was very supportive of what we were trying to do. After many discussions with health care professionals, the project started to take form. It was agreed that I would go out and interview administrators and let them tell us what they needed. We settled on six hospitals. How did we possibly think we could do six projects in six months? I don't know, but it clearly was an overconfident aspiration. In the end we did six, but it took us two years.

Our first visit to an actual hospital took place just before Christmas. Phil was the administrator of Good Hope Hospital, a 10-physician facility that had both inpatient hospital beds and a long-term care unit. It was very rural, very poor, and very anxious for any help we could give. Phil was one of the more progressive administrators of the day, embracing new technology whenever he could. He identified tracking of DRG (Diagnostic Related Group) classifications as his biggest priority. The DRG classification was relatively new, and it was a federal attempt to better utilize hospital beds and associated costs. I saw it as a way to get people out of hospital beds as soon as

WHIM OF IRON

possible. If you had a hip replacement, for instance, you might be classified with a DRG that allows a length of stay of five days. If you had a baby, your DRG might only allow three days; if you stayed for only two days, great. The hospital made money, because they got paid based on the DRG. But if you stayed longer, the hospital had to be able to justify it, or they did not get paid for the extra days. In a small hospital like Good Hope, it was critical that Phil have a program that would tell him as soon as a patient's DRG time ended. In retrospect, the timing of the project was perfect. Everyone wanted to use computers to save money, but they didn't know how. Jane and I would walk into a meeting, confident and experienced, and everyone was prepared to cooperate. They respected and liked Jane, and because they didn't know anything about computers, they accepted me as a guru of sorts. I didn't disappoint them.

By mid-December, I had met with three hospital administrators and had made appointments with three more—Alamance County, Iredell Memorial and Carteret General. I felt excited and in full control of the sprawling project. Jane and I had come to realize that we were biting off more work than we could accomplish in six months' time, but she didn't seem concerned. The foundation wanted us to help the small hospitals, so that was what we were going to do.

Between the meetings with hospitals and the meetings with Duke programming staff, my weekdays were busy (full time, by the way). In the evenings, I spent a lot of time learning software programs: Multimate, the word processor chosen by the programming staff, and

Lotus, a spreadsheet. Weekends were taken up with learning, designing, thinking, and mushroom hunting. Other than Jane, I had no friends. Most of the students living in graduate student housing were married, and I had little in common with them, anyway. I spent a good deal of time walking or biking around Durham and learning that I liked the sleepy little town. I lived in Durham very much like I had in Pass-a-Grille—walking around, talking to people, dancing and playing pool—who could ask for anything more?

An incident occurred one day that really impressed me with the culture of Durham. I had rented a bike and was riding down 9th Street. I had just turned a corner, when I saw an old man fall forward, hit his face on the sidewalk, and just lie there. I threw my bike down and ran to him, asking if I could be of help. He mumbled something to me and looked up and I saw blood on his face. People passing by said we should call the police, but the man became so upset, I told them no, I'd stay and get him home.

I helped him up and we found a nearby bench. As I wiped his forehead, I saw that it was only a small wound, thankfully. I held his hand while we both calmed down. I asked if he would like me to walk him home, he nodded yes and pointed towards Broad Street, one block away. I helped him up and we started walking past my bike. Then a man in a business suit who had been sitting in his car on the side of the road leaned out his window and said, "I'll wait here until you get back so no one takes your bike."

WHIM OF IRON

I was very appreciative but couldn't believe he would wait more than a few minutes. It took about fifteen minutes for me to get the man home, explain to his family what had happened, and then get back to my bike. Sure enough, there was the man sitting in his car, patiently. That was just the first of many such occurrences I had in this lovely Southern town. Nevertheless, other than a few shopkeepers I could say hello to, I didn't meet anyone I could call a friend. These were some very lonely times for me. Family and friends had been my best form of entertainment—cooking for them, talking, walking, and biking with them. To be so completely alone was very difficult.

When Jane brought me my first phone bill, she said something to the effect that Duke wouldn't be willing to pay these kinds of bills (it was for $600). I told her to tell Bob that this was for the cost of keeping me happy, and because I wasn't living in a hotel at quadruple the cost of my apartment, he could just consider himself lucky. Neither of them ever said anything again, and I kept it under $300 from then on. The phone calls to family and friends did help keep me sane. I called someone whenever I would get moody or blue, which on weekends, could be often. I always knew that when I called Hazel, she would be home, sitting in her recliner, happy to hear from me. I can still hear her voice say, "Hello Baby. Where are you?" She became my center. She was always full of wisdom and she would listen for any length of time as I described what I was doing. Even though she didn't understand most of it, she listened, said, "Uh huh," and then I didn't feel so alone anymore. Often she would remind me "It's a long lane that doesn't ever turn," or "Don't you get down now, girl. You know God's with you."

I wanted to spend Christmas with my family, so I decided to go home again for a visit. The drive to Princeton flew by. My head was so full of thoughts of programs, people, computer software, and my new community, that I hardly noticed it took eight hours. So much had happened in such a short time. How wonderful it was to be with my family again! Until I saw everyone, I hadn't realized how lonely I had really been at times. I had had no one to talk with, no one to hug or to hug me, and especially no one to laugh with on a regular basis.

Dan barbecued a 22-pound turkey on his Weber grill and it turned out to be the best I ever ate (it is still my favorite way of fixing a turkey). All the children came home to join in the celebration, and they were all happy to hear how well I was doing. They seemed to miss me as much as I missed them. It was a wonderful Christmas for me. I finally had the money to buy Lisa, Gary and Randy real gifts, and my stepsons, too. They, as always, gave me wonderful gifts, and we had good times together. Dan had put up a tree, and my dog was very happy to see me. It was good to spend time with Hazel, too, who was so very proud of me. I saw all my old friends, and they were proud of me, also, but still scratching their heads and wondering how this happened...Cleo's overnight success!

Hazel and I spent some good times together. She took me to her favorite bar, the American Legion, and it was fun seeing all the people I had met over the years. An incident happened on this visit that I shall never forget, nor will a few other people. One day in the mid-afternoon, I took Dan to the American Legion to have a beer and show him where Hazel and I hung out. When we walked in, the black men looked us over, and it wasn't with friendly eyes. We sat down at the bar, however, and I was sure they would remember me, at least. We ordered beers and they asked for Dan's ID. He showed it to them, but they started to give him a hard time. I soon saw that things were not going to improve, so I signaled Dan and we left. That evening I mentioned the experience to Hazel. Her eyes became slits for a second, and then she went on to talk about something else. On Sunday, Hazel suggested we go for a drink, so of course we went back to the American Legion. As she walked in the door, I could see that she was working herself into a fit. I tried to stop her to tell her I didn't care, but it was like trying to stop a steam engine.

She walked up to the bar, slammed her purse down, and said to the room at large, "Okay, who's the son of a b___ who wouldn't serve my friend a drink?"

The room went silent. The bartender, who was the culprit, looked at me and suddenly, understanding came into his eyes.

"Speak UP," Hazel bellowed, "or I'll cut your c___ -sucking balls off!" I tried to tell her it wasn't that important again, but she wasn't listening to me.

She said loudly for all to hear, "Listen to me, Baby. **No one, do you hear me, no one** treats my friends the way they treated you and Dan. That's not the way we treat people here."

By this time everyone had come around to see what was happening. I was so uncomfortable, I walked out the back and sat on a picnic bench to stay out of the heat. After about ten minutes, the bartender came out the back door and walked right up to me and apologized. He said he truly hadn't realized it was me. They didn't get that many white customers, and he said he was really sorry. I accepted his apology, of course. Things had calmed down, I was invited back in, and there were drinks all around. What I learned is that blacks discriminate as much as whites do. I also learned from Hazel that they have a lot of pride and sense of honor in their community.

All in all, 1983 was a pivotal year for me. I left home, again, but this time I went to Durham, North Carolina. I directed a project, successfully, and I loved the small town I lived in. Money was tight, but not like before. All in all, I was handling the Small Hospital Project well. That pleased me. Although I was quite lonely without my family around me, I had always said, if that's what it took, then that's what I'd do. And doing it, I was!

1984 — The Duke Project Begins in Ernest

As much as I had enjoyed the great reunion with family and friends, when January 10th came, I was eager to get in my car and drive back to Durham. I was on a roll and enjoying every moment of it. The six hospitals that Jane and I had targeted were each different, and each had its own priorities, and each perceived it needed something different. After many interviews, we identified the following software applications that we would develop for each hospital as required to complete the Small Hospital Project:

Alamance, a rural community hospital... Medical Staff Credentialing

Carteret General, a beach community general hospital...Inventory

Granville, a rural community hospital... Emergency Room tracking

Good Hope, a 10-physician rural hospital... DRG tracking

Cleo B. Robertson

Sloop Memorial, a rural mountain hospital… Personnel tracking

Iredell Memorial, a community hospital… Nurse Scheduling

By the end of the second week after my return to Durham, I had visited all the hospitals and had identified each programming challenge. Only Alamance and Good Hope had PCs, which were being used primarily as word processors. The secretaries and coordinators had little time for learning new things—their plates were full with day-to-day crises.

It was interesting to work with so many different kinds of hospitals and attitudes. By the third week, the Duke staff and I were well into programming. Main Menus were being developed and tested. My weeks were full of setting up meetings, traveling to the hospitals, and working with the Duke programming staff. On weekends, I generally hung out with Jane during the day cutting wood or talking about the project—neither of us could think of much else. I spent most of my evenings at a place called <u>Your Place or Mine</u>, a mixed bar of rednecks, college students and locals. Playing pool was the main activity, and dancing was secondary. Well, actually drinking beer was the main activity but after that, came playing pool and dancing!

Sometime during all this activity, Randy called. I was glad to hear his happy voice, and when he asked me how things were going, I said, "Fine, scary, busy."

He said, "Well, Mom, why don't I come down and help you?"

Randy was 20 years old at this point. He had done well in high school, taken a few college courses, done well and said, "There, I can do that. But that's not what I want to do," and promptly left college to try his hand at a few different jobs—his last was for a pizza store. He was sleeping in his car that he parked at various places. Things were so bleak that even his beloved cat deserted him. The great thing was that none of this dampened Randy's enthusiasm for life one iota. Chip off the old block, I'd say. I remembered the project in Washington that he and I had done for my brother and how well we had worked together. In fact, Randy and I had always had fun together.

I finally said on a whim, "Okay, come on down and we'll see how it works out."

When I told Jane, she was less than pleased, feeling that Randy would only distract me. She could tell, however, that there was no changing my mind. Having Randy around would at least relieve my loneliness. Randy arrived in Durham on January 21st. He arrived with his motorcycle and a backpack, which were all his earthly possessions. We decided he would sleep in my kitchen on a foam chair that made into a bed on the floor (Randy was 6'4" and the kitchen was 4 x 8, but he managed, all in all, for five months).

We spent the first day walking around the Duke campus and talking about the project. Randy was easy to talk to, fun to be with and had absolutely no knowledge of hospitals or PC's...but that didn't bother either of us.

"Together we can move mountains. I'm tired of moving them alone," was my philosophy.

By this time I had bought a Fuji bike and an Aiwa headset and spent a good deal of my weekend time riding around town listening to great music. I also started taking a woodworking class at a local high school. Tools had always fascinated me. When things would break when I was young, I learned how to fix them. Even when my little sewing machine got plugged up when I was 11 years old, I just took the whole bobbin mechanism apart, cleaned it, and reassembled it, much to my brother's chagrin. He was sure I would never get it back together. The woodworking class kept me busy in the evenings for a while, but I was always looking for something to do to get out of the apartment. If I stayed in, I worked.

Randy and Jane got along great, so we would visit with her often. Randy liked Durham, or more precisely, he liked Duke's campus and the parties. He would join the programmers and watch what we were doing, but he didn't seem to be catching on or to have any interest in computers. I was just glad to have him with me at first. We soon had issues though, because I was sharing a very small apartment with him, giving him spending money, and not getting any work out of him.

It was about this time that Duke offered me $30K to go to work for them. They offered me less than they would someone else, because I didn't have a degree. I understood their strategy—it hadn't taken Jane long to realize I was a workaholic. She also wanted to give me some form of security in my life. The fact was, however, that I couldn't have worked in a big place like Duke full time. Too many politics, too many personnel issues, too many rules. I turned them down and was never sorry for my decision.

For the month of February, I traveled almost daily, visiting the six hospitals. At the same time I was questioning the employees on just how the software for personnel, inventory, medical staff credentialing, emergency rooms, Diagnostic Related Groups (DRG's), and nurse scheduling should work. It was not easy, because no one really knew how it was done on paper. That became my job—to figure out how it would be done on paper and then move it to a computer.

Between the traveling and the learning, I was pretty tired by the end of each week. That didn't keep me from playing pool, of course, or dancing every chance I got, but I often worked weekends as things started to get busy. Randy and I discussed my moving to Durham permanently.

I think I want to move to Durham. I like it here, there are lots of opportunities and Randy likes it as much as I do. Feels like I'm coming home; my great grandfather and great uncle were both governors of this state in the '20's and '30's. Who knows? A big decision to make with no money, but life is a challenge.

Cleo B. Robertson

My father's mother (my grandmother) married O. Max Gardner (my great grandfather). He was governor of North Carolina for four years, followed by Clyde Hoey, who was married to my grandmother's sister. I felt I belonged in North Carolina.

Within a week I had written:

I'm falling apart. I'm a child inside, and everyone sees that, which is why I don't get backing and support. Even my son questions my ability. I hurt inside because I know if I can't/won't grow up, I'll never be able to run a business. I can't sleep again. Another cycle of down. Randy needs direction, and I'm not giving it to him.

How could I give *him* direction? I was moving forward in great confusion myself; so much learning, so many personalities to manage, so little money. But I was managing enough to please Jane. Jane arranged for many things, including a trip to a well-known endowment. This endowment was the main source of funding of projects in health care in North Carolina.

Going to Charlotte with Jane today to talk to endowment people and another group who donates to hospitals. We were not very well received at either meeting. Everyone is amazed I can think, but Jane and I know we are a good team.

We were surprised at how unaware the men from these two organizations were. They didn't have a clue how difficult it was for hospitals to manage all the data they collected. Once we educated them, they didn't seem to think Jane and I could do anything about it. We had hoped to get support from them so they would allocate some money to the hospitals to buy computer PCs, but that soon fell flat. Jane said there were other avenues, and since she was a master at finding money and getting people to cooperate, I left it to her.

My diary entry reflected my decision to move to Durham, permanently.

Woke up at 2 am and sleep won't come so I worked on nurse scheduling. Jane and I talked business today. I'm so in awe of her that I'm always amazed she listens to me. I have to move by June 1, because I can't pay rent in two places. Randy says he'll help me move.

Dan came down for a visit about this time, and I had to break it to him that we were moving, permanently, to Durham. He was very upset, both because he would miss us, but also because he couldn't afford to stay in the house in Princeton alone. My decision to move was made on a whim—and it was to deeply affect several people far more than I ever imagined. When Dan left to return to Princeton we were both sad, but my decision had been made.

Sleeplessness had never been a problem in my life, but now I had it with a vengeance. Of course, there was always work to be done, and I began a habit that stayed with me until 1989—I would wake at 4 a.m. and get started on the day—paying bills, writing letters, getting myself organized. By 9 a.m., I would be working with the Duke programmers or off on the road for a visit to a hospital. After dinner I would test what the programmers had done during the day, so they could fix problems before the next evening, when I would test again. It was a busy schedule, and I thrived on being busy. Keeping busy seemed to keep me from being moody, but nothing seemed to be able to stop my self doubt.

Am I a braggart saying I know hospitals so well? No, I'm confident I know more than most. An aching stomach reminds me of pressures and stress and yet I'm having fun too!

On March 19th, Randy turned 21 and we had a small party at Jane's. The programmers at Duke liked Randy a lot...they just didn't see him settling down to program any time soon. Good kid, Randy was, but still no interest in the project. He watched us all work at the dining room table; he just didn't know how to help.

By the end of the month, the stress on my body was showing:

It occurred to me today that I need a doctor, or someone to help me discover why my body hurts so much. Bones ache to the touch and nerves pounding in pain. Bursitis, sleepless nights, and headaches—what does it all mean?

What it meant was that I was pushing myself too hard, but I continued to ignore me and to push on with the project. The project was busy, hectic, well organized, and proceeding rapidly...towards what? I wasn't sure. We were learning as we went along. I really think I just needed to go home and touch base with my friends.

Towards the end of March, I decided to go visit Tom and Sandra in Washington after which I would then go on to Princeton. I wanted to assess what it would take to move. When I left the apartment, I told Randy, "Here's a computer, Lotus 123, and a book on how to use Lotus. Do something with the checkbook manager I've started, or don't be here when I get back—I simply can't afford both of us, if only one is productive." I was tired and I needed his help. I headed up to Washington, not knowing whether Randy would be there or not when I got back.

When I arrived in Princeton, Hazel and Dan were both glad to see me and hated that I was moving away. It was wonderful being with Max, and I couldn't wait to have him with me in Durham. As always, I did my rounds of Nassau and Witherspoon Streets. Bill at The Annex always remembered that I drank Bud Light. Harry at the office supply store was always amazed I was still doing so well—an attitude shared by most.

The short trip to Princeton had been good for me, but I was anxious to get back to Durham to house hunt. I called the apartment and Randy answered the phone. I told him I would be in the next afternoon. Driving back to Durham, I felt like I was "going home."

Cleo B. Robertson

As I drove up and parked my car at the apartment, I could see my tall, good-looking son standing up against the doorjamb of our apartment, arms crossed in front of him, with a "I just ate the mouse" grin on his face.

As I got close to him, I said, "Oh, so you think you did something, huh?" referring to my demand that he do something with my checkbook manager, or not be here when I got home.

He said, "You'll see."

What I saw was that Randy was finally challenged by Lotus 123. When I sat down to see what he had done, I was truly amazed. Something in the book had turned Randy on by helping him understand *how* Lotus thought. He made Lotus do things even the support people didn't know it would do. I was most happy. From that day on, Randy was listening to and learning from the Duke programmers, and he couldn't have had a better education.

Within the month, I announced to Jane and the programmers my hope that Randy could take over the programming at some point. Oh, the hullabaloo that caused! No one thought a college-less kid with one month experience on a computer could accomplish such a feat, which didn't change my feelings at all—I knew Randy could take over the project. I just didn't know when.

Money was a stress again, but I was the optimist, as usual:

WHIM OF IRON

I'm almost all caught up and at least my money is going into the business—computer, software, incorporating, and marketing. Feels great.

The truth was that I was getting caught up in the *trappings* of owning a business—incorporating, expensive marketing brochures—instead of focusing on just the software and the project.

Over the next few years, until 1989 to be exact, I spent a lot of time and energy on trappings when I would have been better served staying more focused. But heck, everyone I talked to told me it was important to do these things, so I did them. On April 15th Randy and I went to look at two houses in Durham—the second one at 2121 West Club Boulevard would become our home for the next seven years. When we walked through the big, airy rooms and sat out on the old-fashioned porch, we knew we were hooked. When the agent told us the rent was $400 per month, we set August 1 for our move date.

By this time Randy was proving he was a quick learner. Based on my design of the nurse scheduling application, he programmed Lotus123 to schedule up to 200 nurses, on three floors, over three shifts daily. All the nurses had to do was simply follow the easy menus. That meant the nurses didn't have to learn Lotus, they just learned our software program. He also incorporated the ability for the nursing staff to set their staff needs by shift and unit and then flag when the schedule didn't meet these needs. It was a terrific program. It was used at Iredell Memorial Hospital for many years. If there had been more of me, I could have probably sold it to other hospitals, but there just wasn't time to do everything, and nursing needs were pretty low on administrators' "to do" lists.

Lisa flew in for Mother's Day and enjoyed exploring Durham. It was wonderful talking with her about her life and our life. It occurred to me it would be great if she could come run the business—pay the bills, do all the correspondence, write the user manuals—and that would leave Randy and me free to program. It was a thought that did not leave my mind, partly because I wanted her company and partly because she was an accountant. I hoped she would have the business sense I lacked.

June and July were spent programming, testing, visiting hospitals, and generally keeping busy with the project. By now, Randy was into it big time, so we both worked harder, because we both wanted to do well. Even the Duke programmers saw that Randy was learning their programming language, Knowledgeman, and started to take him seriously.

With much excitement, we went back to Princeton July 20th to pack up and "get out of Dodge," so to speak. We rented a large moving truck because I had collected a lot of stuff. Over the 10 days we were in Princeton, Randy, Gary, Dan, Dave, and Tom were around, saying goodbye, telling "I remember" stories and generally having one long party. Moments before the moving van was totally packed, I heard a ruckus outside, and my dog snarling. The scene outside was filled with excitement. There in the street were Max and Blackie, Big Butts' dog. They were face to face, while hoards of people gathered round to watch the fight. The last thing I needed was a fight and a bloody dog, so I remembered what a dog trainer had taught me once. With all my children behind me watching, I quickly ran down to Max and reached down and grabbed his balls. Max froze. I told someone to grab Blackie's balls too, and some brave soul did as I said. Blackie froze. I grabbed Max's collar and led him away, as Blackie looked on in stilled silence. Best way to break up a dogfight I ever heard of. My children were appalled that I would do such a thing as grab a dog's balls, but, hey, I'll do whatever it takes.

My two sons and three stepsons packed the last items into the truck, gave us one final hug, and we all three took off, Randy driving the U Haul, and Max and I following in my car. I didn't look back. In later years I realized that I left Princeton the way I had left home at 17—I said goodbye and never looked back. I now know that cost me a lot emotionally, but I didn't know what else to do. Nothing could keep me from going where the action was.

The trip from Princeton to Durham went all right for the first few hours. We couldn't go very fast because of the size of the truck. The temperature was in the high 90s, and we had no air conditioning. Somewhere outside of Washington, D.C., about three hours into our trip, we stopped to get gas.

As Randy put the gas nozzle into the tank, I watched in horror as flames shot up and caught everything on fire around Randy. I screamed for him to stop pumping. He quickly withdrew the hose and threw it on the ground. Someone ran out and quickly extinguished the fire. We called the truck rental agency, and they very quickly had a mechanic come out to look at the truck. It didn't take him long to tell us that what was wrong. When the exhaust pipe was installed, it had been incorrectly positioned *facing* the gas tank, and the heat from the exhaust had caused a spark. We were lucky we had not blown up.

We had two choices. We could wait until they could find another truck, which would take a day or two, then transfer everything that had taken us two days to pack into the new truck. Or, we could go on, slowly, very slowly. By this time it was 100 degrees outside, Max was restless, Randy and I were tired, and all we wanted to do was go home. We decided to go on.

When we saw the <u>Welcome to North Carolina,</u> sign we were hopeful we would get home without blowing up. Randy had driven about 40 mph for the last nine hours but he never lost his cool. Inside his head, however, he was raving mad. When we pulled up at the house we had rented, Randy turned the truck around and backed the end into the yard and up against the porch. It was about 4 p.m., and we were exhausted from a very stressful drive. All I wanted to do was go lay down and sleep. I asked Randy if he didn't think he should leave the truck on the street for the night, and his response stunned me.

"No. I'm going to unload the truck now. I want it away from this house and at the station."

WHIM OF IRON

I knew immediately he needed to vent his fear and anger and that this was his way. In the biggest show of determination I had ever seen, Randy single-handedly unloaded a full-size moving van. When it got down to the refrigerator, washer and drier, I went over to the basketball court across the street in the park and asked for two volunteers to help, and two men immediately offered their services.

As soon as the truck was empty, Randy and I drove over to the drop off station for U-Haul. I vented our fear and anger by letting the station manager know in no uncertain terms that his company had just put us at risk of our lives for an arduous 12-hour drive. I filled out a complaint form, and then we drove home.

By 8 p.m. the refrigerator was humming, we had wolfed down a pizza, and we were ready to crash. (We received a full $560 refund from the rental company and a letter of apology. All in all, it worked out okay.)

That first night in our new home was a big event for me. I walked Max slowly around the small park across the street from us and thanked God for our new space. I was in love with my new home already. I could see Randy through the kitchen window as he drank a glass of milk. He had behaved like a true grown up man the whole trip. I felt such a surge of pride. He had taken care of scary stuff and done it well. That night as I went to sleep in my bed in Durham in our new house, I thanked God for all my blessings. But, I especially thanked Him for my son.

On Monday morning, I was back at work, and I met with Jane for several hours to review where the project stood at that point. All in all, things were looking very good. Six programs were in progress. Randy was getting very adept at programming, quicker than anyone thought was possible. The publicity from the Hospital Association was getting good press for Duke, and the foundation that had put up the money for the project had expressed their pleasure at our progress.

By the second week, Jane had arranged a trip to Morehead City to meet with the administrative and inventory people to review their particular project. On the drive down I could feel tension between Jane and me, but I didn't know what was causing it. It was a long drive; we ate a light dinner and checked into a motel. Jane and I always shared a room when traveling, partly because she liked to save money, and partly because I think she liked having company. Usually this arrangement worked well, but this time I could feel dis-ease between us. It didn't occur to me until months later that she might have been having a tough diabetic time. Jane gave herself insulin daily but sometimes it wasn't enough. This may have been one of those times.

In any case, I didn't sleep well, so I got up very early the next morning and went for a swim in the motel pool. It was not very satisfying for an avid swimmer. I walked over to the Channel Marker Restaurant nearby and sat on their dock, dangling my legs towards the water. It was about 6:30 a.m., not a soul was stirring and the fresh new sun was just rising to brighten another day. I was just slightly startled when I heard footsteps behind me. Then a black man appeared, walked by me, and went to the restaurant to open up. Before he went in, I asked him if he thought it would be safe for me to swim to the marshy beach area across the bay. I had been looking longingly at the beach and wanted so much to just jump in and swim, but my fear of sharks kept me from doing so. In addition, the marsh was about ¼ mile away, and I was a little nervous about such a long distance. I hadn't done any long-distance swimming since high school.

He walked over to me and said, "Yes, I don't know of anything that would bother you." He then added, "You swim over. Call me when you get back, and I'll pull you out."

At the time I wasn't sure what he meant, but I was happy to get the okay. I swam over, heart in mouth even though I knew I wasn't on a shark's menu. I was very happy to reach the beach. I walked to the farthermost reaches of the beach facing the sun and bathed for a while. As was my habit from teen times in Pass-a-Grille, I took the time to talk to God and say thank you. I always think of God as a depository for all my joys and fears.

The day was so beautiful, I started singing the Star Spangled Banner because I was so moved by it all (that's the only song I remember the words to). When I was ready to go back, I walked to the other side again and whistled as loudly as I could. The man appeared on the dock almost immediately and stood there as I swam quickly back. When I got to the dock, I finally understood his statement about helping to pull me out. There was no ladder, and it was about four feet to the dock's edge. I hated to have to ask an older man (he was at least 70) to pull me, dead weight, out of the water. I must have weighed 170 at the time. Without hesitation, he put his strong, solid hand down and very slowly pulled me up over the edge. I was amazed at his strength.

He said, "Dry yourself off and come over and have some coffee. I just made a fresh pot."

We sat on the dock drinking fresh, robust coffee in the fresh, early morning. He talked of 20 years in the Navy and of his retirement—as the sun broke colorfully on the horizon, and sea gulls cawed good morning. He told me he was 72, had never been in a hospital, and was still a very healthy man. We had a lovely half hour together in a magical place, and then it was time for me to go. We shook hands and that was the last I ever saw him. I know that wherever he is today, he's still in good health and stretching out his wonderful hand to help others.

When we got back from the trip to Moorhead City, I dove right back into developing the programs.

Business going well. Hard work to wear ten hats. I love seeing someone I'm teaching at a hospital slowly realize what the computer program the Duke programmers have created will do. Most satisfying work I have ever done. Gary is in college—thank goodness. He's coming to visit for a week soon. He's been living with his dad.

WHIM OF IRON

It was actually a relief to me that Gary was in college. He had been drifting about without a passion in his life. My hope was that he would find it in a structured environment.

The beauty of keeping a diary is that it keeps showing how one repeats patterns. In September things were going well. On October 31st my entry shows a different story. It wasn't that what I felt in September wasn't true, it's just that the combination of trying to do too much with too little money by someone who didn't know how to handle money, caused crisis after crisis:

Can't pay my bills so Lisa is loaning me $1000—it will help but it's not nearly enough. Randy gave me a pep talk because he can see I am scared. Got State contract to work with people using their computers. Barbara feels I can help her, and I think I can. Bills scare me because they remind me of Mom when she would be scared she couldn't pay bills. She got drunk to escape her scared feelings. Not me. I'm going to make this software into a product and sell it. Asked Mike to join CBR but he said no. I have to get Randy to be my Mike. Mike and Jane would laugh, but not me. He can do it. I need Lisa here too, so she can run the business and I can sell.

Barbara, the Director of Health Planning for North Carolina, was a bright, energetic, gutsy woman who didn't always do things by the book. She believed in quality and would go a long way to get it. The role I played in Barbara's life was focused on her need to use computers well so she could get the data and information she needed for her studies and projections. When I realized I needed more income, Jane suggested I talk to Barbara. She was immediately enthusiastic and got me a contract, at $40 per hour, to work with her staff optimizing their use of their computer systems already in place. She certainly was ahead of her time and a visionary. I started adding days at her offices in Raleigh to my busy schedule. When the money started coming in, I could breathe again.

Mike, the lead Duke programmer, had degrees, experience, and knowledge, but he didn't want to leave Duke for some two-person outfit that didn't have any security. Mike was a family man, and although he didn't always love things at Duke, he loved working at Duke. The thought that Randy could be my Mike scared Jane, and made Mike smile. Little did they know of Randy's breadth and willingness to do whatever it would take. I was also still hoping Lisa could come save the day.

The State project actually helped me see how the Duke project was suffering from "scope creep." Of course, we kept thinking that if we just had more time, money, and people, we could get everything done. I had not learned yet the "50-50 rule"—if you need more people, make a list of everything the people are doing, cut it in half, and suddenly the people you have can pick up the extra work. It applies to everything—if you need more money, make a list of what you spend money on, cut it in half, and suddenly you don't need more money. It applies to space, time, and particularly, project scope. In retrospect, it is easy to see how I

WHIM OF IRON

could have cut back expenses enough that I wouldn't have had to do the State project, but the education I got from that work far outweighed the extra work.

By October I had learned enough about local customs to know how to have fun. There was a large lake twenty miles away which had been a quarry until they hit water. I was told it was 300' deep in places. I started going there on weekends and spending the whole day swimming and meeting people. I met a couple that came every weekend, grilled great food and floated around the lake all day—we became good friends.

I was still alone during most of my personal time, which suited me just fine. My childhood as a beach kid allowed me to play alone for hours and be happy. It was lucky for me, because I was too busy to have any relationships. Max, of course, kept me company as I walked three miles each morning around the golf course. Nights I would spend in a nearby gay bar, where there was a great wooden dance floor, great music, and everyone left me alone. I would dance for an hour or two and go home feeling happy. In the fall I would spend leisure time looking for mushrooms.

By November, I was waiting for a renewal of my contract with Duke, yet I continued to work. Finances were desperate, so I decided to take a gamble.

I went to Jane and Bob and said, "Here's my proposal for completing the Small Hospital Project. I'm going off to Princeton for Thanksgiving. When I get back, if I have a signed contract and a $15,000 retainer, I'll go to work but until then, not another meeting."

The next day I had a signed contract and my check was on its way. I should have said that months ago, because I could see that Jane and Bob were glad for the direction and clarity the contract gave them. Once again, we were flush and breathing easy!

In November, Barbara asked me if I would go to a telecommunications workshop in Atlanta, Georgia, on the 16th, just a few days away. I was thrilled. Outside of the little traveling I had done around North and South Carolina with Jane, my traveling had been minimal. I was broke (down to $100 according to my diary), but the Duke check was promised by December 1st...the old "check's in the mail" routine. Barbara arranged for the ticket, I borrowed $300 from Jane and I flew at 6:30 a.m. to be at the Atlanta meeting by 9.

The meeting was of marginal benefit to Barbara. What she had wanted to do was connect her NCR computers to the Wang system, which they used for word processing, in order to transfer text between the two. Although I learned a lot about communications, I didn't come back with any real solutions she could use.

After the meeting, the Project Officer in Atlanta asked me if I was flying back later in the day. I said I was. He asked if I'd ever been to Atlanta and I promptly said no, but that I would love to see the city. He made a quick call and then told me that he could get me a hotel room at State prices—about $50 per night. He also checked my ticket and found he could get me a return on Sunday. I was flabbergasted and excited at the same time and, on a whim, said yes. By 3 p.m. our meetings were over and I was walking over to an old hotel that was located blocks from the Peachtree Center. I put my purse away, changed into jeans and a T-shirt I had brought for the return flight home, stuffed some money and my driver's license in my pocket and headed out towards downtown Atlanta.

Someone at the meeting had told me that the Limelight was the happening place at night. The Limelight was all about dancing, so I was determined to find it. By this time it was about 5 p.m., and as I walked past the Peachtree Center, I decided to stop in there and see if I could find out where I could catch a bus to the Limelight. As I pranced down the stairs into the main lobby, I bumped into a tall, good-looking man in a business suit who very graciously said, "May I help you?" I immediately told him I was in for the weekend and wanted to go dancing at the Limelight. He looked me over from head to toe (I weighed about 150 at this point and still had a very good figure). He finally said, "Well, if you'll go back to your hotel and get something on that is a little more dressy then be back here by 8 p.m., you may join me as I host some friends at the Limelight tonight."

Cool. He seemed like a professional man to me. I liked his directness and I wanted to have fun, so off I went to change. I sort of combined what I had to make it look like an upbeat outfit, fluffed up my hair and put on some lipstick. Off I went at 7:30 to see where this adventure was going to take me. I took $100 with me just in case.

Red, as I later learned he was called, was good to his word. At 8 p.m. he appeared, took my arm and led me out the door to a limo that was waiting. Inside I had the shock of my life. Mary Lou Retton, the Olympic star, was sitting on one of the seats. Of course I didn't actually know who she was because I don't watch TV, but someone soon filled me in and I was duly impressed. Red told me he had invited the Olympic team for a party, and what a party it turned out to be! We made small talk among the six people in the limo until we arrived at the Limelight.

As soon as we pulled up, it was obvious we were not the usual guests. Men in suits immediately opened the limo doors and some side doors to the Limelight also opened. All of us were ushered into a reception area. It turned out that the entire US Olympic team was present. The Limelight had arranged for them to all come as their guests, and by some miracle, I had been included. In addition to tables set up with a fabulous spread of food (I hadn't eaten since lunch), we were given a private area, which turned out to be a Godsend. When I got tired dancing, I could come back, eat, sit, catch my breath, and talk with champions (even if I didn't know who they were). It was a wonderful time. I danced with Mary Lou, Red, and many other people. I watched in amazement as the magic of the Limelight glowed.

The Limelight, to my recollection, was one huge room that had piped in disco music. Around the sides and in front of the large main room was a four-foot high platform, which was about four feet wide. On this platform people came to perform. Dressed in every kind of outfit one could imagine, they would jump up on the platform any time they felt like it and bump and grind. In some cases they made fools of themselves and in other cases, truly entertained. I was enthralled and danced as many dances as I possibly could. The frenzy created by the costumes people were wearing (leather tops with little to them, bleached-streaked hair, skirts with slits to the ass) added to the thumping music and gyrating bodies to create an "atmosphere" that was popular in Atlanta for a good many years (the Limelight is gone now).

Slowly over the evening, I learned that Red was the Sales Manager for the Peachtree Convention and Guest Center, and it was he who had thought up this promotional stunt—bringing the Olympic team to the Limelight. It was obvious over the evening, that Red liked me. I certainly was having a good time with him, so much so, that by the end of the evening we were sitting together and talking a great deal. After the party, Red drove the limo and party back to the Peachtree and let everyone off, saying goodnight to everyone right there. He then transferred me to his car, and we drove off to his house for a wonderful night together. He had Saturday off as luck would have it, and by noon we were on a raft drifting down some river with a cooler full of beer. Many laughs flowed out over the water. It was a great day, great weekend, and more of an adventure than I could have ever imagined.

Cleo B. Robertson

I got back to Durham on the 18th, had some meetings with the Duke programmers, finished editing text for my new brochure (which I was sure would bring in tons of work), and by the 21st was on my way back to Princeton for Thanksgiving. It was good being home, but Princeton felt too academic, too rich for my blood, and I was glad I had moved to a smaller town.

Events occurred early in December that were to de-focus us for a few months. First, Randy had a friend, Robert, who was a programmer and very bright guy. Randy and I figured if we could get Robert programming, too, then we could do twice as much work and start earning money twice as fast (we didn't know yet that speed in programming could be a nightmare). Robert had agreed to work for no money until he came up to speed—thank God, or we would have been broke in no time.

Next, Diane came to live with us in the house at 2121 West Club. Diane was an old friend from Princeton who had moved to Albuquerque for a few years. She had sent a letter to me in Princeton (not knowing I had moved to Durham), to tell me she was *moving to Durham.* Her plan was to work and save money to go to the University of North Carolina. Her original housing arrangement wasn't working out as well as she had hoped, so I thought it would be great if she lived with us. Diane was organized, helpful, and hard working, plus an extra pair of hands would be a big help.

At the same time, I was still thinking about Lisa joining us. Somehow I thought if there were more hands, we could move forward faster. Security was something I needed, and if I couldn't have money, then people would do just fine. Randy was trying to work with Robert and having his problems. It was hard for Randy to understand medical staff credentialing—teaching it to others was almost impossible. Because things were going fairly well (meaning no creditors were banging at my door), I got optimistic again.

Finally going to be okay I think. Should we go public and sell stocks? Yes. Soon.

The first two statements were so unrealistic. I can't even imagine thinking them then. I guess I thought that businesses get to a point and then are okay. Period. No more fears and no more cash flow problems. The second statement naturally followed. If we were okay, then we should grow. And, if we were going to grow, wasn't going public and selling stocks the goal of all businesses? It would take four more years for me to understand that businesses are never static, neither positively nor negatively (if they're static negatively, they die). It would take even longer for me to understand that if your goal is to enjoy your business, make enough money to keep some in your pocket, and have some fun, then going public and selling stocks should not even be on the list! As I watched businesses go public, they confirmed for me again and again, that being on the Stock Exchange is not fun. They lost all control and often lost their businesses to boot.

At the end of 1984 I was feeling very happy. Randy and I liked how the programs were developing. We found we worked well together. He had discovered that I have to go through A, B, C to learn, while he could do A, C, Z. That helped a lot, because he would wait until I understood, before he would go on explaining complex ideas. We both wanted perfection and were willing to put the time in to get it. We were both, at this time, putting in 15- to 20-hour days for weeks at a time. We were also both glad for all we had and felt the tide had turned!

1985 — Money Comes and Money Goes

By January, I was starting to install the software we had designed under the Small Hospital Project into the hospitals we had selected. This required me to drive up to five hours and then spend two to five days training the new users. Some were resistant. Some wanted to learn. Some couldn't care less one way or the other—they were just putting in their time. It was frustrating and difficult work. Training was exasperated by the fact that I taught at the hospitals, and the chaos of phone calls, doctors questions, interruptions from other staff members, and day-to-day emergencies made concentration almost impossible. Often the day ended with me having a splitting headache (and sometimes the student had one, too). Nevertheless, we had begun to install the software and that kept me going.

Training at the State was also progressing. I ran into the same obstacles there. From the start of the project I had been sure that we would find a star who would want to learn the software. I was wrong. Those that did learn it well, learned it through long hours and hard work. Technology was just not something to which they had been exposed, nor was it easy.

My 4 a.m. risings were consumed with learning the KMAN programming language well enough to be able to talk intelligently with Randy and testing the medical staff software. About this time Randy decided I didn't know anything, and he and I started to have clashes. It was strange—when he didn't know anything, I was pretty bright in his eyes. The more he learned, the less he thought I knew. The fact was I didn't know *anything* about programming, but I knew a lot about what was needed in design and development. I knew what the hospitals needed. I suspected that Randy's exposure to Duke programmers was not working to my benefit.

Late in January, I found an apartment about a mile from us that I knew Lisa would love. I told her about it and she seemed interested. Her job in California was getting more and more stressful, and she wanted a change. I was hopeful. We had been talking for months, but now she started to ask questions. Early in February, Lisa called and said she'd quit her job, and she'd be here by March! I was ecstatic. I felt so alone most of the time. Having my daughter around seemed like the perfect solution. It turned out to be a mixed blessing for everyone, especially her.

Diane was still living with us, and an incident happened that was quite funny. I had gone out for a day of training and had left Diane to test a DOS manual

WHIM OF IRON

I had written (DOS was the original PC operating system instead of Windows). When I got home, Randy met me at the door and told me I'd better sit down. I saw Diane standing in the kitchen doorway crying, so I knew something big had happened. Randy told me that Diane had been testing my manual, and when she typed in "format C:\" she typed it as my book said. What she could not have known was that such a command would erase everything on my whole hard disk, and all my data would be gone! I looked at Randy a moment, as I went through my head remembering all the work that was on that disk, and then said, "Oh, that's no problem. I backed up the whole hard disk before I left." It was a lesson for everyone—Randy learned to back up often, Diane learned you can't trust anything in computers, and I learned to write manuals more carefully.

Randy was doing wonderful programming and taking over more and more from the Duke programmers. He continued to think I didn't know anything but I just ignored his demeaning remarks, perhaps incorrectly. I needed him so badly, both for his work ethic and for his connection to me. I didn't dare draw the line. In retrospect, I see that because I didn't draw a line he assumed he was right. By this time, Randy and Diane were clashing badly. Diane had her way of doing things, and Randy thought his way was right. Finally, he decided to move into his own apartment. He shared a house with a Duke friend for a while and then moved to Duke Manor, where he really had a good time. It was undoubtedly good for him to leave work at night and go home and play. I was paying him enough that he was able to enjoy some comforts, and it was about time. His absence gave Diane room to blossom and she slowly took over the management of the house. She had four cats that she had brought with her, and it was a stand off between them and Max. Max was willing to be friends—the cats would hear nothing of it. The house felt full and alive.

When Duke's "powers that be" started to see we were really doing something, they asked if we could develop an application for Personnel for them. I spent weeks learning how a place manages personnel and found it quite involved. The basics, such as previous employment, education, and salary, were easy. The questions they wanted to answer about pensions, health, job migration and continuing education made the program tough to design. Duke had 16,000 employees at the time. It was quite a task to get Randy to understand the process of personnel management. He had never been a secretary that was required to manage vast amounts of paper and minutia, a skill vital to database development. Because Duke was interested in the personnel program for the hospital, it was even more complicated. [It's one thing to develop a personnel system for a 100-staff hospital, but quite another for a major university and medical center with 16,000 employees.] To add to the complication, I wanted to please everyone, which I came to realize was impossible.

In my diary mid-February I mention a subject that had plagued me since I got married the first time...weight:

WHIM OF IRON

I'm losing weight finally and feeling good about my body, so I went out for a bike ride and got hit by a car!

It's funny to me that I connected the two events…losing weight and getting hit by the car. I think I thought I'd better not get too happy and the car accident was to keep me in my place. A young woman hit me in the leg while I was riding my bike. She was going 35 mph in a 20 mph zone and she didn't stop at the stop sign. I was thrown in the air, hit the hood of her car and bounced off, with legs running to keep from spilling my face onto the asphalt. The woman took off without leaving any information. My only injury was a very sore leg, but since I had no health insurance yet I decided, in my shocked state, to walk for three hours. The next day it didn't hurt at all, so I came out of it fine. I continued to lose weight, thankfully, but I was more careful riding from then on.

My personal life was still a mess.

Met a man who likes me and I'm a dither! It was the beginning of just one more scenario to end in sadness. We went out, had a wonderful time, and he seemed to enjoy me. We drank wine and talked for hours. As he left he said he'd call me the next night around 9. It was a long evening. He never called.

I have never been able to figure out what happens. Do I not open my eyes and see that he is not having a good time? Did he not respect me because I went to bed with him the first night? Did I just want to think he enjoyed me, and that his laughter was genuine, when in fact he was miserable? As I say, I still have not figured men out. I repeated this scenario so many times, I cringe inside just at the thought.

Lisa was now ready to come join CBR. Before she left California, she suggested that we demonstrate our software to hospitals that she had connections with through her work. I agreed. Because I was in the midst of the Duke project, we decided that Randy would go to California to get Lisa so she could come home and run CBR. At the same time, they would demonstrate personnel and medical staff software programs to four hospitals. I was tempted to go, but I had too much to do. Besides, I decided that the maiden voyage presenting to clients would do them both good. I figured Randy wrote the code, he could surely demo it.

They called me after their first meeting at a Santa Monica hospital. They told me they did great presenting the medical staff software to the hospital staff. It was quite an experience having my children representing me in California! At this point it appeared to me that business was very good. I had attended a State meeting and people agreed to loan an XT computer and to input data for Barbara's group. This was wonderful, because without the equipment, there would be no pilot project for the State Department of Planning. In addition to the State Project, I was running the Duke Project and trying to see as many hospital people as I could to show them what we were doing. Diane was working out quite well for me. She had started helping me write user manuals and it felt like a good team effort. Life felt very good, if overwhelming at times.

WHIM OF IRON

She is here! She is here! Randy and Lisa drove from LA to Durham in 3.5 days. We wallpapered and painted her bedroom in her new apartment, and it is lovely—1023 Wells Street. We are on our way. Bank account perilously low, and we're all excited anyway. I drive to Princeton Sunday (8 hours) to be with friends. DOS manual is being printed.

On March 19th, we had a wonderful birthday party for Randy. Lisa brought croissants; Diane gave him Brie; I gave him a shopping spree at Burlington mall (with Lisa contributing $75 and her plastic card!). We left Durham for the mall at 1:30. Halfway home, Lisa discovered that her diamond ring was missing. She was horrified to realize that she had left it in the bathroom at the Western Sizzler in Burlington. We drove all the way back to find out that some woman had turned it in! Thank God for honest folks.

Those were the good times. The not-so-good times resulted from the house being too small for all of us. It was most difficult for me because I lived in one room with other people in the other four rooms, day and night. If I wanted to take a bath at night or a shower in the morning, there simply was not enough hot water for Diane to do the same. The pressure was starting to show.

I want my rock music loud! I don't have enough space, and I must make it soon. Ulceration on my face expresses my exhaustion. Yet I go on working hard. The kids are working fine together. We are fighting, working, supporting, caring and learning about each other. We are all so alike and so different. Some differences are nice; others not. We are de-focused at the moment—decorating the office, building a team. Projects are on target but we'll run out of time because we're busy building a team. CBR Associates is on its way to success and now has three associates!

The stress of having others in my house showed physically:

Ulceration on my face continues into second week. People are always here, leaving or coming—I am NEVER alone! I shall crack. I feel responsible for Diane, and yet I need to live alone. My face won't heal until I resolve my living situation. Had dinner with Lisa, and she and Randy are having a good time working together. I feel so tired. I am so tired. Tired of trying to resolve so much!

Each day was like a ping-pong game—we're up, we're down, we hit the bottom, we come around. My job was to see that the programs were easy enough for the end user and comprehensive enough to satisfy administration. We disagreed a lot, but we also innovated a lot. Randy had a hard time seeing me as his leader in the development of the software, and the better he got at programming, the less he wanted to listen to me. But I needed him. Unfortunately, when we disagreed, we both tended to get hysterical and it was a strain on everyone.

WHIM OF IRON

One day Lisa and I went to the Eno River with a wonderful lunch and lay out on the swinging bridge high above the river for four hours. We slept, talked, got sun in 75-degree weather and relaxed. It was a much-needed break.

Diane had also come to realize that the house was too small for all of us and decided to find an apartment. I was relieved, and I knew she had done a lot and I'd miss her. She was one person I could count on to be on my side. My consolation was that she would still be in town and we could visit, and she would listen to me moan—all my friends eventually got tired of hearing me talk about the business except Diane. She stayed a good listener and supporter all through the years.

While Randy was working very long hours on the software, Lisa and I were working on designing and typing training manuals. I had a vision of the perfect training manual that was easy to read, had lots of examples and taught the users what they wanted to know. I had chosen XY-Write, a word processing software designed for the newspaper and book industry. It allowed us to do very complicated formatting so the manuals would look easy to use. Lisa, thank goodness, picked it up quickly and was soon writing the manuals, which gave me enormous relief. In fact, she turned out to be very good at lots of things. Her accounting mind was organized and clear and we worked well together. It did, however, take a lot of my energy to do my work and train her, too. There was nothing else to do but move forward.

Gary came for a nice visit. It was the first time all three children had been together in awhile and we had a wonderful time. One day we took a picnic lunch to Duke University's Duke Gardens and sat around eating, talking, and sharing stories. It did my heart good to see the two boys wrestling on the grass and see them all laughing together. No matter how I may have screwed up raising them because I was so unconventional, they all turned out tops as human beings. I truly could feel proud for my part and their father's part.

Money continued to be a concern, but I was learning to take low cash flow in stride. At the end of March 1985, we were down to less than $300 in the bank, which would disappear in a few days when we had payroll. Randy and Diane always got paid, but very often Lisa and I didn't. We were broke and working hard; life felt very good. The challenge and excitement of what we were doing provided all the energy we needed. Or at least, all the energy I needed. Jane E. was always in the background, calling to see how we were doing or inviting us over for dinner. Along with all her responsibilities, she managed to keep tabs on us, to help us when she could and to see that the money continued to flow to keep us alive. Thankfully, she had taken to Randy a great deal and respected his skills.

My role as designer continued, as I worked with the head of Duke's microcomputer unit to get the Inventory software into shape. Because Duke had an interest in it, I frequently reviewed this software with Jane and members of the Material Management Department. It was looking good.

I was going through another period of feeling physically achy and sore. I lived in a perpetual state of being scared and was thankful that Lisa and Randy appeared calm. Of course they were not responsible for covering all our bills. Lisa had not gotten her teeth into anything other than our word processor, but I had plans to teach her Lotus so she could keep our books. I saw us being at the forefront of a whole new service—microcomputer support and training. I felt that if we could survive, we'd be dynamite.

Up at 4 a.m. to work on medical staff manual. Did very good work. Randy is getting programs bug free and I'm confident we have a good market. I have to get going even more. I need to finish the Inventory program and Personnel manual, test nurse scheduling, finish medical staff manual and finish the DOS manual. Took Inventory to Duke to review and that went well. Also want to send our marketing brochure to Dave to have him make it up. Lisa taking care of taxes thank goodness, a big load off my mind. No stomach aches and it's tax season. No State money yet, and I'm in my 5th month of working for them! Meet with Wilson next week. I'm a born salesperson just like my dad; I just haven't blossomed yet. 10 p.m. to bed.

Years later I laughed at my comment that I was confident we had a good market. What I based that on was the fact that hospitals *should* be using our software. I had not yet learned that customers only buy a product when *they* perceive a need! But the constant optimism was the only thing that kept me getting up at 4 a.m. and dealing with so much at once.

On April 17th I went to meet with Mr. Wilson at the State Department of Human Resources to talk about the project I was working on, and for which I was not getting paid. He gave me the okay to continue to computerize the planners and assured me the money would soon be on its way. My pride and inexperience wouldn't let me show or tell him how desperate we were.

Playing politics was never one of my strong points (in fact, I didn't have a clue how to do so), but it did finally occur to me that it would be good to get to know Barbara and her chief statistician, Ruth, better, so I invited them for dinner. It was a good idea. Sharing ideas with Barbara, who had a vision of the future, gave me confidence in my ideas. Ruth, who was very practical and down to earth, also showed support for the software we were developing. I discussed with them my idea to market our software myself, since I knew how it worked and who could use it. Both thought that was a good idea. Our ignorance was never in short supply.

By April 27th my diary noted that we had received our last Duke check under the grant proposal and that if the State money didn't come through soon, we'd be bankrupt. My optimism carried the day; I was sure the money would arrive any moment. About this time, I started talking with Jane E. about training North

Carolina hospitals in the use of computers. Since it would mean income, I put my energy into trying to make that happen. Unfortunately, hospitals didn't see the need for computers, much less training, but I didn't realize that until I had put way too much energy and time into it. Staying focused was not a skill I had learned yet, and it's a wonder we didn't fold because of it.

At this time there was a discussion going on around me that stressed me a good deal. Jane had decided it was time to start marketing the credentialing, nurse scheduling and inventory programs to hospitals. Lisa and Randy agreed. What they didn't understand was the cost in time— *my time*! I didn't feel ready and I used the excuse that the products weren't ready (which was somewhat true). I felt we had to have good manuals. Without good manuals, I reasoned, trying to train people could be a mess. I tried to figure out *how* to market, but my brain just couldn't figure it out. And I had no one to guide me.

Finally, the first State check arrived for $12,000 to cover three of the five months I had been working. It was a Godsend and just in time. People had started to remark about how awful I was looking and sounding— tired, drawn and monotone. I started having dreams that I had sores on my face (a sure sign of stress) so I started sleeping in until 7 a.m. and tried to take the days a little easier. I was very encouraged when I did our billings. We had $3,000 more due from the State, which, with the two additional months we would work for them at $4,000 each, would see us through to August.

Cleo B. Robertson

With money in the bank, I gave Randy the okay to order a larger hard disk so he could store more data. He'd been working on inventory and was being slowed down by his lack of storage space. At the same time that the software was going well, or perhaps *because* it was going well, Randy began to really question my decisions and direction. He, Lisa and I had a meeting to discuss direction and his disrespect for me was so obvious, I barely kept control. We did resolve that they were to call me Cleo at work. Randy also agreed that he would try to calm down. I tried to get him to see that I had the vision. All he knew was that it was his programs that were running and he saw himself as the leader. This was an issue that never did get resolved.

In another attempt to get more business, I did a demonstration of our software on tracking physician appointments to the Health Systems Agencies (HSAs). HSAs were created to coordinate health resources by area of a state, but it soon became apparent that they had no equipment, no budget and no power. Another unfocused path I went down for too long.

Socially, my one saving grace was the Carol Woods community. Aunt Peg had been a resident there for many years now and had many good friends. Jane P. would invite me to dinners at her house, which is where I met two wonderful people. Both were academic icons in their earlier years and now provided an enormous amount of learning for a fledgling like me. They were also fun. By this time Lisa was catching on to Lotus, creating macros, and writing letters and manuals.

WHIM OF IRON

Days are long and intense. Lisa and I agreed we never want to write manuals for a living. Both ready to train and market. Randy is doing a remarkable job of putting inventory together. He and Mike work so well together. I am tired and very happy.

One of the biggest blessings in my personal life at this time was Max. He always knew when I was down and he knew when I needed to rub his head—he was such a good and faithful friend. Another example of God smiling on me. I talked to Hazel almost every day and especially liked to be the first to wish her a happy Mothers' Day or whatever the holiday was. Often I cried when I thought of her, because I missed her positive attitude toward me.

Mid-way through May, Jane P. asked me if I would help her with a computer project. She had started a very ambitious book on herbs and their medicinal equivalents. She started it on an IBM machine using their first word processor, Easy Write, which was like going back to the dark ages. Jane had used it because it was easy, but now it was time to transfer the long, complicated book to a format that a modern word processor could use. That's what was required, if the Duke University Press was going to publish it. I knew from the beginning it was a difficult job, but I decided I would do it because Jane had done so much for me. I rationalized that it was something I could work on at night.

My emotional stability was pretty shaky. I would do well until something went wrong (usually something very minor). Then I would fall apart. I remember one day I couldn't find my keys anywhere. I started crying first and then I just went right down in my old spiral of thinking I'm stupid. Sometimes Randy would save the day. This time he came back and helped me look for the keys, and as we talked, he found them. Then I could become an adult again, feeling life is good. Sometimes these bouts made me think I was crazy.

In mid-May, Jane E. and I went to the South Carolina Hospital Association to demonstrate the medical staff software and see if they had an interest for their hospitals. After my presentation, we all talked and they seemed to understand the need. They did not think, however, that small hospitals had any money for equipment and training. We left feeling pretty discouraged. Randy and I were working long and hard to get four medical staff software marketing packages sent out. I had no doubt in my mind that as soon as hospitals got our packet, they would be calling in orders.

Lisa came home from her trip to California to visit her friend, Cindy. She had the flu and is tired. Oh God, will she ever find what we do interesting? Or did Peat Marwick burn her out for good? Good to see her, she is so lovely. Both she and Randy are. Randy has moved into Duke Manor and is a changed man. No mother to nag him anymore. He put my office together using doors for worktables and it looks terrific.

After weeks of trying to carry all the balls, I finally caved in.

Got the flu and really got sick. Lisa and Randy agreed to pitch in more with the stuff that has to get done, but no one wants to do… writing marketing letters, following up on sales calls, and putting marketing packets together. It's pretty clear to me that Lisa has little energy for what we are doing. Randy says the work's too menial for her. He's probably right, and I think she misses the excitement of the big office, lots of people to interact with, dressing up—the whole corporate scene which is what she's been doing since Penn State. There is nothing "corporate" about CBR!

At this time I was still trying to get motivated to sell, but it was difficult. One day I read in a magazine that because I'm a woman, I don't jump out there and sell. Well to heck with that, I thought. I'm going to sell the products based on reporting capabilities—reports that told management where they had problems (turned out to be exactly right). Only problem was I had no idea how to begin, where to begin, with whom. By June the pressure was starting to show:

Having a breakdown. Can't stop crying. Saw a doctor who said it's stress. Slow down. Right. Atmosphere lacking enthusiasm around the house. Lisa must not be happy, but I can't imagine going on without the help she does give. Using hot baths at night to ease away the aches and pains.

Cleo B. Robertson

On June 11th Gary called from New Mexico where he was celebrating his 24th birthday. He seemed to be having a great time, and I was happy for him.

Two of my stepsons put together our training brochures for the medical staff software, and they were wonderful. One was a graphics artist and the other a photographer, so they did a great job. The fact that it was free also helped.

Toward the end of June, the SBA began bugging me for more money on my loan. The interest of 16 percent was killing me, and yet I didn't know what else to do but keep paying. I knew that at that interest I'd never pay off the loan, but I had no way to pay it off in a lump sum. Lowering my stress level was becoming a high priority. I attended a workshop on meditation but the leader *wouldn't shut up,* so that didn't help. Our bank account was down to $800, but now I knew that it was going to be like this. Couldn't sleep most nights, feeling exhausted and fired up at the same time! By the end of June my diary shows my workload was just beginning!

Jane has gotten me scheduled to do eight workshops in six weeks—four at Duke, one in Ohio, two in South Carolina and one in Florida, where I will stay some extra time and visit with my family.

Actually, I learned a lot from the presentations. The Ohio presentation to HSAs on microcomputers in hospitals for medical staff credentialing went well. I was called a powerful and dynamic speaker! The next week

I ran an all-day session with four Duke coordinators of mainframes to turn them into coordinators of PCs and did a good job. I learned that I was good at making presentations, which was reassuring. Being called a powerful and dynamic speaker did my ego good, but didn't do a thing for my checkbook.

> *I feel so foolish in so many ways. Am I just a bag of wind? I've been talking about making it, and we are at a critical point. I can't work any harder and there's no money. What to do?*
>
> *State project getting very complicated but I'm figuring it out. Designed Home Health database for software called Focus.*
>
> *Inherited a 7-week old black kitten, and Max has adopted her as his own. She bites his tail, and he picks her up by putting her whole head in his mouth and walking around with her dangling out. He's exhausted from chasing her. We're down to $93. Oh well. Going to South Carolina next week and both days are fully booked. Jane can't go with me so Lisa is. I am only one on show, so I have to be good. All on me. I can do it.*

On July 25th, Lisa and I drove to Columbia, South Carolina, loaded down with a computer, printer, overhead projector, and screen projection unit. We got it all set up just in time and had 30 people for two different presentations. Fifteen minutes into my show, programming code or gibberish started to scroll across the screen. Everyone could see it. These were novices trying to understand credentialing of physicians, and here were strange symbols confusing their minds even more. It was awful. I kept trying to clean it up, but finally asked Lisa to call Randy and see what he thought. He said to turn the whole damn thing off and start again, which I did, and it worked. God, the pressure was about to put me under, but I think I handled it well. I told the audience that when all else fails, turn the darn thing off—and they laughed.

About this time, a Duke legal advisor recommended a woman named Laura to me. Her expertise was marketing. I stopped to see her on the way to Washington, D.C. She assured me we'd be selling in no time. In retrospect I can see how often I thought someone else's idea would save us. Marketing was the key, but I didn't know a thing about marketing or selling. Hope rose.

We are down to $500 but this time there is little billed out. I have to SELL! Went to Florida to meet with Price Waterhouse about the personnel software. Then did the same presentation with two hospitals, but they both had very little interest.

At the end of August, Randy and I went to Atlantic Beach to install the inventory software at Carteret Hospital as part of the small hospital project. I rented a motel room and we set up our computer on the night table. We worked together to debug and put in things that people were requesting. Then I would debug again. Lisa had debugged a lot, too, which made a big difference. We spent nine days there in that little motel room, but the result was impressive. Although the hospital wouldn't buy a faster computer, the staff seemed happy. We had designed lots of good reports, which would make a big difference in their lives.

One funny incident happened, which we still laugh about today. Randy and I decided we needed a break and that renting a jet ski for an hour for each of us would be just the trick. The Visa card Lisa had loaned me had no balance on it, so I used it. Randy is a motorcyclist and he was soon spinning doughnuts. I had water skied as a teenager so I stood up and really flew forward, thumping and banging on each small wave. We had a wonderful time. The next morning when I woke up, I heard Randy say lamely from the other bed, "Mom, can you walk?" At first I thought his question was silly, and then I tried to get out of bed. No, actually I could not walk. My muscles were so torn up, the best I could do was shuffle. We spent a very painful few days paying for our adventure.

When we got back to Durham, we spent time getting a demo disk ready for the personnel software program to send to Price Waterhouse. After we had sent out ten, we learned that they all had big problems caused by the software we used to develop our software. We were learning very hard, yet valuable, lessons. I had wanted to send out many but it was Randy who saved the day and said, "Hey, Mom, let's wait and see how we do with 10 first!" Very wise! [And a rule we followed from then on]. Randy soon made the changes necessary and we sent out ten new copies.

As I looked at my workday, I was beginning to understand why I was so stressed. It wasn't just the money, or lack thereof. It was all the learning. I was learning mainframe data language such as machine-readable format, fixed length, record format, and much more that I had to understand so that I could interface our software (that means the hospital can move data from our system to theirs and from theirs to ours.) I was also learning Multiplan (a spreadsheet), NCR equipment that the State used, IBM equipment that Duke used, and the State software, Focus. As if that wasn't enough, I was also trying to learn conversion programs so I could convert Jane P's book from Easy Write to a format the Press could recognize. In the end it took four software programs to do the conversions, but she finally was able to publish her book.

By mid-September, Lisa and I finally had to go to my Aunt Peg and ask to borrow $1,500 for three months at 6 percent interest. Peg wrote us a check without any fuss.

The next morning she called at 6:30 a.m. and said, "You really put one over on me. You must think I'm a push over. You two came in here and got what you wanted."

I was so angry. I think that her friends had talked her into making the call, filling her with apprehension about my ability to repay. I immediately called Jane E. and she loaned me the $1,500 and just deducted it from our next payment from Duke. We were down to rice and vegetables, but everyone was still pitching in. My efforts at marketing were fruitless. I had tried marketing the personnel and quality control software to Carol Woods Nursing Home, but they had no one with any time to learn something new.

After many months of working with the Materials Management people at Duke, we finally installed a system in their office, and I felt that was promising. The fact that we did it for free didn't help the bottom line, but I was sure sales would follow. I also did a demo for a large group of Duke managers, but nothing came of it. There always was lots of interest initially, but soon comments such as "no budget, no one to run it or simply no time to learn something new" would filter out. Everyone seemed overworked. I was making lots of calls to hospital people and talking to people in every business where I felt I could get my foot in the door, but still no sales. People, time and again, mentioned their need for risk management software, but at the moment, we had to sell what we had.

By this time, Lisa was getting quite nervous about money and was not used to the "down to $80 bucks" routine that Randy and I had learned to live with. My dilemma was that I needed to sell, but it took time away from development or hourly work that did make some money. I didn't know that selling is an art that must be practiced often.

For my birthday, Lisa made an avocado, chicken and grape salad for lunch. Randy brought over his VCR and we watched videos. It was difficult having the children share these lean times with me. I felt that I was letting them down and yet I would not give up. In the evening, I went to play pool, a sure way to rest my mind and relax, if just for a few games.

In September, Iredell Memorial called and said they wanted to buy the medical staff credentialing software. I was thrilled, but said I'd believe it when I cashed their check. It was at this time that someone told me that hospitals don't pay their bills, so I made a decision that all sales would be cash up front. It didn't occur to me that I couldn't demand cash up front because hospitals didn't pay that way. I decided that if they wanted the software, then I wanted the cash. Iredell argued with me briefly, but they finally agreed to pay cash. When, was not tied down.

By the end of September, I knew that Lisa was not part of our team. When we went to lunch one day I said to her, "So how come you haven't quit?" She cried and admitted that our small, struggling business was just not for her. She was trained as an accountant and accustomed to busy, secure environments. Although she didn't know what she wanted to do, it was clear that staying with us was not a good option.

I awoke on the 30th with a strained back, pinched sciatic nerve and upset stomach. Was it the stress of Lisa leaving? Marketing? Bankruptcy? Probably it was a combination of all the above. I just didn't know how to slow down. It was as if slowing down meant quitting—and there was no way I was going to quit.

I had gotten a call from a woman named Marion at Baltimore Hospital. She had an interest in our credentialing software. I had met Marion through a consulting friend, and she seemed to have the power to approve the sale. Slow as I was in learning selling techniques, I had at least begun to see that if the person I was talking to didn't have the power to say "yes," then I was wasting my time. She assured me she did. Since I would be driving to Baltimore, I decided to see if I could talk to other hospitals along the way. After a frenzy of calls, I set up 7 appointments in 5 cities! My body reacted so strongly I started shaking and having stomachaches during the night before I was to leave. I was also nervous because my car was old, and I had a hard time reading street maps. I tried to tell my body everything would be okay.

My first stop was a pleasant one. I stayed with my brother and his wife, and because we got along well, they helped to reduce my anxiety about selling. I presented to Hadley Memorial and Children's Hospital in Washington, but it was obvious very early on in our discussions that they had no money and very little understanding of how to automate quality management. I had not checked them out enough. Somehow, in these early days of selling, I thought if I could just *show* them the wonderful software, they would want to buy it. Wrong!

My next stop was Baltimore. I'd never been to Baltimore, but I arrived on time and was quite thrilled to have an opportunity to sell to such a large, prestigious hospital. I got all the equipment set up, did my demo, and knew in my heart that there was not a person in the room who could make a financial decision. One more bust!

I couldn't stay the night; I had so little cash with which to travel. So, I drove on to Princeton to stay with a friend. I met with people from the New Jersey Hospital Association (they didn't "get" what I was talking about, and I didn't know how to make it clearer) and people at Princeton Hospital. Princeton Hospital was an interesting interview, because the administrator did know what I was talking about. He was just sure that his information systems people could build a better mousetrap, so to speak. I tried to show him how impractical it would be for them to do what it takes to develop application software for credentialing, but he would hear none of it.

The next day I drove to Hunterdon Medical Center, where I was lucky enough to get an appointment with the head of information services. As it turned out, they also felt they could build it better, and all my visit did was to show them better ways to do it. That afternoon I went to Hamilton Hospital where I was told flat out that they could do their own.

I rested on Sunday, but by Monday was on the road to Philadelphia, where I met with PHA, a hospital-consulting group that had an interest in using our software in their hospitals. It was fruitless from the beginning because they wanted to credential physicians *for* the hospitals, and that would mean tracking physicians in the software by *hospital*, something we could not do at that time. That afternoon I went on to Baltimore again, this time to meet with a man from the Daughters of Charity who had heard about us through Marion. I showed him the system, all the while noting his total lack of interest. When I was done, he told me there was no money. I guess it was just a tip he had to check out.

I went back to Washington to meet with PHOA (can't even remember what it stands for), but my notes make it clear there was no interest. Stayed overnight with my brother and sister-in-law again, where I got a call from Marion. She wanted me to come back and demonstrate to the medical school. I was ecstatic. Of course I said I would, so the next day I drove back to Baltimore and set up all over again. This time there were good questions, and I left feeling hopeful.

When I finally returned to Durham on October 17th, I was a little more broke, but not discouraged somehow. Clearly, I needed to work on my sales assessment skills. I promised myself I would screen requests for my time better.

Hazel turned 77 today and she sure misses me. What a support system she is for me. She always tells me to keep on going. "It's a long lane that doesn't ever turn," she reminds me, or, "It can't rain all the time, the sun got to shine sometime." I love her so much.

We owe $2,000 in back taxes. Oh my, no wonder my colon is spastic. When we are successful we'll always be able to say, "We paid our dues." Randy says we must persevere! How right he is.

Marc, a marketing consultant, met with Randy and me and says we have a good product, and he'll put together a marketing plan. I'm so excited. Marion has agreed to $1,000 per day for me to work with her staff. I have to send her a proposal. Richland Memorial Hospital *called and said they were buying credentialing for $4,000! Great.*

Marion's Baltimore job seemed too good to be true—and it was. She ended up having no money power at all, and nothing came from all my work.

Lisa's leaving meant that I now had to go back to keeping the books, something that stressed me out a lot. I also had to start testing again, something that she had seemed to enjoy and which I did, too, when I wasn't worried about selling.

My excitement over the sale to Richland Memorial Hospital was short lived. They called in November and cancelled their order—they had gotten free software from someone and would use that. At first I panicked. I had a fear of failing at selling. But I knew we needed cash. SELL, SELL, SELL as Randy said.

November brought some bad news and some good news.

Gave keynote address at Food Service Institute's annual meeting. I was so so. I have so much to learn. I called my stepson, Dan, because I was so upset that I hadn't been great. He was so supportive.

Laboratory at Duke bought our personnel program! We will live another month! Also, State contract turned on. Finally. Went to play pool and then danced my ass off. I would love to be somewhere warm right now. My dog

Max's hips are starting to give out. I had taken him for a long walk and he moaned all night. Hope it passes. I'm not ready for a life without Max.

I am tired, happy, scared, excited, and having my period again. Will menopause never come? I am 47. Down to $200. Made a lot of calls but no cigar. To bed at 8; up since 5:30 a.m.

Once money came in, the first priority was always to get Randy more equipment. By this time I had learned that I had to make marketing calls every day, and I did. I hated it. I didn't know to whom I really should be talking to, and I wasn't getting sales...*but I made those damn calls!* In mid-November, I drove eight hours in two days, gave six hours of training at Iredell Memorial installing inventory, and made no money off of it. This installation was still part of the Duke project, so I felt it was important to have someone using the inventory program—hard to sell without any users.

Thanksgiving was coming up, and I desperately needed to have family around me. Dan had already said he was coming down, and I knew Carl, my children's father, was going to be in town, so I just decided to invite everyone—Lisa, Randy, Gary, Dan, Carl, Ralph, Jane E, and Dick, a man from where I played pool, who had no place to eat that day. We had grilled turkey and oysters galore that Carl had provided. The house at 2121 West Club was full of laughter and good cheer, if only for one day.

Right after Thanksgiving I sold our Inventory program to the pharmacy at Duke for $4,500! That meant we could live through January.

Margaret Knox is doing an article on me in The Leader. Marc wants us to go on a national selling tour and go sell millions. Why not? But of course, those are just words.

The Council for Entrepreneurial Development (CED) in the Research Triangle Park seemed like something I should join. I had heard about it from my lawyer, and because I needed some business direction, I had joined back in the summer. Now I received a stockholder's meeting notice and decided I would go. When I showed up at the little one-room office where the proxy votes were being counted, everyone was stunned when I asked where the other stockholder's were. I had never heard of proxy voting, and when I told them that, they all laughed.

Luckily, one of the men realized I was naive but serious and suggested that I go to the next meeting and volunteer for the Planning Committee so I could learn what the organization was all about. The first meeting I attended was rather daunting. When I walked in to the auditorium at a local company at 7:30 a.m. in my only suit, I was faced with a sea of suits, 99 percent men. The presentation was interesting, however. I started attending meetings and became more and more involved in what was going on. It took time away from marketing, but I figured I would be networking, and that would give me leads. Besides, I reasoned, I was learning how to market, sell, and grow, and wasn't that what I needed to learn?

The Council was made up of some 400-600 businesses that ranged in size from one person to thousands, from thousands of dollars in income to millions, and with a range of services and programs that certainly looked like they could help me with my small business. I joined the Planning Committee, and my life changed. I met Peter Bechtel, a young entrepreneur who had already started a hardware business and soon launched his physician-billing system. I met Jack Hunnel, a president of two companies that made medical prototypes for manufacturing. These two men became my allies, while the whole CED became my second home.

On December 5th, I held Max as he moaned while the doctor gave him a shot. He softened into my arms and was gone. Dear God, take his wonderful soul to spread goodness amongst the stars! I cried. It hurt so badly. He was so much a part of my life every day. He was a good dog, good friend, and a good protector. As much as he brought into my life, I did not think I wanted to replace him. First of all, he was irreplaceable. Second of all, I was putting more energy in to the business and didn't feel I had time for a new dog.

By this time Randy wanted to get more out of the business—he wanted to be paid in shares of stock. Even though CBR wasn't worth anything, I understood. After talking with my lawyer, I knew that I had to be very careful. Having stockholders would make the business less attractive to lenders, investors, and buyers! In the end, I decided to give Randy 88 shares. How we arrived at that number, I don't remember, but I do remember Randy's reaction.

Had lunch with Randy today. Marc and David (lawyer) came and we gave him a stock certificate for 88 shares. He appreciated neither the luncheon nor the stocks. He wanted more. I thought he would be pleased. Oh well.

I couldn't get him to understand that I needed to retain stock as a negotiating tool, and that his owning it lessened my ability to negotiate. The tension between us started to escalate.

Christmas was coming upon me fast. I decided, because I couldn't afford to buy Christmas gifts, I would do a family tree for the Robertson/Zahnizer families (my father's and mother's families) using Lotus123. It took many more hours than I anticipated (of course), but when it was done, it looked great and was very comprehensive. I mailed it off to everyone for Christmas. I felt good about my gift, but depressed about Christmas.

About this time, one of the Duke programmers raised the question of who owned the credentialing, inventory, and scheduling software...Duke or me? It was a good question. By rights, since Duke had provided all the programming power in the beginning and set up all my sites, it belonged to them. That meant I had to negotiate some kind of lease or royalty arrangement with them. After talking with Duke's lawyer and my own, I decided to get everyone together and talk about it.

> *Today I hosted a luncheon at Bakasias's for Bob, second in command at Duke, Jane E., Max (Duke's lawyer), Marc and David (my lawyer), and both Duke programmers. The subject of discussion was CBR having the rights to the six software programs we had developed. While everyone was sitting around talking, Bob walked in and sat at the end of the table and had me sit in the corner seat next to him.*
>
> *In a very low voice, Bob asked me what I wanted to do with the software. I said, "Make it the best ever and sell it." He said immediately, "Have a dollar?" I said yes, and handed him one. He said, "Okay, you now own all six." He then got everyone's attention and said he valued CBR Associates and wanted to maintain a good relationship, because he knew his departments all benefited. He told them that as of this day, CBR now would own all rights to the software. Everyone was surprised, toasted me, and that was that. God bless Bob. Only the lawyers looked disappointed.*

Christmas came and was a great success, despite my swinging moods, as usual. I got lots of good things from my children. In fact, overall, things seemed to be going pretty well. Life was very different without Max. Mornings, especially, I missed him. We had taken walks together almost every day. I didn't feel as secure at night either, when I was alone. Max's death changed the whole structure of my life. I stayed in bed, loafed, got fat. I finally realized I would have to get another dog.

I spent New Year's Eve alone and went from desperation to satisfaction. I worked a little, talked a long time with Jane E., who continued to be my personal advisor, and finally got all dressed up and took a taxi to my favorite bar and dance spot. I played some good pool, drank too many beers by winning, and decided to walk the mile or so home. My thought at the end of 1985 was that "alone is not bad." I also had confidence we would make it....somehow!

1986 — Many, Many Road Trips; No Cigars

One of my presents from Jane E. had been a book of inventions by Will and Ariel Durant. And it had this great quote:

> *"The past is the present rolled out to understand.*
>
> *The present is the past rolled up for action!"*
>
> *Will and Ariel Durant*

As the year began, having not learned from my other lessons, I decided to string together a whole bunch of presentations and go on the road. My summary of those visits was not very encouraging:

Back after driving 1,538 miles alone, I met with:

ROI in Wilmington, Delaware, who had an interest in credentialing but no money allocated for it.

Medical Center at Princeton wants credentialing but doesn't feel confident it will do enough for them.

St. Francis Hospital, Trenton. Wants credentialing but has no money.

Robert who has his own business doesn't see a need. No help there.

Stephen, AMICUS. No interest.

Columbia Women's Medical Center liked credentialing but no money.

Howard University Hospital doesn't understand the need.

All in all, absolutely nothing came out of an expensive, time-consuming and tiring trip. I still had not learned how to qualify a buyer. In fact, at that time I didn't even know I was supposed to! Sometimes I began to think I planned this trip so I would feel important.

I sit here and cry from time to time. I hate doing the taxes. I don't want to do them. Called Randy. He thinks I'm crazy, that it's a snap. Let him try to figure it out! Max, I miss you following me around saying, "I love you" with your eyes. Yesterday so high, today so low. So what?

The space shuttle, with six people aboard, blew up today. Oh God, if I miss Max, what are those families going through?

The space shuttle disaster reminded me that my problems weren't really all that bad. In fact, as awful as it may seem, I think it settled me down. I finished my taxes and payroll, caught up on all correspondence, and felt satisfied I was doing the best I could. My weight, however, continued to creep up…by this time I weighed 158 and was feeling awful, and panicked.

I had a history of yo-yoing on weight. I gained 30 pounds during my first marriage and lost it all soon after I divorced. I gained 90 pounds during my second marriage and lost it all soon after I divorced. I had kept it all off until now, and I didn't know what to do. Divorce the business? NEVER, I said.

I was always trying to make myself go more slowly. "Just do 30 things a day instead of 60." But I couldn't. The way I looked at it, it was the 60 things per day that kept the electric on, the water flowing, the phone working and a roof over our heads. Food was available most of the time, and we dressed fine. Compared to what I grew up with, we looked rich! Slowing down was tantamount to quitting.

Good day. Found a deposit I hadn't recorded of $2150, which helped my panic. Lisa moves to Greensboro Sunday. Helped her pack. She has a new job, a new apartment and a new start. I shall miss her daily presence, and I'm happy she's happy.

Cleo B. Robertson

How to market our services and products? I don't have the answer, yet. Learning Dac-Easy, an accounting program. Should help me keep books straight and taxes too.

5 a.m. and wide awake and anxious. Just about everything. For a person who can't relax if money is a problem, I'm sure in the wrong business. I still believe in what we're doing.

Whenever I began to doubt whether sticking with what I loved made sense, I would remember the book on millionaires. The book had helped me answer an important question: "Would I do better in another field?" The answer was clearly no. I was doing what I loved. Not only did I love developing software, I loved the thought that I could prevent errors in hospitals. So here it was, 1986, and I was still broke, but I believed I should stick with it.

Events were soon to take place that would change everything dramatically. Over the past two years, Randy had grown enormously in skills. He was very important to me. With a lot of time, hard work and help from Duke programmers, he had become exceptional at writing software code. With my tutoring and direction, he also learned how to listen to what it was people wanted and then make the computer do it. He had a natural desire to please, a wonderful curiosity about making things work, and great pride in accomplishing any task. Who could ask for a better person to work with? He had even learned to work with me on difficult ideas.

Randy soon proved that he could design, too. He didn't always know the ramifications of what he was doing because he didn't go into the hospitals often to talk with staff, but he could hear their needs and was soon turning those needs and desires into reality. He would take anyone's ideas or mine further and make it work fantastically.

Another area of his new expertise was hardware. Something was always going wrong with something, but Randy would just pull the box off the central processing unit (the big box with a computer) and look inside to see what needed fixing. I never had to use technical support for hardware because Randy was it. He also learned all the other software we needed to develop—communications, backing up, managing large files, repairing disks—probably 30 or more software programs!

So, in the spring of 1986, when Randy told me he wanted to talk with me, I felt we were an unbeatable team. He started out the conversation very slowly. He had been talking to a lot of people at Duke. They liked his work. And finally he broke it to me. Duke wanted to hire him directly. He would be part of the microcomputer support team, working with the top programming professionals at Duke. Because Duke had been an IBM development site for years, the amount of professional expertise that would be available to Randy was unbelievable.

I remember telling myself to breathe. I also felt pissed that Duke had so little faith that CBR could make it, that they had decided to hire my *only* programmer away. And, it had been those very same programmers who had said I was making a big mistake by bringing him down to work with me in the first place. Shit! After all that had passed through my brain in seconds, I said, "Randy, if Duke wants you and you want to go to Duke, go. It's a great opportunity." He was first and foremost my son. If this was what he wanted to do, then I could only support him in his quest.

Randy and I came through a crisis today that would take most people a lifetime. If I had known that Duke was courting him to go work for them, I would have panicked about it. Well, today he told me he's leaving CBR. They offered him $20,000, which is more than I can do. I was destroyed AND I knew he had to go, so I gave him my blessing and best wishes as my heart pumped heavily and my stomach churned. He'll go to work for Duke by June 1. He said he needed to get his education. I am terrified of life without Randy.

Over the next few months, I tried to get to a point where I could operate without Randy. The programs at Duke would not be a problem, because Randy would be their support person on site now. But the other software I had out in four hospitals was an issue. What would I do when there was a problem? Call Randy? (He said yes at first, but after a month or so, he said he couldn't take support calls at Duke anymore. From then on, every time the phone rang, my whole body reacted.)

WHIM OF IRON

During these months I was tired a lot, working hard, and trying not to think about AR ("After Randy"). The State project was going well, and Randy and I were making good progress on getting Inventory debugged, so all was not at a loss.

I was in Atlanta at a hospital conference when I ran into Herb, a salesman I had met in Princeton. Herb knew Atlanta and he wanted to sell. He was particularly comfortable with hospitals, so it seemed natural for us to do sales calls together until he was comfortable with our product. He went ahead and set up some hospitals appointments with people he knew, and we did a good job presenting. I came away thinking we had made two sales.

Upon my return to Durham, I made a trip to Stokes Reynolds Memorial Hospital in Danbury, North Carolina. They had a 55-bed skilled nursing facility and 40 long-term care beds. As their director of medical staff said, they were tired of being shut out from the computer world. After a long conference, they decided to order an AT computer, a word processor and our credentialing program. After all the times I had heard that and it didn't happen, I decided to hold my excitement until I cashed a check. They did confirm for me that the smaller hospitals understood the power a computer on a desk would bring to their fingertips, even more than the large ones.

What the trip told me once more, however, was that the software was needed. Even in a small hospital, it was needed. Although they only had 15 physicians on staff, they had no one with the time to credential each physician yearly (credentialing requires re-verifying where the doctors went to school, interned, did residency, surgical procedures they may perform, etc.). If it isn't done, the hospital never knows if a physician's license has expired, or if there is a lawsuit against that person. I saw the need for smaller hospitals to have the same capability as large hospitals and they did, too.

I came back very excited, and my mind could not stop racing. I thought that when Randy was no longer with me full time, he would still work on his own free time to fix bugs, etc. and life wouldn't seem a whole lot different. We needed to finish the product. We had talked about ownership of the software at one point over the years, and I had agreed to 50/50 with him…when we had a product and were selling it. I assumed he would continue to invest his time in the product because he believed in it. I was in for a rude awakening.

Another rude awakening occurred one early morning when I got a call, and it was Randy. He hadn't been able to sleep, so he had gotten up to use a new bottle cutter he had bought so he could make things out of bottles as gifts. When he had pressed down on the bottle to cut the neck off, it slipped, almost cutting his thumb off. I rushed over immediately and drove him to the Emergency Room at Duke. When they took him into an examining room and blood spurted across the table, I fainted. He turned out to be quite lucky, because they sewed it up and he didn't have any loss of motion. I was glad to be there for him; I missed him and his energy a lot.

WHIM OF IRON

Back from fruitless 1000-mile trip to South Carolina. Didn't sell anything.

All the driving was killing my legs, so I finally gave in and made a call to a man in Greensboro who sold dogs. I needed to start walking again. He assured me he had the perfect dog for me. Boude was a 125-pound, real German shepherd, and when I first walked in to see him, he came loping up to me with the biggest head and skinniest body I had ever seen. I asked where he came from, and the seller said a family in Tennessee. From the looks of him, the family didn't give two hoots for him. The price was $1,000. I actually had the money and since I've never been good at managing it, I said yes and gave him $400 down payment. I thought I was crazy, but when this very loving, very lonely dog rubbed his head in my hands and almost purred, I caved in. My heart went out to him because he was as lonely as I was. As we drove home, I kept reaching in the back seat and petting his head so he would get to know me.

A week later:

Got a new dog, Boude. A new dog that shits in the house and doesn't know how to bark... for only $1000. Taking long walks with dog, which I need as much as he does. I think he has heartworms.

Which it turned out, he did. It took several hundred dollars for a treatment that almost kills the dog, and then weeks of his vomiting up worms, but I couldn't let him die. By this short time, he was important in my life.

On the same day the State said they wanted to renew my contract for one year at $50 per hour, and they said they wanted me full time. That computed into $60,000 per year, which seemed pretty good for little old me. So my immediate need for cash would be taken care of, or so I thought. My passion, however, the software, was now entering a new phase. In this phase I would be the designer, tester, installer, and supporter of all our software, assuming I could also sell it. My mind and stomach cringed at the thought.

Randy kept busy in his last days trying to clear up any bugs in credentialing, since that was the program that people had the most interest in. If I could sell one credentialing program, we would be on a roll, I was sure. I was making lots of calls to follow up on leads people would give me, but I didn't know how to qualify a call. I didn't even know how to find out who could make a decision.

Bob had me write an article on credentialing for some magazine, which I most willingly did. At this point in my career, I was trying to get into all journals, talk to all hospitals, and meet with all potential customers, even if they weren't in the hospital arena. Took me a long time to know how to learn and use these skills.

On May 9th, Randy left CBR. I had no idea at that moment how much my life was about to change. I left for Atlanta the same day.

The trade show I thought I had to go to was interesting, but it was not where I should have been spending my money. When Herb and I met for lunch, it didn't take long to know that he was not selling any systems, primarily because he simply was not aware of the hospital's needs and what credentialing was all about. Our relationship fell apart the first night I got there. Herb wanted us to make changes in the software to make it more marketable. I knew I could not do that. Not just because Randy was no longer available, but because what he was trying to do was to solve *all* their problems, and I knew enough to know that would not work—hospitals would always need more. Sell what we have, I told him. He couldn't. We both soon realized we could not work together, and I went back to Durham quite depressed.

Randy's happy at Duke and doesn't want to work for me this week. He says he will next week—we'll see. He's having a blast setting up his new AT they bought him. State project keeping me busy but no money; I need to put some aside for the lean times.

5/18/86 Randy testy with me tonight as we worked on Personnel. It's 9:30 and we just quit. Too long a day for him, and he's having more fun there. What am I going to do?

I could see that once he got out of the daily routine of working 12 hours, he found there was a life after CBR. He began to enjoy himself, have friends and do things other than work. I didn't see a lot of him but I certainly didn't blame him.

5/22/86 Depression weighing me down. Check from State has not come yet, and I've been broke for two weeks already. Randy totally uninvolved in work for me. I'm adrift. Do I sell? Who will support? Oh God, Oh God. Head hurts. State contract may get shot down. Then what do I do? Only Boude loves me, and I'm impatient even with him. Lisa's off on 5 weeks of vacation. Maybe I should have gotten a degree. I keep crying, which doesn't help my head. I'm so panicked. I can't think. I need to rest this weekend. I need to stop worrying. Oh God, how did my mom survive? Poverty sucks.

People came from Scottish Rite Children's Hospital in Atlanta to see medical staff credentialing at Duke—they were impressed but nothing said about buying and I didn't know how to ask if they wanted to buy.

I was managing to go to the State project every day, but my heart was still with the software. I continued to test at night and to write all my comments down for Randy. When he did come over, he was always angry with me. This was no longer what he wanted to do. He taught me Crosstalk so I could support hospitals myself on the phone, then left with no word about when we'd work together again.

Hosplan, a marketing company, had heard about our credentialing program and wanted me to write up the specifications. I desperately needed their help, but I simply didn't know all the answers to their technical questions. I called Randy at work, and he said he would no longer talk to me on Duke's time. My heart stopped for a beat, and then I asked if he could meet with me that night so I could submit our specs to Hosplan. He said maybe. That evening as I wrote the specs, I called him, but his phone was constantly busy. I finally panicked because I was meeting with the people the next day, and took a cab to Randy's apartment (my car was in the shop). I wanted to tell him how much I needed his help, but he was gone. I had wasted six precious dollars to no avail. I decided I must replace him as soon as possible. That night I washed and waxed the kitchen floor to keep from screaming.

Another trip to Stokes Memorial Hospital, and another promise of a sale. No check had appeared from the State yet, and all my inquiries went unanswered. Damn. In the meantime, I was giving them all my day time. I started interviewing programmers and found one that I thought would do. It was very difficult to know what skills a programmer had or needed for our work, but I took a desperate stab in the dark and hired him. With Scottish Rite Hospital in Atlanta saying they were going to buy also, I knew I needed someone to help me, or I'd fall flat on my face.

Randy isn't around much. As someone said, "He's just off on his own path." Oh well, I'll survive, as Hazel said this morning.

Spent day from 4 a.m. to noon setting up or testing inventory, and from 12 to 9:30 p.m. learning and using Reflex, a new software program the State uses. Got my state check and it's all spent, but I feel much better. Problems with Personnel program and lots of debugging with Inventory.

In between my State schedule, I squeezed in meetings with people at Duke to teach them how to use our Inventory program. Luckily, when it had problems, Randy was right there to help. For non-Duke projects, he was less able to help. Duke was working him hard.

On Thursday the medical staff program wouldn't load into my computer. I called Randy, and he said he couldn't help me from work and then left for a four-day weekend without letting me know. I'm supposed to demo to five hospitals next week. What a disaster. I hate being dependent on him. Doom and gloom gathering. Part of me understands his need to separate from the business. Part of me can't, because I worry that if I totally let go of him, I'll fail.

Somehow I managed to get the program to load and was able to get ready for the demos. How I could go ahead and do these demos with no programmer on staff if I did sell one, I'll never know. I did know, however, that when I had gone on sales calls with Herb at hospitals, the administrators invariably talked to him, seldom me. I could see they were more comfortable with a salesman than a saleswoman. What to do?

Sunday evening I went to play pool. As I stood in the crowded, smoky room I looked around. Over the tops of people's heads I could see a clean-shaven, blond-haired, good-looking young man standing near the cash register.

I walked over to him and asked him his name. He said, "Greg."

"Well, Greg," I said casually, "what are you doing on Monday?"

He was definitely surprised. But he answered, "Nothing."

"Good," I replied. "Do you own a suit?"

"Yes," came cautiously from his lips, as I could see him trying to figure out what I was up to.

"Greg," I said very matter-of-factly, "I have to visit with hospitals next week and I need a man to go with me. I'll pay you $50 per day for two days; are you available?"

"Well," he replied in his delightful southern accent, "that depends. What do I have to do?"

A smile broke over my face and I answered, "Nothing. Just shake your head yes or no and say nothing. Can you do that?"

Of course he could, so Monday morning bright and early, I picked him up at his apartment. He looked very business-like in his suit. I filled him in during our drive down to a hospital in the western section of the state, our first appointment. By the time we were all sitting in a conference room—the administrator, vice president of the medical staff, medical staff director and the medical staff credentialer—Greg was primed.

Sure enough, they asked him questions, he nodded, and I responded. This went on for over half an hour. In the end they all looked at each other and the director said, "Well, I think we should get it," and everyone agreed. This was the only time Greg said anything. He smiled warmly and said, "Good decision." I could have hugged him.

The next day we repeated our stellar performance at a hospital ten miles away. We did well, but I could tell that their "head of information services" was feeling threatened. After all, wasn't it *his* job to program for departments? As it turned out I was right, and they didn't order. But taking Greg with me in the end got me two sales (he went on two calls in Durham), and after that I didn't have to use him anymore—I had references so I could go on my own.

When I got back home, I found that Jane E. had called me five times while I was out. When I got back to her, she told me that Duke wanted to give me $25,000 for the right to use all the CBR software we had developed. They had agreed that I could continue to market what we had developed, and that their changes and improvements would also belong to CBR. I truly felt like God was walking in front of me. When I went into the living room to yell and scream and jump for joy, Boude came running in to see what was wrong. For the first time since his ordeal, he looked better and I gave him a huge hug. The heartworms were gone and we had cash…what more could anyone want?

Well, actually what I wanted was to get the check immediately. By September I still hadn't gotten the money, and I was real broke and real scared. My hip and leg were acting up from old injuries, so walking Boude was difficult. My weight was going up, I missed Randy's company and hearty laugh, and I was just simply lonely.

    One morning, when I took Boude on our usual 3-mile walk around the golf course, we were about a mile from home, when my leg and hip just crashed. I fell to the grass and could not, for the life of me, stand up. I didn't know what to do. There was no traffic at 7 a.m. on the side street we were on, so I just sat petting Boude and crying. Finally I realized I had to get help, so I started crawling towards the golf course clubhouse hoping to find someone to help me. It was about 200 yards, and a most difficult crawl up and down over hills and across the macadam parking lot, but I finally reached the main building. I waited a few minutes and then heard a voice. I yelled out, "Help" and within seconds a man was by my side in total bewilderment. I explained what had happened, and in no time Boude and I were loaded in his truck. He dropped us off at home and went on his way.

    I knew what I needed to heal my leg and hip—money. The Duke money or the State money—I'd take either one. In actuality, it took about a week of rest to heal my physical problems. The financial ones took a little longer. Somehow I got through August. I still had a sick car, no credit card, no health insurance, and not even enough money to buy any food other than staples. September was busy at the State, but there was still no word about the new contract or any payment for the work I had already done. By this time I had hired John, a programmer, and had already found that what he knew was too unstructured for what I was doing, so I let him go. Since we had agreed he would work a few weeks without pay to see if there was a fit, I wasn't out any money, thank God.

On my 48th birthday, Duke came through. Jane called me around noon and told me she was coming over. As soon as I saw the envelope in her hand, my stomach relaxed and I took a deep breath. The $25,000 check looked mighty good.

Lisa and I drove to George's in Shelby. He's my relative, and I wanted advice about what to do with the $25,000 and to see if he could help us financially. When he learned that I have no credit due to the SBA loan, he said he couldn't work with me. We were very hurt.

At the time I was angry with George for not having any faith in me. Years later I realized that as a banker, he was not used to taking such a big risk, and couldn't, even for me.

I had met another young man named Jack, and he seemed to be a programmer, so we talked about him trying out. He started hanging around and even brought his old, beat up computer. He seemed to know a lot, but when I tried to get him to look at our programming code, his eyes would glaze over. I soon realized he was not a Randy.

Gary called to let me know that he was going to Virginia Tech. His father had been nagging him to go to college, and I guess it was just time. He was doing real well and interested in microbiology. I was delighted he was challenging his good mind.

The Council for Entrepreneurial Development was taking up a good deal of my time. My name appeared in the newsletter as co-chairperson for the CED expo, an annual event that drew hundreds of businesses and thousands of visitors. Jack and Peter were still trying to teach me what I needed to know to market myself, but of course they had their own businesses and problems to solve. I wasn't sure I was learning anything that would save my business, but having the association with good people in business, who were also friends, was well worth my time.

It never entered my head after Randy left that I would stop developing or trying to sell the software. I was committed, as committed as a pig when served for breakfast. I still had my vision and passion; I just didn't have any money or a programmer. My life was ruled by my whims, and the software was one whim that I was willing to give lots of iron—I wanted to succeed. Luckily, I thought that all success took was a lot of iron.

The year ended with lots of loose ends, financially, but I was managing alone, even when I thought I couldn't. I felt good, and Boude and I were a great team. As I toasted in the New Year, I was confident that 1987 would be a really good year!

1987 — To Sell, or Not to Sell; That is the Question

The New Year began with much excitement. Duke had agreed to put on a workshop I had designed dealing with medical staff management. In 1987, hospitals were quite leery and very hesitant to try to manage "doctors," but the handwriting was on the wall. The Joint Commission on Accreditation of Health Care Organizations (JCAHO) was pushing for more documentation of physicians' credentials, so it seemed like the perfect opportunity. Besides, physicians needed support when they got sued, and good data could help the good doctors. If a hospital could show that Dr. X had the fewest incidents of infection, for instance, then a lawsuit over an infection could be avoided or at least defended.

Besides Jane E., Bob had been my main Duke supporter, and he was most supportive of the medical staff workshop. On January 2, he came over and we had a wonderful time. We sat in front of the fire, ate boiled shrimp, and dreamed up the best workshop in the world. Bob gave me permission to talk with anyone at Duke in order to have great materials and handouts. We felt we were putting together a workshop that would show hospital CEOs how to avoid lawsuits, save money, and compile information that would benefit everyone.

When I checked with Jane, she suggested I talk to the director of marketing for Duke, who she felt could be quite helpful. I called and had no problem getting an appointment. I was being taken seriously, and that made me feel very positive, strong, and confident. My meeting with the director went well, but I could tell that he questioned whether hospitals wanted to know what we were going to present. Were they ready to manage doctors? I couldn't believe they wouldn't be; he seemed to feel that perhaps they weren't.

Changes were taking place in my family that would greatly impact my life. Lisa had met her future husband at a training seminar, and it was just starting to dawn on me that one day soon my daughter would get married and leave me, in a literal sense. I found myself crying at the strangest times—in the car when I thought about her, or walking down a hallway in a hospital, I would suddenly start crying and have to go to the ladies room. It felt very much like when she went off to college. At that time I cried for six months before she left and then totally supported her and adjusted once she was gone. I guess I was getting ready for her leaving me again, permanently. I had a very good feeling about Andy. I truly felt they knew what they were getting in to, and could stick with it, through thick and thin.

When I wasn't thinking about Lisa, my time was taken up with dreams about the Duke workshop. I had visions of hundreds signing up, standing room only, and great newspaper stories about the glorious event. It was great fun. I also was sick with a cold and cough again, something that kept plaguing me through these years. Obviously I needed more rest, but I was driven—driven to prove myself, driven to be someone, driven to be recognized. It's a wonder I didn't drive me right into the grave.

Once again, trying to bring people into my life who could help and share the load, I agreed to have Jim, a young, local man who liked computing, start at CBR. He showed a lot of promise, knew computer jargon, and I hoped with some training, he could take over for Randy. Randy was supportive. His head was at Duke and he would have loved to let go of CBR. But, thank goodness, his conscience wouldn't let him leave, totally. Jane loaned me some NCR equipment so I'd have a computer for Jim. Randy took on the responsibility for getting the "medical staff system" together. He said he would supervise Jim, get the system running, and advise me as to his usefulness after a month or so.

Randy seemed to understand that I couldn't do it all alone and started relieving me in many ways. He also started taking some responsibility for the final product. I was thankful.

Long days, long nights. I wish I were cooler and calmer through it all. Randy seems to be taking more control—I love him for it. Hazel called to thank me again for her microwave—she loves it and uses it every day! Great. Sent Hazel a heating blanket and sheets. Should help keep her warmer.

I overspent at Christmas and gave microwaves to Hazel, Lisa and Randy. I had never managed money as a child, and I had never seen money managed by my mom, so when I got money, I spent it. It seemed to be the only power I had.

What kept me most sane during these times was talking with Hazel, who was always there. I could see her sitting in her recliner, listening to TV, watching out her door at passers by, or waiting for someone to drop in or call. I called her often and loved to hear her say, "Hello, baby. How are you doing?" I always felt like I was the most important person in Hazel's life even though I knew I wasn't. She was a mother to me, and always helped me come out of a funk. God bless her soul.

When I wasn't trying to train Jim or doing the State project, I was busy getting ready for the workshop scheduled for April. I had built a database that I could use to show the audience how easily accessible information on physicians could be. We wanted to show that hospitals would be able to answer the following questions quickly and accurately:

- How many physicians are on staff by specialty, office location, and other variables collected?
- What is the age distribution of the staff by specialty and number of admissions?

WHIM OF IRON

- Who has been trained to perform what surgical procedures?
- Which physicians are not meeting the continuing education requirements?

These were just a few of the questions we could answer with our credentialing software. The point of the workshop was to show the CEO's and administrators what they could do with the data they were already collecting. We didn't add work; we just gave them useful information from the work they were already doing. Seemed logical to me that they'd want to know.

I loaded in data on 50 physicians—office locations, age, specialty, number of admissions, etc.—until I had enough to make the reports meaningful. Then I designed reports and profiles to show how easy it would be to get answers to their questions.

It never occurred to me they weren't asking any questions. It took this workshop to realize they had so many fires every day to handle, that managing the physicians who brought in their income wasn't on the list. In fact, I later learned they intentionally left the physicians alone as much as they could, so the physicians wouldn't get pissed off. I had studied enough hospital statistics to know that in a small hospital, if one physician leaves, half the admissions could go with him. They wanted to keep their physicians producing income—managing them would be of no benefit whatsoever. Of course, it took time for me to get their point. I had developed software on a whim, and I was going to make them use it whether they wanted to or not. Or at least that's what I think I was thinking. How else could I have gone on?

The State contract was going well. I was learning four new software systems so I could teach the staff how to use them. They were complicated programs (Paradox was one), so I decided to learn how to program them (there was a programming language built in) so that I could make the system easier. It took a lot of my time, both at the State and at home, to learn how to make the software do what I wanted, but eventually I got it. People at the State varied in their acceptance of the software, but eventually they started using it.

As part of the State contract, I had been asked to work with small hospitals and health centers and get them using software, too. Stovall Memorial Hospital was interested in the State system I had been building to track patient data. I drove up into the mountains to install the system and show them how it worked, keeping in mind, these were not the days when computers were everywhere. When I walked in with a computer, I could *feel* everyone back away, particularly the women, who would be expected to learn how to use them, usually with little or no training. All hospitals were under financial pressures, but small ones like Stovall felt the pressure most of all.

I spent two frustrating days trying to get everything working, train the timid woman in charge, and get home before dark on Friday, a five-hour drive. By noon on Friday, it was obvious the system would not be ready to go. I was so disappointed, but there was little I could do. The State was tied into NCR equipment and software, and it had a lot of bugs (as all software did in those days). I left by two on Friday feeling I had failed. I would have stayed the weekend and worked on it, but the CED-expo was being held the next day and I wanted to be there.

The CED-expo '87 took place today at the McKinnon Center, and it was a huge success. Met lots of wonderfully interesting people and had a good time.

On the Monday following the CED-expo, I drove back to Stovall Memorial Hospital. After eleven hours of trying to get them up and running, I gave up. Too many hardware problems (eventually a new PC had to be sent to them, and then things finally worked). I felt defeated driving home.

Car broke down on I40—broken hose. Thank goodness for AAA. Came home to dance (alone) with a nice fire and then wrote copy for my brochure. Great night.

By the 21st things were worse again. I had visited Stovall again but still no success.

I'm depressed tonight, along with millions of others. Swam 50 laps last night in Masters swim—I should feel good, but tonight I joined an aerobics class and couldn't follow the steps—I felt like Heloise, the elephant. Dieting would get me my self-image back—so I eat cake instead. My head is screwed up. Called Dan—May Day, May Day. He said to call back in ten minutes. Maybe I will, maybe I won't. I hurt so badly emotionally. God, what is going on? I'm a wreck.

Why I never recognize that I am in the same negative self-image role that I have been in thousands of times before, I don't know. Up down, up, down. What better way to feel you are worth nothing than to overeat and be fat? That's easy. To not overeat, to relax and breathe, to *not* do a million things a day because my work is my worth...those are the choices that I knew would help me feel worthwhile. I seldom chose any of them. Being fat and critical of myself felt comfortable and safe.

When I wasn't at the State project, I was home working on the workshop database. Jane and Bob were helping, because we all wanted the workshop to be a great success. Duke had produced a very professional brochure and sent it out to lots of hospitals. Was it enough? We didn't know, but we hoped so. It was snowing out, which always helped me stay home and focus. In fact, for the rest of January, snow, ice, and sleet were our constant companions.

Scottish Rite Hospital in Atlanta had our credentialing software, which we had named MedstaffPLUS. It was up and running, but frequently had problems. Since their information service people hadn't bought the software, they wouldn't even try to support it. Most of their problems had to do with their hardware, but we soon found we were expected to take care of *everything.* Randy started looking for software that would allow us to dial into a system and see what was going wrong and fix it over the phone line. *Closeup* seemed to be our best choice, so I bit the bullet and bought it.

In February the State project got real busy. I was training people in the use of the computer and software, even though the NCR stuff was full of bugs and very limited. I often wondered why the State of North Carolina had chosen such low-level software to accomplish such high-level tasks, but the only answer I could get was that it was a done deal.

Durham was changing, which made me feel sad. Interstate 40 was being built around the town, and the park by the reservoir which I had enjoyed many a day, was now gone. Changes never sit well with anyone, I guess. Otherwise, Durham was a good place for me. Another advantage was that I was in the hub of things happening for small businesses. A local school offered a class on financial management. It made me realize if I'd saved just a little of what I had given to Jack, Jim, and others, I'd have more myself today. I made a promise to myself to put $200 a month into savings and start to build a pot. To the best of my recollection, I never saved a penny.

The State contract was paying me steadily now, so I decided it was time for a new computer. I bought an NCR PC8 because I could get a good price through the State. I was in heaven. For me, getting a new computer is like a mink coat to another woman or a fishing boat to a man. It turned me on. I was still lost in the thought process that if my product looked good enough, people would flock to buy it. Over time I learned it just doesn't happen that way.

A marketing consultant, who had been supporting me and assuring me I'd be a great success, announced about this time that he was taking a full-time job. That surprised me. It meant that as a business advisor, he had not been able to succeed himself. How could he help me?

I was still struggling along at this point without Randy, who would turn 24 years old in a few days. The State contract was keeping me busy and seemed to be going well. I invited Mike from Duke over to see my new computer system, and he told me Randy was rated first of all the programmers in performance. I was glad for him, and I wrote Carl to tell him how outstanding his son was, but for myself, all I knew was that he had very little time that he could spare for me. I know that sounds self- centered, but survival was my top priority as usual.

By March 15, I had finished the first draft of the case study for the Duke workshop. It had taken three months to put in data that was good enough for the workshop. I sent copies of reports I had designed to everybody involved and felt good about where we were so far.

I didn't understand that, at this time, sales should have been my only focus—and I still didn't know how to sell. Did I go to the CEO or Medical Staff Coordinator? Did size of hospital matter? Should I use Duke's name? Or are they too big for the small

WHIM OF IRON

hospitals to relate to in managing staff? I didn't have any of these answers, so I just kept doing what I loved to do—inventing, creating, and designing. Instead of selling, I just continued to explore "markets," as the Council for Entrepreneurial Development taught me, and prayed a buyer would appear.

Early in March, I had begun working with Duke's Inventory Department to get them up and running on INVENTORYplus. At the same time I was putting a lot of energy and money into a brochure that would describe all of the six software programs Randy and I were developing. It had seemed important at the time. CEOs don't buy from a brochure, but I didn't know that then. I was to learn much later that a principle of Marketing 101 was that you have to put your name/product out there *three times* to get their attention. I didn't have the money to do direct mailings (nor the energy). But I couldn't even conceive of calling the CEO and asking for an appointment. Who me? Little Cleo from Pass-a-Grille without any degrees?

One evening as we were working, Randy told me he was unhappy about what Duke was paying him. They claimed they could not give him more because he did not have a degree. That pissed me off. I called the head of Information Systems (IS) and arranged a meeting where we could discuss Randy's status. The head of IS made it clear that they found him extremely valuable; it was just as clear that without a degree, they couldn't believe he could know as much as someone who had one. I spoke strongly in Randy's favor. They said they would think about it. I wished so much I had the money to hire him back.

At the end of March, I learned the bad news—the Duke workshop was not going to go. There was only one registrant. Duke hadn't known how to market any better than I did. The rule of three mailings having to be made before anyone got interested was unknown to all of us. Actually, the real reason it didn't go was because the administrators didn't want to manage the medical staff—exactly the reason the head of marketing at Duke had told me it wouldn't sell.

I hid my disappointment, but I couldn't hide how tired I was, and my friend Peter told me to take a week off. It sounded like a good idea, but with money so low, impossible. I worked on my income taxes for days, only to find out that I owed $3,000, which, of course, was due on April 15. The good news was that Duke Pharmacy was looking at our inventory program, and a sale there would provide the needed cash. In the meantime, I was wearing thin on everyone.

I'm so tired. I'm crying and I don't know why. Called Randy and he's bored with me and my "I'm tireds." Maybe I should give it all up and work for Duke. I don't know anymore. I'll talk to Bob.

The pressure was starting to make me think I should get a job. The thought of working for Duke, or anyone, however, just made me try harder. The State project had gotten me involved in learning new software, and I had finally gotten it to work correctly. It had been hard to get the printers to work with our software. No one who worked with the State had much time, so training was hit and miss. But, all in all, the

State contract was finally bearing fruit, and people were getting things done more efficiently.

Marketing. Why is it so hard for me to do? I have a new idea for getting money by having CBR Associates consult to hospitals on quality issues.

I was already as lean as I could be, but I started marketing more (which meant more phone calls) and I stopped looking for a management team. A friend had helped me see *I was* a management team. All in all I was feeling good about my life, for the moment.

Lisa came in at 7 and we all went to look at her wedding dress again. It is so lovely.

Just as I have had a "fat" image of me, I have also had a "poor" image of my status in life. If life truly is an illusion, I can be rich as easily as poor. I've tried poor. It sucks. I think I'll try rich. Or richer, in any case.

My house was full. Besides Boude and two cats I took in called Bit and Byte, Randy would stop by, my friend, Diane, was over often, and Duke people working on our project would stop in now and then. When no one was around, I worked.

Anyone reading this must be able to hear, as I can, the swinging of the pendulum of my life. High, then low; hopeful, then on the edge; elated, then suicidal. Only once did I actually think about whether it would be better to die than to go on. I listened only to my negative voices, and they said I was fat, useless, unable to succeed, no friends, blah, blah, blah. Who wouldn't want to kill themselves with those kinds of messages flooding their every waking moment? But then someone would call and want to know about MedstaffPLUS or INVENTORYplus, and off I'd go, ready to tackle the dragon once again. Where did that energy come from? Genes I think. And anxiety.

Just paid as many taxes as I could. Not too bad, about $1000 short. I'll pay soon. Still trying to learn payroll in Dacpay. So tired of State contract. Jeannie came by and we agreed it was time (is time) for me to quit. June 30th I'm done. There. And I can begin here. I have not been free to market in a long time. I'm ready to go.

A woman from Indian River Hospital in Vero Beach, Florida, was here Monday and Tuesday to see medical staff. She has to sell the program to her hospital, and I think she will. Very tired.

I was trying to get the coordinators of quality in each hospital to market the MedstaffPLUS software to their administrators. Most of them didn't know how. I sure didn't.

Jeannie and I had worked together on the State project, and I was extremely impressed with her ability to think. Jeannie knew how to "read" the data and come up with solid conclusions. She's one of the few people I had ever known who knew when she didn't know, and wasn't afraid to say so. I wanted her to work with me. She could design and program the hundreds of reports that hospitals would want after their data had been put in. My vision was that on the first of each month, a whole series of reports printed automatically, which told the administrator where his problem areas were, who was involved, how to take care of the issue, and other important information. Jeannie could build such a report base.

Jane E. kept trying to get money for me to do a project that would pay me while I continued to tighten up MedstaffPLUS. None of them ever came through, however. It was hard to find anyone interested in quality management. Neither of us could understand it. The State project was still paying the bills.

Just back from trip to Stokes Reynolds Hospital in North Carolina, where I was trying to get them up and running on State system. It was good I guess. Not what I want to be doing but… I'm tired to the bone. Long drive back in rush hour traffic through Winston Salem and Greensboro in the pouring rain.

After attending the Council for Entrepreneurial Development (CED) meetings, I had become convinced that all I needed to do was get some capital, and I could sell my products like crazy.

Easter weekend. I have lots of work to do. I am excited. CED has accepted my business plan for the Greenhouse Conference—how wonderful. I'll have my day in front of the venture capitalists.

Another entry shows everything wasn't hunky dory:

I feel anxious. Time to walk Boude. He missed me so. I do have someone to come home to. My face is showing wrinkles finally, yet I feel so young. My body hurts like hell—stress. I need to do something…time passes too quickly.

The reference to coming home to someone stemmed from my experience of growing up. Mom would get off work at 5 p.m., catch the bus to our house, change her clothes and be out the door, headed for one of her favorite bars, by 5:30. She would stay and drink her precious salary away while Nancy and I went without dental help, food and clothes. When I went into first grade, my sister walked me home at first, but she soon found other friends, and I had to walk home to an empty house after that.

I never got used to walking into the empty house. It was better in high school, because then I would have swim practice or a part-time job (or both), so by the time I got home, it would be time to do homework or laundry and then to sleep. My sister worked a lot, too, and stayed away intentionally—she and Mom didn't see eye to eye about the drinking. I tried not to make waves. Only once do I remember pouring a fifth of Four Roses down the kitchen sink. Mom got so mad at me, I never did it again. Now, so many years later, I could appreciate coming home to Boude, who made a big difference.

WHIM OF IRON

Scottish Rite Hospital in Atlanta had sent people to look at MedstaffPLUS and had been impressed enough to buy a system. The question that kept running through my head was, "How does one set up a computer hard drive, install software, and configure printers, etc., when one is *not* a techie?" That question was to haunt me, as I set up my first system, alone. It was at times like these that I felt disappointed Randy hadn't seen or believed in my vision. As far as I was concerned, our 50/50 arrangement for CBR Associates was out the door. To get 50/50 you have to take *all* the risks, lack of money being one of them.

> *Tried to repartition my hard disk, and I can't—don't know how. I leave for Atlanta Wednesday to install a whole system all by myself, and I'm nervous. I don't like it at all. Randy gone. Says he'll help in a.m. Let's hope so. Stressssss is on!*
>
> *8 p.m. Finally got everything back in order— what a mess. Learned a lot though, so that was good. Scottish Rite is my first installation alone, and I have two systems to work on.*

A lot of the stress of travel came from just getting to and from each hospital. If I was driving, I would have to find my way and often drive four to eight hours in a day. If I was flying, I had to have the money, make reservations, and get myself there with my equipment, which, by this time, included a 34-pound Compaq computer. At some point I pulled the muscles in my shoulder from lugging the computer around. Getting taxicabs, arranging hotel reservations, meeting deadlines, and doing it all alone, took a toll.

When I came home, walking with Boude helped me relax. He was my friend. I remember once walking uptown and sharing a spinach turnover and some pea soup with him. Everyone knew him and enjoyed petting him. Often, I would stop at one of the pool halls, and they'd let Boude sit by my side while I played a few games by myself.

After hanging around with CED business people for a while, I had picked up the bug to get investment funding. I didn't know what I'd do if I got it, but I felt I was supposed to want it, so I did. I got good at giving a business plan presentation, but I never got any money. I thank God for that now, but at the time I was upset. I had visions of going big...somewhat like trying to run when you haven't even learned to crawl yet. Even if I had gotten the money, I managed money so badly, it would have all gone for "good" causes, and I would have gone bankrupt anyway. Asking for too little money also was sending the wrong signal to investors. But I was determined to try.

I get to present my business plan to business investors at Fugua School of Business and the University of North Carolina, Chapel Hill. How fun and exciting, I will give five minutes of pure enthusiasm and confidence.

I am asking for $200,000. No, $100,000, but I will ask for some backup money in case it takes me longer to get marketing momentum going. I'm ready and excited to go for it.

Courses at the CED had talked about marketing and getting your word out to potential customers. They never talked about the nitty gritty of doing that. It takes money to go on trips, whether in a car or plane. Even more important, it took my time and energy. I was trying to do too much, and I didn't know how to set boundaries. All I was concerned with was surviving. If this sounds schizophrenic, it is. High, low, high, low. That was my life. I could wake in the morning ready to climb a mountain and by noon be ready to chuck it all in. That was a theme that was to plague me during these years—that I was not worth anything. I couldn't make it, who was I? I often felt I had no value and it had little to do with reality, but that didn't keep me from succumbing to the no-value belief system I had learned as a child. My mother always told me I could do anything I wanted, but that was not what I heard from others, particularly my father, as I was growing up.

Small incidents that had occurred over my life cemented in my mind the idea that I had no worth, didn't belong. It was very hard "to just get over it" as others told me for years. We all have patterns that don't serve us well. We continue to do that which fits our beliefs, like the abused child who grows up to marry an abuser.

My first adventure to install software should never have happened. I had sold to a hospital I didn't have the time, money or energy to support, because they were too far away, in Atlanta. Their check for $6,000, however, obliterated all sense. "A sale is a sale," was my way of thinking. I soon learned that some sales cost a lot more and end up with less profit than others.

Cleo B. Robertson

Even in retrospect, installing the software in Atlanta remains one of the worst days of my business life. Randy and I had tried to prepare for every eventuality, but we couldn't. Scottish Rite had different hardware than we did, and it was old and out of date, too, which was not good. The information management people weren't real happy we were coming in to solve a hospital problem that they really felt they should solve. So, from the beginning, there was no welcoming committee.

On top of that, there was a less-than-enthusiastic trainee who let me know she wasn't happy that she was going to have to run the software. After unpacking all the software disks and instructions Randy had given me, I sat down to install our software on an old computer. Once the hour-long loading of software had taken place, I began to input physicians' data on their names, office address, phone numbers, medical school, etc. and to test it. By this time, it was close to noon and I was feeling tired. The medical staff person who maintained physicians' credentials was standing around, and impatient to get going. Doctors kept coming in and asking questions. We broke for lunch and I could hardly eat. My stomach knew what I was trying not to show—something was wrong. Little glitches kept popping up. I was very worried.

After lunch I really began to try to run the software. Reports would show weird data in the fields, and when I would check on the address or phone number, it would be right in the database and wrong in the report. I kept thinking it was the data that was wrong, but by 3 p.m., I knew I needed Randy. I called him at Duke, even though he hated for me to call him there. I had to act very professional and as though not a thing in the world was wrong, but as I described the problems to him, I could tell that he, too, was upset and didn't know what was wrong.

After an hour on the phone trying one thing after another, he finally said he couldn't help me any more, but that he would call as soon as he got home from work. I went back to loading data and pretended that everything was fine, just taking a little longer than I had thought it would. As I entered data, I could feel tears welling inside, which I quickly pushed down. Then my critical voice started in on me, telling me what an uppity little tart I was, thinking I could do this installation all by myself. Everyone left at 5 p.m. and I continued to work, assuring everyone that when they came in, in the morning, it would be working like a charm. They didn't look like they believed me, and I wasn't sure I did either.

Randy called at 6 p.m. Hearing his voice was like hearing God, I was so happy. Again he told me things to check, and then I'd read back the answers, and then we'd go another route. At one point, I thought all was okay and we hung up. I ran a whole bunch of reports and they were fine at first, but soon errors started appearing again. I was near to exhaustion and mentally crashing, but I called Randy again. It was now 7:30 p.m. and he had talked to one of his co-workers. They had figured out what was wrong. We had the most current version of the Disk Operating System (DOS), and the hospital had an old version. It was like trying to run a car on diesel that wasn't designed for it.

Once we made the decision to reformat the hard disk and start all over again, I was beginning to get my fourth wind of the day. We saved the data I had put in, reformatted the hard disk (that's like erasing a blackboard), reloaded our software with an *old* version of DOS, and within an hour and a half, the system was up and running. It took me another two hours to clean up the data, and then I walked wearily to my hotel. I vowed that from then on I would not install on-site at hospitals...they would have to come to Durham, equipment and all.

That night I was so happy everything had turned out okay, I felt like celebrating. I took a cab to a local mall, and as I entered, a man yelled to me from a bar in the back of the entry, "Come on over, try a new beer on me!" Sounded like the best offer I'd had in a long time. I had a wonderful time in the bar. The man who flagged me down to try the new beer, Corona, kept flagging other people down, until there were at least 30 of us, all drinking, eating great appetizers they were buying, and laughing a lot—just what any doctor would have ordered.

When I got back to Durham, all the stacks of "things to do" were just as I had left them. We had gotten the hospital up and running...but we couldn't go through anything like that again. Randy and I met early the next morning and agreed to find a better way to install and train clients.

WHIM OF IRON

Got State check so IRS check didn't bounce. Sent bill off to Scottish Rite. I am happy.

The comment about the IRS check not bouncing was also part of my pressure. When I had money, I spent it. I didn't know how to stash away for a rainy day, because every day felt rainy in some way. But we kept on paying our bills, which was saying a lot.

A golden day. Met with Jane E. and Peggy on medical staff. We worked together sooooo well. Very stimulating. Also met with Duncan, who then called the administrator at Annie Reid Hospital. I have an appointment Tuesday to see if I can get a contract to do medical staff analysis and management there. Hope so.

Jane was anxious to help me get some steady income. She could see how hard we were working and understood we needed sales, but she didn't know how to go about it any more than we did. Peggy was a very bright hospital professional, and discussing quality management with both of them was just heaven to me.

All the phone circuits are busy, so I have no one to tell the good news to—I sold MedstaffPLUS to Indian River Hospital, Vero Beach, Florida. YEAH! Only took one month for a sale at $6000 plus $1000 for software. Sounds real good.

This was an important sale, because I had gotten the lead by word of mouth. The fact that they were outside the North Carolina area only enhanced the importance of the sale in my mind. I was sure if one bought, they would all buy. Everything I had learned about the difficulty of servicing a client long distance was forgotten, as my checkbook smiled back at me for once.

It's 3 a.m. and I'm sleepless. Big presentation to Annie Penn tomorrow. Cold, rainy. I worked until 9 p.m. on the program and it looks real good. Want tomorrow to be a sale. My first real chance to present my view of my systems to the right people—administrator, MIS, finance, medical staff coordinator, physician in charge of credentialing—a whole team from Annie Penn Hospital and Rex Hospital.

Each presentation made me anxious and sleepless for two major reasons: 1) I was always alone trying to set up equipment and slide projectors, etc. while meeting the very people I wanted to sell to; 2) these people were interested in solving the problem of credentialing physicians and other health-care providers, but they didn't want to spend any money. The fact that I could get an audience at all was remarkable and largely due to my connections with Duke. In the end, I didn't get either hospital to buy, and I was again very disappointed.

Long day. Mind busy thinking about the five minutes I have at Venture '87 to get some money. I'm lonely in my business. I hope I get investors' funds soon so I can share some of the work, planning and excitement with others.

WHIM OF IRON

I was alone because Randy was off at Duke and no one else wanted to or could afford to join me. I didn't have the money to pay anyone. My vision was that with venture capital funds, I could build a team…if I could have had just a few people around to share the workload, I would have been happy. Making lots of money was not important to me. Of course, that's all investors were interested in—making money.

One day, I got a phone call and learned that Barbara, whom I had been working with at the State contract, was run over in her stopped mini van, by a tractor trailer going 50 mph. When I heard about her accident, I was distraught. Barbara had been like a big sister to me in many ways, and I could only pray that quality management was alive and well in the hospital where she was being treated. Teams of doctors tried to put Barbara's face and body back together. She had a new baby who had been with a babysitter at the time of the accident, and I couldn't imagine the anguish she was going through. When I saw her months later, she told me her whole face was metal and that it would react to the weather—what a nightmare, and she was so brave through it all.

It was about this time that I was working on a new brochure. I was trying to do the "right" things in business—hire people, get a brochure, and make sales. Since I couldn't hire anyone, I figured a brochure would be my next step. After spending about $5,000 on this one, I had a few lovely pages that told my philosophy in too many words, which no one *ever* read. I was still learning expensive lessons and feeling like a yo-yo.

This morning I swam 30 laps and was ready to be skinny and happy. Tonight I feel lost again. No one to be with. Called Lisa for help but she's so busy with wedding, I couldn't bore her. Dan was busy at work. Randy's not home. Hazel going to Elks dance. I miss her. We talked. She's so good for me. She has to stay in Princeton for Bobby and the children. I had wanted her to come stay with me. Oh. Well.

Swimming was the one sport I wanted to do and I made time for it. But nothing could overcome the lost feelings, which overtook me on a regular basis. Only Hazel was always there for me, sitting in her rocker, glad I called. I understood why she didn't come to North Carolina, but I sure wished she would.

Cold sores on my mouth and face. Got two important calls today and didn't follow up on either. Instead I worked fruitlessly on my accounting books.

Every moment that I wasn't with Lisa or Diane, or on the State contract, I spent worrying about business, or specifically, the venture capital fair coming up.

I gave my five-minute practice session for Venture Capital '87 to members of CED. In 8 points or less, why should someone put money into CBR? I read a two-page, boring answer. When I was done, my friend Jack took me aside into a room and closed the door. He said, "Okay, Cleo, you're the investor, and I'm CBR Associates." He walked out of the room, and then back in, smiling, hand extended, and said: "Hello. I'm Cleo Robertson, and my company has developed software that is the most unique…" He was smiling, using his hands, no notes. I could "see" what I had to do. He showed me how to do it. I shall forever be indebted to him for teaching me what I needed to know to at least have a chance at the Fair.

The Duke Project was going slowly because the hospital where we were developing inventory had very slow equipment and a very large inventory database. The woman running it got easily frustrated. I agreed with her. The hospital wanted more, faster, but with the equipment she had, it took her four times as long to enter the daily data on usage. We also were still developing reports, so she didn't always have the one she needed. Both Randy and I had spent a lot of time making it easier and easier, but the long input time was sabotaging our efforts. They never did really get it going well because they didn't want to invest $3000 on faster equipment!

My emotions were starting to bounce, along with checks, as Lisa's wedding day got closer.

Bounced three checks. I wrote a check in for $50 instead of $550. Jane E. loaning me money until Wednesday. Presented at the CED Venture fair—did great, but no money.

Get a job? Same old question. Won't give up!! NO NO NO!!!

In evening walked with Boude and thought of new ideas for what to do. Cried and cried and cried. Can't go to Boston to meet Lisa's new in-laws to be. Better Carl go alone. I always overwhelm everything. No money to go, and my Pass-a-Grille pride will NOT allow me to have Carl or Lisa pay anyway, even if they would. Tears. I hate not being able to carry my own for my daughter's wedding. I won't get a second chance. Lisa here to pick out a DJ for reception.

So sad I am. Tears. I can't stop crying

The Venture fair was very disappointing because I could finally "see" that the only businesses in which the investors invested, were those with BIG potential to go public and have millions of dollars in sales. This was typical of my behavior. Set a goal to get some money, work hard to do a good presentation, and then not get it *because* it was the wrong place for me. And yet, getting a job was still not something I could stand to think of doing. As soon as I was tied up in a job eight hours a day, I knew that all hope would be gone. I had to keep on going.

Not having the money to pay for Lisa's wedding or to fly myself to Boston to meet the family was a great shame to me. That's what mothers are supposed to be able to do and here I was, broke and feeling like a great disappointment to Lisa. By the end of May I had worked myself into a depression. It seemed that anyone I phoned was either not home or busy. Only my dog continued to give me constant love. Whenever I was feeling left out and not good enough, my tendency was to shut the door and not let anyone in.

> *People wonder why I never went to college. Pride. I wouldn't accept money I couldn't earn myself. Same reason I won't go to Boston with Lisa and Carl to meet everyone. Pride. I am going to accept the challenge and market medical staff management. I hurt badly because I feel so alone. I am alone. I even gave Bit and Byte away. The neighbors wanted them and will take better care of them. I am alone by CHOICE!*

Knowing why one is alone and being okay with it are two different things. I chose to be alone, I said. But in fact, I wanted someone to say, "Hey, come with us and have fun." When someone did say that, I was ready to go and enjoyed myself. But on those days when the phone didn't ring and I didn't see anyone, depression would creep in and I would be crying, as I tried to make calls and sell. A lot of this emotional starving was a carry over from childhood. Mom seldom had an interest in my life, and I was most often alone in making decisions and doing things. I believed I was crying now for the emotional support I never got. Knowing this, however, didn't help.

I knew that once Lisa went to Paris, I would see very little of her. (They were moving right after the wedding because Andy had been transferred there; he spoke little French, she was fluent.) Even though we weren't always together, I had always felt she was around and supportive. Once she fell in love, her focus changed, as it should, and she was *really* leaving home this time.

In my dreams, God spoke to me. A bolt of lighting came from the sky, and I was so frightened, I ran away and hid. When I woke in the morning I looked in the mirror and saw more power in my face than I'd seen in a long time. A thin, strong face. I'm going to use all the power that's available to me to win. Walked two miles with Boude in the rain—a delight. Tomorrow, 50 laps again. I just have to solve my loneliness from 5 p.m. to 9 p.m.

From depression to elation in one easy dream. Actually dreams had a way of changing my moods, and this one was very powerful. In fact, I identified with the lightning as a sign of *my* power, and it gave me courage.

Walked 6 miles today and put in full 8 hours at State. Up at 4 a.m. Just walked home from YPOM. Played some good pool. Still no money from State or Scottish Rite. Trial by fire. Lisa hates to hear it. She's right.

By the beginning of June 1987, life seemed to be coming around.

CED asked me to be on their Board.

Lawyer got me off speeding ticket with no points.

Duke asked for a proposal to do Quality Assurance program.

Friend at Duke is supporting my drive to get AMA, AHA and JCAHO to endorse medical staff program. Life is great!

Joining the CED Board was a big deal to me. I was part of a professional team, and I felt very excited to have friends to talk business with. The fact that I was such a small business and knew absolutely nothing about taking my product to market didn't bother me at all. I figured I could learn how to do anything, a hold over from my Pass-a-Grille days when I *did* learn to do anything I wanted.

I remember when I was nine and I found an old Singer sewing machine with a foot pedal in the garage of the house we were renting. I got someone to help me lug it up to the bedroom, and I began to learn how it worked. I oiled it with stuff Bill McArthur gave me from his garage and soon the foot pedal was moving freely. I was in business. In the old Oshkosh trunk we kept in the garage (one that Mom had used to move our belongings), I found some cloth. I cut it into strips and then pinned the strips together and sewed them up. After adding a waistband and some snaps—Voila! I had a new skirt. I wore it very proudly to school until someone said, "Oh, I see you made your skirt, Cleo." I was surprised; how did she know? "Well, you have one panel running up and down and all the others are sideways." I looked at the skirt and saw what she meant. I never wore that skirt again, but I made many more.

Early in June I went to visit Barbara:

Cleo B. Robertson

One eye bulging, one eye half closed! Her whole face replaced with metal. A beauty reduced to surgical solutions. Thank God my only complaint is tiredness.

Barbara's condition was a shock to me. Her life, and that of her whole family, was forever changed. I felt very vulnerable. She amazed me with her determination to get the right help, yet even with all her connections to health care, it was an uphill battle. In the end she saved herself with pure determination. Years later I saw her at a conference, and I was amazed. She looked chic and professional in a slim suit, her face totally lovely again. Only her glasses gave a clue as to what she had been through—one lens had a half patch on it since her vision had been altered badly. She taught me what courage looks like.

Feeling motivated, I started marketing again. The idea that I had to "put an organization together" was what I *thought* I should do. I didn't know how. Whether it was getting money or choosing the right people, I didn't know how to get anyone interested besides me. I kept reinventing and relearning the same lessons, but didn't know really what they meant.

June 11th my son Gary, turned 26. "*Oh God, please be with him*" was my only comment in the diary that night.

The pressure of getting to the wedding party up in Boston was weighing on me heavily. All my life I've wanted to "belong." Mom and Dad both told me, at separate times when I was a teenager, that they weren't sure who my real father was. Dad said he thought he was, because we both had gaps in our teeth. Little comfort to a girl who wanted a dad who said, "Yes, you are mine, I love you." For years I wished he had lied. Now, the thought of being left out was quite depressing. As the time got closer to the meeting of wedding families, I somehow managed to squeak out enough money to buy a ticket to Boston. I simply had to go. Being part of my daughter's wedding was one of those milestones in life that was immensely important to me. It said I belonged, I was part of the family, I was important. I went. Andy's family turned out to be the kind that makes you feel at home instantly. Carl, my first husband, Lisa's dad, was there, and we got along just fine. It was a great time.

Back home, I had to face reality...again.

I was invited to do a demonstration to Computer Intelligence, a company nearby, and within minutes I knew they would not buy. Even after all this time, I still had no idea how to screen a potential buyer. I was still wasting lots of my precious energy with no results. No wonder I would get discouraged, but it was my own fault. I just didn't know it at the time. There were other ways I wasted my energy. Selling to a hospital far away was much harder to support and train than I had counted on. The traveling, alone, exhausted me.

Flew to Atlanta to fix Scottish Rite's credentialing and do more training, and then flew back at night. Long day. Working on cleaning up privileges for credentialing, writing letters for marketing, trying to find an equipment distributor, writing letters for custom menu, and learning Ktext to edit program with.

The above entry said a mouthful. Scottish Rite had been a difficult installation from the beginning. A mixture of poor equipment and bad attitude will always fail in computers. Somehow I got it running again, but I had stopped using them as a reference. They blamed all their problems on us. It was a nightmare.

The second statement about cleaning up privileges was also a nightmare. From the very first day that physicians started keeping track of what privileges they were allowed to perform at a hospital, chaos reigned. Each hospital's medical staff sets privileges. This means that Hospital A may grant a privilege in <u>open heart surgery,</u> while Hospital B will grant privileges in <u>pediatric open heart surgery</u> and <u>adult open heart surgery</u>. Hospital C, however, gives privileges in <u>surgical heart repair</u>. As long as it was specific to one hospital, it didn't matter what they called it. But physicians started having privileges at more than one hospital.

At some point, it became important to have a standard list for all hospitals. With standard lists, any doctor could schedule knee surgery, for instance, and the computer could check to see if the doctor had privileges in knee surgery. If he didn't, he'd have to refer the patient to someone else, which is why many doctors didn't want automated privileges. What our system did was protect the patient. But particularly, in small, rural hospitals, doctors did what needed to be done, whether they had the background and education to do it, or not.

The reason I felt the hospital world should be excited about a standard list was that during analysis, focus could be put on those privileges where adverse incidents were creating risks for both the patient and the doctor. It took me one day at one hospital to realize the magnitude of the problem, because even within one hospital, different lists existed. The Surgical Suite might use a list they got from the College of Surgery, while the Emergency Room might use a totally different list. The worst part, of course, was that terms and phrases crossed from area to area, so when the Medical Staff Coordinator tried to put apples and apples together, it was almost impossible.

Our goal had been to take a large university hospital's list (Duke's) and clean it so that we could offer a standard list to all our customers. I spent a lot of time on this task, and I never got anywhere. In the end, we built the software so each hospital could enter the name of *their* privileges, knowing that each hospital's would be different. So much for standardization.

The worry of appearing too small as a business was always with me as I marketed, although it really didn't matter in the end. But I spent money and put a lot of energy into trying to appear "big," whatever that meant.

Rick, Bob, Jane E., and Bert all agree to be on my Advisory Board. Setting up meeting for July 23rd. Setting up demo at Duke also in July.

State contract ends Tuesday. I will be free to get this balloon off the ground because others will be helping.

When someone at CED first suggested I have an Advisory Board, I jumped at the thought. Here was just what I needed—people to listen to my ideas, to give me advice, and to help me make decisions. Only it doesn't work that way. These were wonderful and caring people who gave me their time, but they didn't know exactly what I was trying to do. Since no one was doing it, they couldn't visualize how to sell it. We only met once, because it was obvious that what I needed was sales. I put together a plan to call 10 hospitals a day and talk to the medical staff coordinators.

Wonderful day and evening. I'm finding I'm good at marketing and glad to have the time to do so. Fun talking to people in hospitals and finding out their needs.

In evening, walked from Papagayo's to Cameron Stadium on Duke campus to see old Duke stars play USA team. USA won but Duke gave it their usual style. Even got Tommy Amaker's autograph!

Durham was a good place for me to be at this time in my life. Nothing was too far away. I loved sports and following the Duke basketball team. I had met enough people who worked around town in stores that I could talk to along the way, wherever I was going, and take care of my need to be with people. I also was spending a good deal of time working on Jane P's. book.

WHIM OF IRON

The State project had been scheduled to end in mid-June. They wanted more and more from the hardware and software, so I kept right on working. I needed money and I worked hard, but I also wanted to give the staff tools to make their work easier. It was not easy to do. IBM equipment had finally been purchased, but there were lots of bugs in both the software and hardware. Tiring.

Duke demo of our software for several hospitals bombed. I bombed. I'm going to go talk to Dennis at the American Hospital Association and tell him my dream for hospitals to manage their risks and patient needs.

This was typical thinking for me. I'm at the end of the rope. Who can I get to help me make my dream come true? Dennis was a bigwig, and I didn't know the bigwig wouldn't even give me an appointment. I kept thinking, if anyone saw a demonstration of the software, they would want it to be everywhere, like I did. I never even got the chance to talk with him.

The State contract, which was supposed to stop, started again and was adding to my daily pressure. I didn't want to go to the State every day. I needed to stay home and make phone calls and write letters. But I also wanted to eat. Randy was doing really well at Duke, blossoming into a full programmer, and I was happy for him. For me, I kept struggling, appreciating the time he did give me after hours and on weekends. Supporting customers by phone was hairy, though. I always dreaded the sound of the phone ringing. My gut would turn and I would hesitate before answering it to take a breath and get my butterflies to stop fluttering. Often my dread came true, and there was a problem I could not fix. I would make up some story about Randy being out with a customer. All I could do was sweat it out until evening and hope he came by.

New businesses are told to "market," but no one sits us down and says, "Ok, first you get a list of all the hospitals, then you find out who makes decisions about software, and you call them to see if they have the power to write a check or cause a check to be written. If not, find out who can." This is the kind of direction small businesses like mine need, but we seldom get it. I finally got it, in 1989.

On a few rare occasions, Randy invited me to go water skiing from the boat he had bought. He had no idea what a change in my mood such an invitation would make. I would go from feeling alone and lonely to elated and excited in about one millisecond. I think water skiing made me feel younger than my 49 years, and I always enjoyed being around Randy...he had good energy.

By mid-July, nerves were starting to jump on another front. Lisa's wedding loomed ahead and I had invested a lot of time and energy into making it successful. I wanted it to be all that she wanted it to be. I insisted on joining Carl in giving our daughter away...I was so proud of her. I often thought back to the day she was born and all the hopes and dreams I had for her. One of them was happening, and I felt good inside.

The pressure of presenting to an Advisory Board also caused me anxiety, but cash coming in always provided relief.

My advisory board meets in two days. I have my presentation together and ready. I will go through it with Randy to see how I do, if he has time. He did a fantastic job of making the tracking system better. He doesn't know how good it is. Everyone *needs to track something. My head is spinning with ideas. Indian River Hospital finally agreed to buy MedstaffPLUS. That's a welcome $6,000. I am ready for my presentation. I am ready.*

The money caught me up to date, with little to spare, but I was confident my Advisory Board would solve my problems. On July 23rd we met.

So…I spent $108 to ask five people what I should do, and from what I can tell, I should find someone else to run this business. Period. Jane kept emphasizing I care too much about the product. I'm tied to it by an umbilical cord. She doesn't know how good I am at cutting it.

Shit. I learned that what I am doing is not what I should do.

God, why did you create me? I will die of aloneness. No one sees my vision. If I died today, a few would miss a heartbeat for a moment, and then I would be gone. Oh, if it were so <u>easy</u>!

I was feeling desperate. What I thought would work, didn't. I needed help and a plan of action, and none of the people on the board had any more skills than I did. So when I began to feel I was failing, I also began to feel the world would be better off without me. My lack of faith in God was pitiful.

My feelings of being worthless, a piece of shit, of no use to anyone would become so strong, and I would feel so much anger, that I started beating myself up. Physically. I would look in a mirror and hit my face with my open hand again and again and again, until my face was red and my heart purged. Then I would cry and go through days of not being able to do anything. Depression would keep me from thinking or moving. But then I would go to a meeting and perk right up. It was a crazy existence.

I had been attending the CED meetings regularly but had met few people I wanted to get to know better. Most that I did befriend were men. Most owned businesses, some successful, some not, but all far larger than CBR in staff and income. It was clear they measured success by the bottom line, and mine didn't even exist. But because of my interest, I was asked to join the Program Advisory Board, and I was flattered. I wanted to be involved so I could feel I belonged. At the first meeting, I met Peter Bechtel for the second time, and he soon became a business advisor and friend.

As with all humans, most of my problems stemmed from my behaving like a scared three-year-old a lot of the time. It didn't help that I was overwhelmed with responsibility for hospitals' systems, and for paying bills, too. Handling money scared me. The only money discussions I ever heard in our house were about there not being enough. When I was five and six, Mom would send me to the Post Office to see if there was a white envelope in our box. I would run down and climb on my tippy tippy toes and look. Again and again. But I never saw a white envelope. Only years later did I learn I had been sent to see if there was an alimony check from Dad. We went through some very lean times, but somehow we always ate. Mom never failed to provide housing, utilities and some food.

At the end of July 1987, I flew to California to meet with a private, well-endowed hospital. They had seen our system at Duke and were interested. They felt they were better managed than other hospitals and therefore needed the most up-to-date tools available. I admired that they wanted tools; I was surprised at the weak quality assurance system they had in place. They bought finally, but the system never was used terribly effectively. No one really knew what questions to ask, or else they didn't want to ask them.

Finally, my daughter's day had arrived!

Wedding Day! Today my daughter was married at Duke Chapel, with a reception at the Brownstone Hotel. Everyone here and having a wonderful time, even Carl's Mom! Most lovely wedding in the world. Beautiful bride, lovely people. Andy so good. I gave a toast! They have a wonderful start into the future.

My only daughter was married. It was so final. She wouldn't turn to me anymore; she'd turn to Andy. I was glad and sad.

I spent August taking care of taxes, bringing my books up to date, and writing a draft proposal for a Duke/Moses Cone workshop I had dreamed up. Randy was beginning to get tired of Duke. They overworked him and undervalued him. He wouldn't have minded the overwork if they had given him value back in the form of salary. When they didn't, he started to lose interest. Randy worked hard, and he wanted to be appreciated (as we all do).

We started having conversations about where the software could go and how big the market was. Peter continued to advise me and be my friend, which carried a lot of weight with Randy. I think he took me more seriously because he respected Peter so much. Jack had joined our group, and along with David, we had others around us with whom we could talk business "to our hearts' desire."

In mid-August, Randy expressed an interest in coming back to CBR...if I could pay him more than Duke. We had been working together really well again, and that helped. He had agreed that if I could start him at $40,000 a year, he would work for me. The State contract was barely covering expenses, and sales had been too few for me to pay him, so I decided to find some money. My contacts through CED had educated me as to the availability of money from the State, and I wanted to apply. Then I could get Randy back.

My days were busy with work; my slack time was busy with thoughts of Lisa.

The installation at Catawba Memorial Hospital went superbly well. I was there for three days and also set up four PCs! Evelyn Travis had data in and was printing reports and designing her own reports before I left. Long three days, and worth the effort. God is so good to me.

I think often of Lisa and Andy traveling in Europe, and I smile. God be with them both in their joy! Lisa and Andy—having fun? Oh yes!

The recurring theme in my life of being alone reared its nasty head again and again. I knew I made a choice to work on my own, but I so much wanted someone else to care. Randy cared about what he was doing wholeheartedly at work, but outside the office he lead a separate life.

Slept well all night. So much to do. Up at 5, and got first draft to Catawba written offering medical staff consulting to implement the information they will have from MedstaffPLUS. So much I can do! Scared and excited. Wish I had a real partner who would call to see what happened at Catawba, and cared.

9:07 p.m. Randy and I just quit working on the software. Both tired. We have worked hard to please people, and it is starting to take effect.

We both continued to do what needed to be done—Randy, programming while he continued working at Duke; me, fulfilling the State contract and marketing our product.

Great day at State doing good work. Then to Sheraton for CED Executive Board meeting. Talked with Peter and Jack. I learned a lot. Learned even more when I played pool with a successful businessman. 15 percent top, 5 percent low. Go!

Pool had become a passion for me. Durham was "hick" enough to have good country players who could "shoot a good stick." They taught me a lot night after night. I honed my skills.

Don't like doing the State job, but it pays the bills. Or I hope it does. I feel good, ready. Do a presentation soon to investors at University of North Carolina. I get to sell myself and what we've done. Randy and me—we've done one hell of a job and <u>all</u> I have to do is sell it.

10 p.m. Very good day. Got physician recruitment under control at the State, and got turned down by a friend that I had asked to loan me money in exchange for stock in CBR (he'll be sorry). A professor at Duke asked me to teach three hours in Health Administration program. Great!

I loved teaching, something I knew a lot about. Students asked good questions and often hard ones, which challenged me. Often Bob and I talked about teaching a course in medical staff analysis, but nothing ever came of it.

I'm like a ping-pong ball. Up, down, up, down. Went to Kenan Center and was happy as could be because my presentation went well. Went to Duke to meet on quality assurance, and crashed. Home to work on business plan. Alone. So tired of aloneness. No money. No anything. Except hope. Will the electric company take hope in payment? Silly me. Lisa wrote from France—life is good.

Didn't sleep all night. Got up at 2 a.m. and did financial projections, but couldn't get back to sleep. Tired inside and out.

The Kenan Center presentation was an important one. Over eighty investors, all men, had been gathered together to hear business plan presentations and so they could decide if they wanted to invest or not. It was an honor for me to be allowed to present. I practiced and practiced. I made people listen until they were sick of it. Then I gave my presentation to the mirror one more time. The actual presentation was a great success. I had ten minutes to tell these men what my business was all about. Public speaking was something I had always been comfortable with and I did a good job. When I was done, there was a question-and-answer period. A gentleman asked, "Ms. Robertson, have you found that being a woman in the hospital business presents any kind of difficulty?"

I knew exactly what he was asking. He wanted to know how I could sell to administrators when even men had a hard time. I told the story about hiring Greg to go on hospital calls with me, and by the time I was done, I had this very dour group of men laughing in stitches. But his point was made. I didn't get any money.

Bob said I made Duke look good when I presented at Kenan. Rick bragged to Randy about me, too. He sees I am doing all I know how to do.

Bob's opinion of me was also very important. Bob had hired me for the Small Hospital Project purely based on his instincts and Jane E.'s recommendation. He backed me 100 percent of the time. For all of that, I worked very hard to make him proud, and I did, and I was glad.

Randy and I were both working very hard, and I appreciated his persistence and abundant skills. He didn't like to hear about my visits to hospitals, and I bored him with my hopes and dreams, but we worked well together and that was enough. For now.

Randy and I worked from 8:30 a.m. to 10 p.m., and then I called Caroline. I'm so glad I acted on instinct. All life is about is being in the right place at the right time and knowing it! Caroline has an interest in joining CBR. I know it. She knows it. Good energy flows. We are soul mates.

And here on my wish list when I said I wanted a soul mate, I thought it was a man. No. A woman! We have the same caring and desire to succeed; we have high standards and bright minds. Mostly, though, we both care. Caroline is going to see that caring can pay off—BIG! Caroline, all right!

As I write this, I don't remember who Caroline was. I do know she was one of many I tried to interest in sharing the boring job of keeping books and paying taxes, of meeting with administrators who didn't want to meet with me, and of being there when I came home from a trip to listen and care. But you can hear the words I used to keep me from buckling under… "instinct," "being in the right place," and "we are soul mates."

How would things have been different if I *had* recruited a partner? At this point, I didn't know. What I did know was I had now been working with Randy and doing all the office, administrative-type work as well as marketing and sales for over six years. I was getting tired. Having hope that someone would join me kept me going.

One great diversion for me was when Rollie would invite me to the University of North Carolina at Chapel Hill to tell my story to inspire business majors. He knew lots of business people,—he taught graduate courses on business at the University of North Carolina in Chapel Hill. He was well known in the investment community, so if he thought well of me, then I felt I must be doing a good job. That gave me a measure, and I worked hard to improve on it.

CED expo went very well. I have so much energy, and Randy, too. He heard again from Bob and Rick how well I'm doing. Seems so unreal. I know I'm capable of being anything I want. As Hazel says, "Look at Mrs. Reagan. She's only where she is 'cause of her husband!"

People around me, encouraging me, turned me into a confident, do-it person. And then I'd remember something my father had said when I was young, and I would crumble inside. Usually these crumblings took minutes, sometimes days, but mostly I got my act together and forgot I was depressed in short order. I simply didn't have time to be depressed.

My 49th birthday. Did lots of work, walked Boude at Eno, Randy came with flowers and presents—a headphone to answer the telephone! And socks with batteries to keep me warm; wonderful gifts. We then went to YPOM and had a great birthday party. Lots of State people came and two from CED. Wonderful time. I feel young again. At 1 a.m. went to hot tub at Metrosport and relaxed. Life is incredibly good!

My memory of this party remains very happy. YPOM, or Your Place or Mine, was my favorite hangout. I could walk in at any time after 5, play pool with some very good players (I had been taught to always play with better players, because they would make me better), talk, dance, drink beer, and laugh until 1 a.m. YPOM was known as a redneck bar, and the reputation was justified for the most part. There were a lot of rednecks, some tough, some not so tough, and this was their place. Seeing these very straight, business-type people drinking beer and having fun at YPOM did my heart good. But somehow the old saying, "Everything changes...the good and the bad," kept coming true, and my good feelings would turn to bad.

Felt ten yesterday. Today, 94! Achy (damp and cold outside). Muscles ache. Walked three miles this a.m. with Boude. May go to hot tub. Yes.

Thank goodness for the hot tub.

I have had aches and pains since I was eleven. The first ones started after a two-month bout of pneumonia and centered in my shoulders. Slowly over the years, muscles hurt in arms, legs, neck, and back to such a degree that I was often going off to someone to "fix" me. But the pain is still with me. I've just learned to manage it better.

A large trade show for hospitals was taking place in Orlando, Florida, and I thought I should be there.

Got computer off to Florida for $220! My God...Found out Visa card full so Piedmont never gave me a ticket. Paid cash today, and they were okay with that. Tired, lots to do and convinced that I can do it. My money has evaporated but I hold on.

Surely anyone who "saw" my system would buy it. These were the early days of computers, and in order for me to be sure that what I needed was on my computer, I had to bring my own. Originally, I had started out with a portable (or luggable), but after awhile I needed more speed, hard disk and larger monitor, so I started taking my own fully loaded PC. It was a pain in the butt and always ran the risk of not working once I got it there, but it beat trying to rent one, which was never successful. Money was again scarce but as long as I had things to do, I could keep my stomach quiet.

Up at 8 a.m., walked 2 miles with my Boude. Cleaned out tomato plants, put in 30 flower bulbs, and got yard and porch in order. Cleaned house, did the dishes, vacuumed etc., all before noon. I am greatly overdue for a business partner who will share the good and bad times, the boring and mundane issues. I think I'll look in Florida for a partner.

My body aches so much, yet I feel healthy inside. Stress. More exercise, Cleo! Not doing enough. Go for a bike ride. Flat tires, oh well. Went for a swim instead. Doing a new dance tape, which is a lot of work. Off to the Eno in afternoon. Boude loves the Eno but likes to keep walking instead of sitting along the bank watching the water go by, like I do. He's so good for me.

Summer is gone. Tomatoes out, bulbs in. I had a good summer. Not enough at the beach, but a good time. Maine, Boston, Vero Beach. I am a lucky lady.

*I told a man I was stressed about doing a demo for 500 women, and he said, "A lot of women and men would give their right arm to know enough **to demo** to 500 women!" He made me feel good. Said to take two aspirin four times a day to relieve my pain.*

There were times when I knew I had billables coming in, and I could keep panic at bay. Then there were times when I had few or no billables...then I panicked. This was one of the latter times.

12:23 a.m. Bills are paid, for the most part. This Florida trip is draining my money pockets. Wrote Walter (a CED member whom I had become friends with) and asked him to help me find money. Going off to find Randy and talk. Feel sooooo anxious inside.

2:45 p.m. Here I am again. Drove to Marina to talk to Randy but he was busy fixing his boat. Came back to pack and have a drink. If I don't get someone to share the pressures soon, I'll be an alcoholic!

The last days of September 1987 were spent cleaning up the State project, doing last minute errands, and seeing friends like Jane E. Randy was so engrossed with his new boat, he had little time for anyone else, but it was a great diversion for him. Sometimes I would wonder if I should go fish in Florida and give up all this struggling, and then I read in Illusions:

In order to live free and happily, you must sacrifice boredom.

It is not always an easy sacrifice.

When I returned from Orlando October 4th, I was not a happy camper.

Just back from Orlando trade show, shaken and in need of a friend. Asked Randy to come over and talk over dinner, and he did. No one will ever know how much I need my family around me. I hit every insecure feeling in my 49-year-old bones during the trade show. My ulcer is ever present to assure me of how scared I am.

The trade show was a reality check for me. After I set up my makeshift booth, I stood by, waiting for the world to flock to see how MedstaffPLUS would work wonders. Next to me was a million dollar company that had spent a lot of money on a posh booth. They had similar software, but we looked like Mutt and Jeff next to each other; I was obviously Mutt! All around the whole room were professional-looking booths, and the sheer number of participants overwhelmed me. Reality #1: Do not try to compete with the big boys at trade shows! All the medical staff software was consigned to a side hallway, where no one wanted to walk. Reality #2: People do not come to a trade show to buy. They come to look. Each competitor was trying to get a look at the other competitor's software, so we were all involved in a cat and mouse game. Reality #3: All a trade show does is give your secrets away.

All in all, I came home broke, scared, and very insecure. It took the combined help of Randy, Gary, Hazel and a few Duke friends to help me get over it.

Randy turned a sick, depressed night into a productive one for me. He set up my computer, which made it back from Florida okay, and then, while he worked on Committees, I got organized. Committees is looking great. Randy's wonderful.

Gary called and was great to me too. They all understand I'm going through my mid-life crises (who am I, have I done <u>anything</u> with my life?) and are being very supportive.

Hazel turned 79 on October 13th, and I sent her a mink hat that Jane P. had given to me. I knew Hazel would enjoy wearing it to church. She was still a constant in my life, and I was now calling her several times a week, if not more. I knew she would always be there for me. During one conversation she said that her friends were wondering, "Who is this white woman who Hazel keeps talking to." We laughed over that one.

40 degrees—awful. Where did fall go? I need sun. I miss my daughter. France is so very far away. What shall I do with my life?

9 p.m. What am I doing? Drunk and lonely. Hell, I'm in the same boat lots of people are. Why not? Why should I be happy? For years my kids made me happy, and then work. If work stops…

Cleo B. Robertson

Work had become my life, and everything revolved around it. For the first time I really began to question if I could go on. Jane had told me that she could get me hired at Duke. I asked her about the starting salary, and when she told me, I laughed. Because I had no degree, they would hire me for $25,000 for a 40-hour week. As a consultant I was making $50 an hour, so for a 40-hour week, that equaled $2,000 per week or $100K+ per year. Of course I didn't work 40-hour paid weeks, but I always thought big. I asked her if they thought I was crazy or what? She said that they couldn't do better, so being hired permanently by Duke was not an option, in my mind. It turned out to be a Godsend that I didn't go to work for Duke.

Progress is being made, I hope, in the State project. If people don't want to make it happen though, what can I do?

My answer for everything was more work, but with the State project, I had a feeling that more was not enough. Computers took a lot of work and attention, and the State just didn't have the support system—and they didn't want to pay for one.

Lisa is in Brussels for three weeks. She is really having a time. I envy her a little and I am proud too. She has been a big influence on my life.

An 18-month old girl was brought out of a 22' well after 58 hours in Midland, Texas. We all prayed, and God heard. Along with some very good Texas drillers!!!

I have big dreams and write them down, and then re-read them, and find they didn't come true. Am I just full of big dreams like my father? Can I be so pompous as to think I can do what seems impossible?

Doubt was my constant companion towards the end of October:

People say suicide victims don't reach out, but sometimes they do! Nobody answers their phone when they're needed, desperately needed. I need to talk to someone.

I called Hazel again, and I upset her with my upset. I AM HURTING INSIDE.

Suicide was something I grew up with. One of the brothers from our local gas station shot himself in the mouth, and his mother had killed herself by cutting her wrists on the roof of the gas station I visited often. Their dad had also killed himself, and a woman who rented a room from us also killed herself. I understood that suicide was a choice some people made. When I got depressed, I would often mull it over. Not so much how to do it, but how would everyone feel? I realized much later that I did this to feel someone would miss me.

Alone, bored and broke. Lots of testing of MEDSTAFFplus. Tried to get tracking done. Slow. As I walked into CED meeting from the rain, my right shoe slipped on the wood floors. I did a complete split right in front of everyone.

At the time I thought I had split apart my groin, but I recovered amazingly well.

Lisa just called from Paris! They are fine, busy, great. I miss her so.

Snowing!! Went from hot to cold, a change of 30 degrees, yesterday. Awful. A roller coaster I am on again, emotionally. I swam 50 laps in 30 minutes today. I quit drinking. I feel terrific. Dan marries his love tomorrow. May God bless them both abundantly.

I was still trying to learn what I was supposed to do to succeed.

I was on the panel in a CED meeting on "Getting clients when you're a nobody." It was very good for me. I realized insurance companies won't listen to me because I'm a nobody. Selling direct to hospitals is too confusing. Multi-hospital systems like HCA only want to work with a someone. What does that leave? Not much that I can see.

Tomorrow I go visit at Pitt Memorial Hospital to present a proposal to do their medical staff analysis. At three, I meet with a private investor.

Two opportunities. I'm going to sell both of them!

What I didn't know was how to really begin selling. What was the smallest step I would have to take to succeed? I remembered a Gestalt workshop in the '70s, where a man in his late '60s waited until the last day to work on a problem he had. When we were just about to close the workshop for the weekend, he spoke up.

"Neil, I want to tell you why I'm here. I'm 65, and there are so many things in my life I haven't done. I feel like a failure," he said quickly.

Neil waited a moment and then said, "So, what's one thing you'd really like to do before you leave the earth?"

Without hesitation the man said, "Go around the world!"

"Oh, good," Neil said. "So you know what you want to do. What's the smallest step you have to take to do it?"

The man thought awhile and then said, "Decide where I want to go."

"Oh, no," said Neil. "That's too big a step. Give me a smaller one."

The man then said, "Find a travel agent."

"Oh, no," Neil said again, "that's still too big a step. Think of a much smaller one."

After half an hour of the man trying to find the smallest step and Neil saying, "Oh, no," again and again, he finally hit on it.

"I need to buy a new pair of shoe laces," he said matter of factly.

"YES!" Neil answered and everyone clapped and the workshop was over.

Two years later in Philadelphia, at another Gestalt workshop, Neil and I were standing outside the building. A man walked up and said to Neil, "You don't remember me probably, but I was in a workshop here two years ago."

Neil said, "Well, so you've come back?"

"No," the man said. "I just wanted you to know that I bought the pair of shoe laces, and I've been around the world twice and going again." The smile on the man's face was a delight to see, and Neil congratulated him. He said goodbye and was soon on his way to get ready to go around the world again!

Now as I struggled with my marketing and sales programs, I wondered what the smallest step was that I needed to take.

Met with Bob, a venture capitalist. I think he and his group are going to invest in my business. Give us the money to do it right. I am excited. Very responsible, I feel, to make a success of it. We will. A team. I'll finally have a team.

This was another way I kept on going. Someone would show interest in the business, and I would dream about the wonderful success we would become. They all went away in time. Very much like my private life. I kept looking for someone and I would fantasize how great we'd get along, and then they'd go away. I wanted someone to come save me (CBR). As anyone who has been there knows, you can't look to other people to solve your problems. It took me years to learn. While Randy was working incredibly hard when he had time, he was proving to be less of a partner than I had hoped. He would not talk "business," and it was business talk that I needed.

11 p.m. Randy worked on tracking program and did all I wanted and more! He's so patient. I'm in a funk again. Feeling low. Still not drinking though. At least I'm not a mess. A sale would make life perfect.

I sent out hundreds of letters every month, each one typed by me and individualized by my conversations with the recipient, or others in the hospital. Over the years I had developed a contact sheet for each hospital client. On it, I recorded all the pertinent information about the hospital at the top and then entered in the journal at the bottom, every call, letter, and meeting I had with anyone at that hospital. That way, when someone would call, I knew immediately everything that had transpired on that account since it began. My contact sheets saved my ass more than once.

Unfortunately, all my organization was aimed at the wrong people. I was trying to sell to the whole 50 states, and I didn't know that could not work—it's one of the laws of sales. You can't sell to an area bigger than you can get around easily, if presenting your product was required. But I didn't know, so, I was killing myself trying. No one in CED, or any of the workshops, told me how to focus on my market, and how to reach that market, which would have been invaluable information for any beginning business.

My friend, Mitch is here. Can he tell how panicked I am? Am I? I made a lot of sales calls and got through to no one. I'm looking old. Old to my eyes. Maybe it's just how I look with $200 in the bank! I refuse to resort to booze or anything else. I'm going to tough it out.

Will I ever historically make sense of all these writings?

Mitch was a miracle to me when he came into town. His passion was journalism. When he was around me, he wanted to know how and what I was doing. I loved his attention. He had a wonderful wife and two children, so they gave me a sense of family. Whenever he came into town he would give me a call, and we would catch up. Sometimes I would even meet him at the airport for an hour layover. He always had his family's progress to report, and then business. I had plenty of time to tell him what I was doing. He never failed to give me more confidence and hope. Mitch came into my life at the beginning of CBR, and I have forever been thankful. It was in the early years of my business when no one understood what I was trying to do with hospitals. And he didn't either, but he understood my passion, and he understood that there was a lot I didn't know. He helped me learn a whole lot.

WHIM OF IRON

I met Mitch through a Washington consultant, Jim. It was Jim who had introduced me to microcomputers. Jim worked with a Princeton group with whom I had done a very early project (early in my business life) that dealt with editing copy on some pharmaceutical products. Mitch was also an independent consultant, so when the Robert Wood Johnson Foundation (RWJ), a Princeton-based company, asked Jim to do a project, he brought Mitch and me together. Mitch's role was to write copy for a physician practice patterns report. My role was to see to it that the report went out without errors.

It was an interesting project. RWJ Foundation funded a very large survey of physician practice patterns, and thousands of physicians filled out questionnaires. Mitch took the results, had them statistically analyzed, and then wrote up the results. The report was filled with graphs and graphics of all kinds, plus lots of lists such as, "Where do you practice medicine from most often?" "Hospital," "Private Office," and "Clinic" would appear, for instance, with percents for each. During this project, I met very high-level people in health care. I also met working professionals, who very generously shared with me what they had learned so far. In fact, it was Mitch who told me hospitals don't like to pay their bills, which resulted in my taking upfront payment *only* when I started selling. People said I couldn't do that, but I did. There was no way I was going to go through all the work of setting them up, and then not get paid. I had to live, after all.

Jane had decided that it was time for the North Carolina Hospital Association to get involved in selling the MedstaffPLUS software. She believed it was good and that there was a need. In fact, she became my champion and got me some meetings with very big foundations and associations. At that time, none of them could understand what we were trying to do.

About this time, I began talks with Durham General Hospital about our software. I liked the management people at Durham, and they sincerely seemed to want to do the best job they could. Duke had some kind of loose affiliation with them, so that kept it all in the family.

Randy was busy working on one of our client's data, which had been a nightmare for over a week now. It was not easy to take sheets of paper with names and addresses of physicians on it and get that data into the computer, clean and correct. Phone numbers had changed, physicians had multiple offices, privileging lists were not up to date, and getting their entire graduate, resident, intern, and practicing history was a big job. We learned that the initial loading of data was always difficult, but having people work with you who didn't even want to be doing it, just made the job harder. Much later I realized that there are some sales you simply don't want.

It's cold out. Spent five hours canoeing on the Eno River yesterday for mistletoe—great fun. I was in canoe with the leader of expedition, and we both went to reach for some mistletoe at the same moment and our canoe rolled right over. He came up out of the water sputtering and yelling that I shouldn't have done that, etc., etc., etc., and I said, "You know, you're not really helping at all. Why don't we just get back in the boat and keep going?" He did, but he wouldn't talk to me the rest of the trip.

Christmas was marching closer, and I felt so unprepared. Lacking money, I made some presents, but my heart was not in it. I needed cash, and I needed a rest. Lisa and Andy were coming home for Christmas, so that was the highlight for me. I couldn't wait to see them.

Great day in Durham. Carolers came by, and the whole neighborhood lit luminary candles. Lovely. They put up a thousand all around the reservoir. Lisa and Andy called. They can't wait to be here. I can't wait to see them. Talked to Gary. He'll be here for Christmas, along with Carl.

Holidays were always great events for me, and having the family around eased my stress.

State work finally coming to fruit; nice things happening. Jeanne is pregnant, Barbara is doing well with half vision, my Aunt Peg is well. Lisa and Andy here Saturday—what a Christmas present they are!

As the next entry shows, I was still handling money poorly.

Wonderful day. I bought everyone presents with money I should have used to pay bills.

Maybe I can tear a dollar in half and make more money, perhaps?

Randy saved Christmas Eve. No one else would be here until the day after Christmas Day.

Randy came over, built a fire, started the grill, and I put water on to boil and we sat down to fresh 1½# lobster, grilled leg of lamb, sautéed carrots and beans, fresh bread and wine. Lovely. The lobster was a great surprise for Randy. The jacket I made him fit PERFECTLY! And he loved it! He gave me eel skin manicure set, which is spectacular for the eel skin as well as the precise tools. We then sat by the fire and talked. Missed midnight mass but the evening was a wonderful memory anyway. We are very lucky people.

Woke to the sound of Randy in the kitchen—he brought bacon, eggs and lots of loving energy. We're going to bake!

Terrific day. Baked bread, pies, rolls and talked, played computer pool. House ready for Lisa and Andy.

Christmas dinner was a great success. Carl (my children's father), Gary, Randy, Lisa and Andy all indulged themselves royally on a great roasted turkey with all the trimmings. Everyone pitched in, particularly Randy, so it was easy. We all enjoyed hearing Lisa and Andy tell us their experiences and how well they were doing. Lisa knew French before she went, and Andy was in the process of learning, so the fact that they had adjusted, was wonderful. It had taken a lot out of Lisa because she was more fluent, so she had handled all the apartment details, getting services, and learning the shopping (which is quite different in Paris). She did it all well, and Andy could not praise her enough.

New Year's Eve was a quiet night, but an enjoyable one, too. I made chili and took a large batch to the firemen who had to work that night, and then home to sit by the fire and think back on all the activities for the last week. Lisa and Andy had left, as had Carl. Randy was busy partying and having much-deserved fun. When I counted my blessings, they were many. When I counted my cash, there was none, but that didn't seem to dampen my view of the New Year.

The New Year—what's ahead? Relationship amongst CBR, Duke, NCHA and NCHT. A growing, thriving business. Friends. Lisa and Andy back in Paris. Finding adjusting harder than they thought it would be. They get one pizza, 4 beers and 2 coffees for $50! They were fun to be with. They are happy together and will have a long and fruitful relationship. I am feeling very good. New Year's resolutions: Exercise more, eat less, relax more, worry less, love more, and then some more. Welcome, 1988!

1988 — One Step Forward, Two Back

The New Year started out with many thoughts about work. The <u>Leader</u> wanted to take pictures and do an article about CBR, which was exciting. It never occurred to me that local news about a local company would do little in terms of sales…I prayed *anything* would help.

A friend called and invited me for chili. When I got there, the "sled team" showed up, and I went for a wonderful evening of riding around in a Blazer with good men in two feet of snow. At one point they all jumped out, tied an old car hood to their rear bumper and turned it upside down. They told me to get in, which I did without hesitation, and they took off through the paths below the power line. There I was, swinging from one side of the path to the other, snow blowing every which way. I had no control whatever, and it was a blast. Later we all went to play pool.

When I wasn't playing, I focused on procuring money.

Met with Bob for second time regarding investing in CBR. My hunch the answer is no. There are other avenues and I must explore them. I'm done with crutches. Swam 50 lengths and feel great. Still at 154 pounds. Now what? Sell systems. I feel so anxious I can't right now, but maybe in an hour or two. Nothing ever happens as a mistake so I'll make an opportunity out of no investor. Meet with Trust and Hospital Association next Tuesday. Hope lives on.

And the following shows the lengths to which I was going to keep the faith:

When I opened <u>Illusions</u> to answer my question, "What to do about business because I can't sell by phone?" I read:" The original sin is to limit the I. Don't.

Okay. I won't.

Early in February, I went to Fuqua's School of Business's Entrepreneurship Day. I had a great time, met lots of people, but didn't learn how to sell my software. Entrepreneurship is a wonderful thing, but at some point cash flow and profit have to be realized. And I just didn't know how to do that. I had been paid by foundations and Duke for so long, I didn't know how to market and sell the product. Even knowing that didn't give me the knowledge. Randy felt that all

WHIM OF IRON

CBR was, was his software. I was slowly learning that product was not enough.

The State project was running out of funds. I heard rumors about cutbacks. I prayed that I wasn't going to get cut. My work seemed too important to their efficiency to cut back, but I waited, as did everyone else, to see what would happen. I took my pleasure from small successes: I was quoted in a new business magazine in the Research Triangle Park, the Hospital Association/Trust deal looked like it might go through, and lots of people were hearing about my work.

During March I put a lot of energy into finding sales people. I figured they would know what I didn't know. An idea I had to create a Center for Hospital Computing or something like that was obviously not a vision others shared, so I was moving on to simple sales. The NCHA and Trust wanted to get money from two endowments and have me build the Integrated Administrative system. It was a great idea, but I knew it would be a hard sell—hospitals were still slow to appreciate the advantages of knowing what was going on quality-wise.

Towards the end of March, I learned that the State contract would end April 15th, after three years. I felt glad/scared. I knew that if the Duke project didn't go through, I would have to do it on my own from sales. That would be hard. Nevertheless, I was optimistic.

On April 8th, the bottom dropped out:

Went in to work on State contract and John asked me to come in and see him. He told me straight out that there was no money left in their budget for me. Someone needed it elsewhere, and they just transferred it.

The news, though halfway expected, rocked me hard. I drove home in shock, knowing I was now really on my own. I was in no position to have no income.

Visa payment bounced—have asked Jane to loan me $800 today. I felt sick in my stomach as I drove home and feel frozen even though I keep working. I have lots of alternatives: Hospital Association project comes through; sell many packages; get a job; pack it all in and hit the road.

Life is certainly never boring.

By mid-April, I was again desperate for money.

Asked Mitch to loan me money, and he is going to, in small amounts. Rick gave me good advice today. I'm going to prepare a Prospectus to sell shares for CBR. I'm having a hard time going. Being alone at home with my work, trying to get the business moving, MedstaffPLUS not working, Randy involved with work, boats, skiing, motorcycle, I come last, if at all. I need to get him out of Duke!

Mitch saved the day by sending $1,500 (I didn't know it at the time, but he would send me $1,500 every month for four months). I was very careful with his money because I knew I had to pay it back. The Prospectus to sell shares for a company that had a new, untested product, no sales, and no income was, in retrospect, stupid, but I didn't know that then. Randy being gone was extra hard on me because he had always been the one to cheer me up when things got bad. I sorely missed his confidence.

About this time the inevitable happened: my hard disk crashed on my NCR PC. Because I didn't have a recent backup, the crash was very bad because I lost a whole lot of spreadsheets I had been designing for administrators. I finally decided they must not have been good enough and redid them in a better format. I had a meeting with Duke Endowment May 19th, and Bob from Duke was coming on Sunday to give me advice. I felt very excited that my ideas would get a hearing.

By the following week, life had changed… again.

I want to feel great. Right now I have a lump in my throat and don't feel so great. But feeling great will come. Won't it God? If I work hard? I'm trying hard. Trying isn't good enough. I'm such a wimp!

Someone suggested that I didn't know how to "close" a sale, and I gave that some thought. It had never occurred to me that there was an "opening" or "close" to a sale. I asked some CED friends, and they agreed to come over and give me some tips. I worked hard at it, but truthfully, I didn't know how to shut up…I loved my product so much I was sure if anyone learned enough about what it would do, they would buy. I still didn't know that love of a product does not sell it.

After many months talking with the Technological Development Authority (TDA, which was operated by the State of North Carolina), and presenting to a panel of business people under very competitive conditions, I finally was given a $50,000 loan. The following entry belies my happiness in getting the loan from TDA. Part of the reason was that it would take all of it to hire Randy back, and I truly did need more; part was that the loan carried a 50 percent yearly interest rate, which somehow I had ignored during negotiations because I needed money, and no one else would loan it to me. But 50 percent interest!!!

Met with Ed of the North Carolina Hospital Association and still have hope. Other times I'm panicked. Got the TDA loan for $50,000 but that's not enough! God, send me some help!

By June…

Mitch loaned me another $1,500, and I paid bills, but I am flat broke. Randy also overextended at work as well as in money and time. Doesn't want to work on program. Neither do I. No energy to finish it.

On June 22nd, Lisa's birthday, the North Carolina Hospital Association Board gave positive approval to proceed with a project that Jane and I had been working on for some time. What I needed was exposure, and Jane had come up with the idea of having me do demonstrations to hospitals around the State that were sponsored by the North Carolina Hospital Association. Hearing they were willing to go forward with this plan gave me great hope. Jane was confident the exposure would solve my problems.

By the end of June, I told Bob and Jane that I was hiring Randy back. They both knew there would be problems within Duke, because even though Duke didn't want to pay Randy the same as the "degreed" programmers, he was doing the job of three of them. Duke had evaluated what Randy was doing as "easily replaceable" and had never trained anyone to cover his job. They would not be happy to hear he was leaving.

Randy and I talked a great deal about where we were trying to go. I wanted him back, and I wanted him happy so I offered him $40,000, and he agreed to leave Duke by August 1. He knew I was on borrowed money, but he said he couldn't leave for less, and I knew better than anyone that I'd have a hard time finding anyone cheaper. It meant I would have no salary. But that was nothing new. That's what the person who starts a business has to do—go without, in the hopes that in the long range, money would come. It was a big risk and I understood Randy not wanting to take it.

I then asked Jeanne to join CBR because of her incredible ability to interpret data, and she agreed. She came on board full time in September at a salary of $40,000, too. What I had done was split the $50,000 between the two of them and figured I'd have sales before six months passed and could then cover the rest of their salaries. By this point, I wasn't taking any cash out, or very little, to buy groceries. The math didn't support what I was doing, but I didn't know how to do the math, so I moved forward. I'm glad I was so ignorant and gutsy.

When the Duke programming department learned Randy was leaving, they got really upset with me. Bob and Jane stayed supportive and got me an appointment with the head of Information Services. We met, I listened to why he felt I was unfairly offering Randy too much money to take him away, and I very calmly told him that $40,000 is what Randy was worth. He disagreed. I just stayed calm and assured him Randy would give Duke fine support with their MedstaffPLUS software, and that seemed to calm him down. I didn't really care they were pissed…they had underestimated Randy simply because he didn't have a degree, and I was glad to show them he was worth a lot more.

My son, Gary, was once again traveling around, and he called from northern California when he turned 27. Seemed impossible that 27 years ago, I was a homemaker, and now, here I was, out selling, something I never thought I'd do (well, I wasn't really "doing it," but I kept trying). <u>Triangle Business Weekly</u> took my picture for an article they did about CBR. Nice, but it didn't help sales really, just more energy wasted. Despite all the stresses, this was truly an exciting time for CBR and for me. I was waiting to hear from Ed at the North Carolina Hospital Association about how to proceed with the project to do demonstrations around the state. I was excited that once we started, it would put a whole lot of things into place.

Waiting for the Hospital Association to sign, is wearing me out. I'm ready to GO! I can sell the software to 20 hospitals by the end of the year!

Part of my enthusiasm came from knowing Randy would be on board August 1. Jeannie would also start August 1. Now, not only would we be able to do so much more professionally, but also we would be a team, and I would have a "family" around me.

My days were exciting. Randy's girlfriend, Sara, had become my good friend. We would go for long, three-mile walks in the Duke Forest, and she would let me rattle on and on about what was happening. I was brimming over with happiness. All the documents for the North Carolina Hospital Association agreement were together, finally. On July 14th, I went to Raleigh to finalize the agreement. A funny incident happened prior to signing.

One of the men representing the Hospital Association was quite leery about signing the contract with me. He arranged for a luncheon with himself and a few other people from the association. As soon as I sat down, I knew he had something on his mind, but I had no idea what it was. We chatted about a few things and then at some point I said, "By the way, Randy is going to be joining CBR full time in August." The man in question turned quickly towards me and asked, "Is Randy your significant other?"

I burst out laughing. "No, no," I said with great enjoyment. I now knew why he was hesitant about signing a contract with CBR. I added, "Randy is my son." With that, the whole table relaxed and from then on we talked about the project without the tension in the air. At the end of the luncheon he told me they would be getting in touch with me soon to finalize the deal.

About the same time I had a new brochure done for the IMSSS systems (Integrated Medical Staff Support System). Somehow, acronyms seemed important in the business world, and I tried to think of logical ones. IMSSS represented to me all that could be done for the patient and the health care industry to lower costs and improve quality. How could anyone *not* buy it, I wondered?

I was sure that with all the sponsorship, I would succeed big time. Didn't everyone want to manage quality? Save money? Get good PR? The fact was, it wasn't that easy. Hospitals were struggling with how much control they could exert over physicians, physicians were scared management was going to go on a witch hunt, and the boards were afraid to upset the apple cart. I didn't understand all this at the time…I was sure my superior product would sell itself—probably the most common belief of new entrepreneurs. We're wrong, but often we don't find out until it's too late.

Every time anyone showed any interest in the software, I would hop in my car and go talk with them. Greensboro Hospital asked me to talk to them, and I did, but I could see that I was not getting through. Each person listening was figuring out how they could design the same software in-house and save a lot of money. This was a common theme. What data processing people didn't tell management was the high cost of in-house development. They essentially had to dedicate a development team to researching needs, and then allow the programmers to develop the software. I tried to point out that just because people could learn how to program the software, didn't mean they knew how to design software for end users with little or no experience with computers. Moreover, in my mind, it was the hundreds of reports designed by hospital management professionals that we had incorporated into our product which brought so much value. These were reports that answered critical questions that they weren't even asking generally, but slowly I realized that some didn't want the answers. They didn't even want to ask the questions.

My children continued to give me good support. Gary gave me a sewing machine for my birthday, because I needed to make and mend things rather than buy. Randy was excited about making better money and being back on the project full time. The time at Duke had just been a break, so to speak, and of course he had learned a great deal that would be useful to us. I was delighted to have him back on board. An added plus was that he and Jeannie got along so well, that she started being productive immediately.

The Hospital Association's PR man, Bill, was assigned to my project. Bill was excited because he could see the potential for quality management software. His support and encouragement were invaluable during this period. I was going in front of a lot of people explaining our program, and I was nervous. Bill never had any doubt I could do it, which gave me the confidence I needed.

On August 2nd, 1988 the North Carolina Hospital Association and the North Carolina Hospital Trust signed an agreement with CBR to market IMSSS to the North Carolina Network System. It was a remarkable event for me. These two very staid organizations had never sponsored a company before, and it was a risky thing for them to do. If it hadn't been for the Duke backing, of course, they wouldn't have given me the time of day. But even with the backing, it was remarkable that they took the risk. I was sure that this was the real beginning for CBR.

The very next day I sent out 800 packets to hospitals in great expectations of many sales. I was sure the phone wouldn't stop ringing. Success was mine—all delusions of the novice entrepreneur. By this time August had rolled around and Randy and Jeanne were working with me. Work all of a sudden seemed like great fun. Fun not to be doing everything alone! Fun to see progress made daily. Fun to see their enthusiasm and knowledge. Jane was still very supportive about the project, and she was now ready to help with the marketing.

WHIM OF IRON

Whenever I got scared during this phase of the business, I would go walk along the Eno River. The Eno River walk is a great accomplishment in environmental protection and the vision of a local woman. Every piece of land that became available along the Eno running through Durham and other communities was bought up with money raised through an Eno group, so what we had was miles and miles of unspoiled woods and river to enjoy. It was along the paths that I would find mushrooms of all kinds—oyster mushrooms hanging richly from the top parts of tree trunks; chanterelles, yellow and black, subtly hidden under leaves and undergrowth; sulphur shelfs that were two feet wide and over a foot tall growing on tree trunks; puffballs, which were a favorite until I discovered morels; and a rare cabbage mushroom that turned out to be delicious.

Over the years I had joined mycology forays and learned how to identify the above mushrooms. If I couldn't identify it by sight, smell and taste, then I wouldn't keep it. In the beginning, I would take my findings to a local authority, who would help me identify each clearly. By the summer of 1988, I knew how to collect and eat about eight different wild mushrooms safely. These walks, looking for mushrooms and listening to the river water running, healed my soul. It was here I could talk to God and tell Him how scared I was and how much I was relying on Him to help me. My dog, Boude, would accompany me, and since he weighed 125 pounds, I had no fear of being alone, deep in the woods.

If I was feeling energetic, I would walk the couple of miles to the "quarry," a large lake created when large equipment had taken rock and stone out for commercial purposes. I was told that a dump truck still sat at the bottom, caught when water had been struck, and quickly filled up the entire excavated area. It was here that I could swim in the cold water and reduce my body aches and pains, and clear my head. Boude would swim along with me, and we'd go all the way around the lake. I missed the Gulf of Mexico's warm, salt water, but since going home was out of the question, I was happy for the quarry.

Randy had hit CBR with his feet running. He was totally involved in building good management reports with Jeanne. I would find him still working at 8 and 10 p.m. He respected Jeanne, and she soon learned that he could make the computer do anything she wanted, so they were the perfect team.

Jane and Bill had set up some preliminary meetings for me, the first being with Wesley Long Hospital. The demo went well, but I could tell they thought they could do better on their own. I realized after presentations like this that they had a hard time believing that I, a nobody from nowhere, could build the best quality management software. I always figured that they would find out sooner or later.

By the end of August, pressure was building for me to go out and do demonstrations to hospital medical staffs and management. I went, but mixed with excitement was a stomach-wrenching fear. There was not enough time for me to test the quickly developing software.

I get very scared. Pressures of demos, no time to test, competitors on my neck, and then I sit with laptop on porch and "play" with what Randy has built and I am energized again! Faith burns anew. We are on top. We will do it. I have faith.

Onward Christian Soldiers….

The first week in September I drove to Ashville with Bill to do my first big demo. Most of the time I would take my computer, an overhead projector, a projector that took my computer slides and put them up on the wall, as well as the software. It didn't occur to me that there was an art to presenting, that you don't give people too much, you don't oversell, and you listen for when they have "bought." I didn't know any of these things, so I would just throw everything I had at them. I figured more was better.

I was enjoying having Bill as a partner on the road. He was well read and very knowledgeable, so I learned from listening to him. When I did my first demo, I was amazed at how much Randy and Jeanne had added and fixed in our software program. There were new reports and graphs, new functions, and more data fields. It was very exciting to watch our products mature. About this time I got a letter from another software developer who claimed I had stolen proprietary information. I was panicked of course, until Jane told me that they were just barking up a tree, and that turned out to be true. Duke's lawyer sent off a letter, and that ended that.

Hospital presentations began to go more smoothly. My original clumsiness had been replaced with speed setting up, while I talked at the same time to those arriving to see the show. When I went to Moses Cone Hospital I was very excited, because they had talked about how much they wanted to manage quality. Unfortunately, they too, thought they could build a better mousetrap, so I left knowing there would not be a sale.

Other presentations followed, but it never really got easy.

I am practicing my presentation for tomorrow. 50+ people in Raleigh to hear me and Randy and Jeanne. I want to WOW them and it's hard. I must be spontaneous, yet organized. Explicit, yet global. Short, yet informative. I will sleep on it. God will be with me and show me the way.

Much to our delight and surprise, the presentation went wonderfully. People were interested, asked questions and got us really excited. However, during the question and answer period, questions kept coming up about how they could possibly manage the doctors. Little hospitals were afraid of losing the few they had, and big hospitals were afraid the doctors would take their admissions elsewhere. We drove home pretty discouraged.

WHIM OF IRON

Our days were getting longer. Randy and I would often work until 10 at night. There was always more testing to do, which would result in more programming changes and back to testing. People make jokes about software always having bugs, but when you realize that *every* change can cause a bug, one can only marvel that there aren't more bugs. I remember once searching through some programming code I had written in a programming class. I looked for days and finally found the "bug." It turned out to be an extra space between two words! Because of one extra space, the printer wouldn't print. Often after a long day looking for bugs, I would have to go play a few games of pool to begin to relax.

There were, thankfully, moments of levity. One day as I walked Boude around my extended neighborhood, a beat up-looking red Volkswagen van suddenly stopped in the middle of the road, and a wild-looking woman started yelling, "That's him, that's the dog who got my poodle pregnant! That's him!" I looked incredulously at her and let her continue ranting. When she finally stopped, I said, "It couldn't' have been my dog. Boude never runs loose."

With complete conviction, she said, "Oh, yes he does. Or he did once that I know of. He came up to my chain-link fence and saw my 12-pound poodle, Itsy, inside, fully in heat. He tried to get through the fence, but when that failed, he jumped right over. Itsy was delighted, I have to admit. She had a smile on her face a mile wide."

I looked at Boude. His face had guilty written all over it.

"But how could a 125-pound dog mate with a 12-pound one?" I asked, still not believing.

"Easy," she said. "He just sat down and Itsy jumped right on him and twisted and pushed until she was finally secured on him. They both seemed to have a great time. I tried to break them up, but it was useless, they just ignored me."

"So when is the big event?" I asked. I wanted to see the puppies, but I feared she was going to ask for dog support,

"About a month," she responded. She had been patting Boude's head, so I knew that she wasn't angry with him.

With our dubious introduction behind us, I took a good look at her. She was 65 when we met, with long silver-streaked black hair almost to her knees, a big Jewish face that you so often find from New York City, a face of history and lines. She had a very large nose, but it went well with her big teeth, one of which was capped in gold, right up front. We exchanged names and addresses (we lived within three blocks of each other) and promised to get together for the big event.

Turns out, she was a New Yorker but had taken off years ago to join the Native Americans living in the southwest. Her name was Sunrise. Through her, I learned a lot about Native American belief systems—

very similar to my own beliefs. Everything is sacred. God is everywhere.

Five weeks later I got the call from Sunrise. I went over and sure enough, four dogs had been born. Or we thought they were dogs. They really looked more like monkeys, because their hair was long, very long, and their bodies seemed wrong, but we couldn't say why. Anyway, two finally died, one lived a year only to be put to sleep because it kept biting people, and the fourth became Sunrise's second child. Navajo, as he was called, was white (his mother was pure white), shorthaired, and looked like a mutt, as he certainly was.

Sunrise was a remarkable woman. She had run a very successful florist business in New York City's theatre district for many years and had been of the elite crowd. After she and her husband divorced, Sunrise took up with younger people who had causes in the '60s and '70s. She was a great believer in believing. After a few years of living hand to mouth and working on issues, Sunrise finally decided to leave for a simpler life. She ended up in the Southwest, where she lived on Indian reservations and learned their culture. She stayed for 17 years.

One day she decided to get in her Volkswagen van and drive back to New York City to see her daughter and granddaughter. On her way past Durham, North Carolina, her van broke down. While it was being fixed, she checked out Durham and decided to stay. She moved into a small house and started making lovely jewelry from out of her home.

I learned over time that she was the only daughter of a Jewish New York City chef of great renown, and she had been taught to cook at an early age. Some of my best memories are of us in her kitchen. We had very different styles, but we each respected the other's skills. One time we took veal, vegetables and rice, discussed each part of putting our meal together, and negotiated a final dish. It was beyond imagination, it was that good. She knew the fine art of herbs and spices, and I learned from her every time we were together.

I have digressed from my story to tell you about Sunrise, because her presence in my life became very important to me. When I went to her house, we talked about spirit and faith, healing and being healed. We made things out of feathers and stones, crystals and turquoise, and we honored everything. At one point we even started Sweat Lodges and were instructed in how to build a correct structure, lay the stones, etc. I spent most of my spare time with Sunrise learning female values I had never been given as a child or adolescent. Messages I needed to hear, like "I have value. I am worth something. I don't have to be perfect. I can be creative. I am creative."

Soon it was Sunrise who gave me patience and vision as I went from hospital to hospital, presenting with all my heart and coming home too often without a sale. She didn't know how to help me succeed in business, but she could keep me believing in myself, and that was very important. She would burn incense and say prayers and I would feel God inside me. A personal God, not just…God. I needed to have faith

WHIM OF IRON

in me, and Sunrise taught me that having faith in God *was* having faith in me.

As a child, I had grown up believing I was not enough. But in fact, it was my insecurities that drove me to keep going—I wanted to *prove* myself to my mom and dad. Sunrise encouraged me and kept me from feeling all alone.

Jane continued to be a good friend and someone I could hang out with occasionally (Jane had a very busy schedule at the hospital). One night when I was visiting her, we sat out on her porch overlooking Duke Forest and talked about the problems facing small hospitals. They knew they needed quality management. They also knew they couldn't afford it. All of a sudden an idea came to me—if we found foundation money to buy the hardware, then the hospitals could buy the software. We both got excited about the idea immediately. Jane was a "pro" at getting foundation money. They all knew and respected her. Jane said she'd get on it Monday.

On September 13th, 1988, I drove to Charlotte and presented to the Duke Endowment people. Our goal was to get money for hardware—we convinced them that the major problem for small hospitals was that, not only did they have to buy the software, but they also had to buy hardware. The response was very good. And just knowing that my name would be associated with a project sponsored by Duke University Medical Center and The Duke Foundation made me feel quite important.

Randy and I celebrated the Duke Foundation success by going to Fishmonger's in Durham and pigging out on seafood. It was wonderful. We both knew that each success just put more pressure on each of us to work 1000 percent, but we were so excited we didn't care.

Spontaneous surprises would happen every so often and relieve the day-to-day stress. One day UPS showed up with a 10-pound, fresh-caught, pink salmon direct from Alaska—shipped on the same day a friend had caught it. He and his dad were off fishing in the wilds, and they were kind enough to send one home. I put it on the grill, and Sunrise, Randy and I truly stuffed ourselves on the wonderful delicacy. Friends continued to make my day in so many ways.

The next day my daughter flew in for my 50th birthday. We had decided that we'd celebrate the big day by going to Emerald Isle on the North Carolina coast for a few days. I could use a break, and being with my daughter was always fun. We drove to Greenville first, where I did an uninspired presentation to a bunch of uninspired health care workers, and then we headed to the beach. I decided to take a shortcut, after looking at the map, and headed off as though I knew what I was doing.

Half an hour later we both knew I didn't. I pulled over on the dirt shoulder of a road totally out in God's country, at an intersection that didn't seem to be on the map. Suddenly we heard the squealing of brakes as an 18-wheeler pulled off the road behind us. A large man in cowboy boots walked up behind us and, after doffing his hat, asked if he could be of help. I explained where we were trying to go, and he laughed. "Well, lady, you better follow me then, 'cause you're going the wrong way." For the next 25 miles we followed his big truck through desolate backcountry until finally, we emerged onto a highway. We waved thanks, he tooted, and we went merrily down the road towards the water. North Carolina is full of nice people like our trucker.

Lisa brought a bottle of champagne to the beach to toast my 50th birthday. We went to dinner at Café Coquina then played pool.

Randy gave me a clock and musical jewelry box! Lisa gave me a lovely frame for their wedding picture, utensils and rack from Paris, bubble bath, and her! She was wonderful to spend time with.

Life was busy. Randy and Jeannie were going great guns creating a wonderfully powerful product, I was busy going to hospitals and doing presentations. I needed to make sales but I was so busy doing busy work, I had no energy for sales. The fact of the matter was I was avoiding making the calls. I hated listening to secretaries tell me when to call back.

The Hospital Association had set up a series of demonstrations for me in various cities and towns around North Carolina. I drove, alone, to these demos, going from city to mountain, through long, lonely roads and fast, busy highways. The medical staff's reception of me and my message at each hospital was generally good, and still there were no sales. Hospitals knew they needed the software, but they were overwhelmed with the implications of getting hardware, training, and even more basically, figuring out what questions they wanted to answer.

It truly was a difficult time for everyone. The hospitals had never managed their physicians. Did they actually graduate from a medical school? What privileges were they allowed, by training, to do? Who had a pattern of errors with patients and could benefit by some continuing education? Once the Joint Commission on the Accreditation of Hospitals told them they *had* to manage this data, they did, indifferently.

As one small hospital executive explained to me, "If we piss off just one doctor, we can lose half of our admissions. Best to be very careful and trust that the doctors, themselves, keep their records up to date."

Into this atmosphere I come along and say, "Manage, your doctors! Collect their data for them!" And the executives are saying, "I don't think so."

By the time I went to Charlotte, it was my ninth demonstration to multiple hospitals under the North Carolina Hospital Association's banner. My presentation had become smoother, I still got nervous showing the software for fear of a bug showing up, but the Duke Endowment people attended, which helped my mood. It was the final demo in Greensboro when everyone really got excited. Wesley Long and Richardson Memorial were very enthusiastic, and I felt we would soon be on a roll. Jeannie had done a great job testing the software, and Randy had done a great job of creating it. All I needed to do was sell it. I was feeling the pressure in my body—I pinched a nerve in my hip (sciatica) and was in great pain.

Towards the end of October, I did a full presentation to the HCA Nashville Hospital. It was one of those times when you are trying to reach a bigger audience than those before you. HCA had many hospitals, and I had dreams of CBR being their quality management software of choice. Big corporations are hard to sell to because it's hard to find out who the buyer is. I left discouraged about reaching anyone.

I distracted myself from the pressure of sales by agreeing to do workshops. The Hospital Association asked me to attend one in Pinehurst, and I always figured the exposure would help sales (it never did, but it took years for me to learn that I was just avoiding making calls).

Off I drove to the famous North Carolina resort and when I got there, I immediately felt out of place. Women were dressed to the 9's, men wore suits, and the whole atmosphere put me off. So, I headed for the gift shop, and bought an expensive watch that I could not afford, and which I lost within a month. The child within me would often act out by buying stuff when under stress. The problem was I couldn't *afford* to act out.

By the very end of November money was getting tight, and all the sales that I thought would be pouring in after the demonstrations, didn't materialize.

Business was not the only thing Randy did well—one day he got to show what a good friend he was, too. A tornado hit Raleigh one night and tore up an apartment complex where a friend of Randy's lived. Tom was an artist and all his paints, brushes and canvases were in his apartment, along with a few finished paintings, when the tornado hit. He told us he woke up in the middle of the night and thought a train was coming through the apartment. His roommate woke up, too, and just as they grabbed each other by the arms, the roof lifted off and they were carried through the air and dumped unceremoniously a hundred feet away. Luckily for them, neither was hurt, but Tom hardly had the money to replace all of his supplies; the paintings were irreplaceable.

The next day Randy and Tom went to the apartments, which were sealed off by the police. Neither Randy nor Tom hesitated for a moment. It was early morning, and the police had not arrived yet, so the two of them climbed down through the rubble, using a chain saw to clear the way, until they found Tom's apartment and all his stuff. Besides the painting supplies and paintings, they salvaged his TV, microwave and some clothing. It was quite an adventure and one that ended just fine, but as Tom was to say later, he couldn't have done it without Randy's confidence and determination.

Each year the Council for Entrepreneurial Development (CED) held an annual exposition of businesses. The purpose was to give entrepreneurs access to information on securing money, running a business, etc. Their emphasis was usually about growth, but that didn't figure in my head. I was trying to survive; growth, to me, would be one sale. I kept going to the meetings and expos, however, because I wanted to learn, and I didn't know where else to turn. For this year's expo I had agreed to be a presenter. My topic was "Writing a Business Plan Presentation."

I threw up just before I went on stage, which is not unusual for me to do. I remembered throwing up before every swimming meet in high school. I carried mouth freshener with me, and I'd just wash my face, freshen my mouth and go on.

This reminded me of a story I heard about Bob Hope, one that helped me out many a time. It seems Bob was getting ready to do a show, and there were only ten people in the audience. A radio announcer said to him, "I guess you don't get nervous when there's such a small crowd," to which Hope replied, "The day I stop getting nervous before performing, is the day I will quit. Being nervous means I still care."

Obviously, I cared.

My presentation went well, but no investors ever approached me.

Up at 5 a.m. to get correspondence done. Worked till 2:30, took a break and visited with Sunrise, and then to other friends. Wanted confirmation that I could do "it," whatever it was.

When I got home it was 7 p.m. and there was a call from HCA – they wanted CBR as a preferred vendor. This meant that every time they made a sale, they would bundle our credentialing and QA software with theirs, giving us two sales every time. I was ecstatic, of course, but part of me wondered how something this good could happen to me. Of course I'd done my homework and worked hard to get HCA, but it was like chasing a tiger and then catching it—what next?

Wanting confirmation, I called Neil, a therapist I worked with for years. "Neil, if I truly work hard and I do the best I can and I succeed, then I am doing what God would want me to do, right?"

"Right," says Neil. "Always do the best you can."

Right, of course.

I was having trouble accepting that I could succeed. I remembered back to one of the few encounters I ever had with my dad. I was eleven, and he told me that it was too bad that he hadn't been in my life to help direct me. He said that my brother and sister had an advantage, because he had been around while they were growing up. I was left with the feeling that I could never be good enough. If you're not good enough, you can't succeed.

This was a major misperception about myself that constantly was making me scared...I didn't want to fail, and I was afraid to succeed (if I succeeded I would be making a liar out of my father). So I went on succeeding, but found other ways to take my power away, like by being overweight and having bad relationships. Or at least that's how I figured it.

Bill and I were spending a good deal of time together as we drove around the state. Often we would talk about marketing strategy. It was wonderful to have others for these kinds of conversations. What I didn't know, and they didn't know, was that there were Marketing 101 rules we were ignoring (because we didn't know they existed). Our plans were born of our enthusiasm, not out of knowledge or experience.

The CED meetings were my fun time, when I got to talk to people about business and they didn't get bored. At a Christmas party with CED members, I talked to my good friend, Jack, and I told him that we were really stretched for money. He suggested that what I needed to do was hire a marketing expert to get us going.

I said, "I agree. So send me one that doesn't need to be paid, because we're broke." I promptly forgot our conversation.

One day when I saw Ed, the president of the North Carolina Hospital Association, I asked him if he would mind if I marketed our quality management system to other hospital associations. My rationale was that other associations would want to be heroes and bring a solution to their hospitals, just as Ed had. He agreed it would be fine for me to do. He didn't say, but I think he knew, it would not be an easy sell. Hospital Associations were not in the business of sponsoring private companies or telling physicians how they are doing.

Drove 240 miles to demo to Duplin Hospital today, coming home with only a "possible."

Lisa and Andy will spend Christmas in Vienna – I am so proud of her. She is teaching accounting to French people in French!

Gary is staying in St. Louis for Christmas. He is doing research he wants to finish. I'll miss him. Randy and I will share Christmas together. Our family has dwindled, temporarily.

As the year was drawing to a close, not only had our family dwindled, but our money, too.

It was slowly dawning on me that, even though the North Carolina Hospital Association was sponsoring us, and even though Duke University Medical Center was our development site, and even if small hospitals could get hardware for free…we still couldn't make a sale! I asked myself "Why?" over and over again, but no answer came to mind.

But it wasn't for lack of trying. New Bern Hospital asked me to meet with four of their QA people, so I drove the two and a half hours there and met with them. The presentation went well, even data processing decided it was good software, but I didn't feel I had a buyer in the room. It didn't matter if everyone in the hospital loved the software; who could write a check? At this point, I didn't know how to find that person. It never dawned on me to ask.

Christmas Day was 65 degrees and sunny. And all in all, it turned into a good holiday. It was not our usual Christmas with the family, but we managed to have a good time. Work was always on Randy's and my mind, so the holiday got very little of our attention anyway.

By New Year's Eve, I had caught up on all the bookkeeping, rearranged my house, and comforted Lisa as she suffered with chicken pox in Paris! I felt ready for the New Year and prayed it would bring prosperity. Or at least enough cash to pay the bills!

1989 — Mr. Beyer Arrives

I spent New Year's Day catching up on filling out tax return forms, typing W-2 forms and generally getting ready for my accountant.

On January 2nd, my life changed dramatically, and forever. I was in the middle of writing letters, when I got a phone call out of the blue from a man who said he knew Jack, and Jack had suggested that perhaps CBR could use his skills. He said his name was David Beyer, and that Jack had told him we "have a good product in a good market," but didn't know how to sell it. Mr. Beyer said he thought he might be able to help.

Not one to turn away help in any form, I asked him, "And what are your credentials?"

His answer was simple. "I'm a turnaround specialist. I take businesses that are going towards bankruptcy or are already in it, and I turn them around."

I laughed heartily right into his ear and then said, "Well, that describes us. We have about ninety days before we go belly up." I felt relieved to be able to say the truth to someone.

David responded by inviting me to lunch at noon, and I accepted. He said he would come pick me up, a courtesy I appreciated very much.

I heard the doorbell, turned off my monitor and went to the door. My first impression was of a very bright faced, happy man dressed in a dark business suit, who truly seemed pleased to meet me. I didn't take him in the house or introduce him to Randy and Jeannie. I didn't want to have to explain anything about David to them. Not yet.

We walked into the Ninth Street Bakery, and David immediately led me to a table where we could talk. I didn't know what to expect from our meeting. I had never heard of a turnaround specialist, but I could easily figure out what he meant. Jack had sent him, so I felt pretty comfortable. And I really had finally faced the fact that we were going bankrupt, which broke my heart. We had all worked so hard—the words many a failed business owner has uttered.

After some introductory remarks and a little background, his first question was, "Do you believe in God?"

Without hesitation I said, "Yes. 100 percent."

I don't remember the rest of his questions, but they all centered around values...what I valued, what I did not value, whether money was important to me, or success, and where I wanted to be in five years. As always, I talked from my heart. I am not a devious person, wouldn't know how to be, so I gave him only straightforward, honest answers.

He asked few questions about the products, but rather focused on who I was, what my vision was, and how I was making it happen. After about an hour he said, "Okay, I have a good picture in my mind. I'm going to get some literature from you on the products, and then I'm going to go away for about two weeks and do my homework. When we meet again I'll be prepared to tell you whether I can be of any help to you or not."

He was so clear. Everything was kept to the basics. I didn't get lost in our conversation, something I sometimes did when I talked business with professionals. He seemed so honest and open himself. He told me a little about his background and gave me a sheaf of 28 testimonials from other businesses he had worked with over the years. Each one was filled out by hand, which impressed me. But what really impressed me later when I had time to read them was how each entrepreneur or business owner had said the same thing—David had made a big difference in their bottom line.

After a little more talk, David brought me back to the house, came in quickly to get the literature on our products, and then he was gone.

I tried to put him out of my mind. I didn't know what he could do, but I knew I had to get busy and sell. I met with a consultant on how to sell/close, and he was very helpful.

Reality has hit. I can last one more month. May have to let Jeanne go. Need sales. Here we go, Cleo, shoulder to the grind. We <u>can</u> do it!

Somehow we always had made it in the past, and I hoped we could again. The difference, of course, was that instead of it being just me (I could always live on a little less money), or Randy (who could be very frugal, too), there was Jeanne to think about. She had a husband and child at home and needed to bring home her paycheck.

Two weeks later, just as I was about to announce to Jeanne and Randy we would have to make salary cuts, the phone rang. It was David. He said he would pick me up in twelve minutes.

When he pulled up outside the house, I noted that he looked handsome in his dark brown business suit. I wasn't attracted to him as a man (thank God), but I did like his clean look. And he seemed so happy and upbeat. After parking the car at my favorite restaurant and finding a quiet place for us to talk, he began his report after a few short courtesy remarks.

"I have made some calls around the country to consultants working with hospitals in the area of quality management. They agree there is a need, especially now that credentialing physicians is mandated by law."

We each ordered our lunch, and then he continued. "There are a few other companies out there with a similar product. With 6,000 hospitals in the United States, there's room for one more."

"We have one problem," he said as he sipped his coffee. "Hospitals don't know they need credentialing. They think it's just government interference to make them credential every physician who joins their staff. They don't realize that the legislation and your software are simply trying to identify problems in the systems that deliver health care. We're going to have to educate the market rather than sell to it."

In less than two minutes he had shown me that he had done his homework. He knew about the National Databank mandated by Congress, which was to ensure that physicians, who had been severely reprimanded and/or sued, would be reported. That would prevent bad personnel from moving from one state to the next.

He knew that the historical pattern in hospitals, and all of health care for that matter, was for administrators to take care of hospital business, and doctors to take care of doctor business. Few people would have listed that as one of the biggest obstacles to success for quality management software, but he was right. They didn't want to buy something that, in all probability, would upset their doctors.

And finally, he had a solution—education. Teach administration what automating the credentialing process would do for them, and they will buy. No longer would their credentialing coordinator have to type up to 30 letters to check on qualifications for every doctor who applied to them for medical staff privileges; or write many specialty boards to verify their certifications. Doctors' credentials would be up to date, and the hospital would be able to pass the JCAHO accreditations more easily. All we had to do was educate them. I knew I could do that.

David had done his homework. Never before had I heard a marketing plan for CBR that was geared just for CBR. I was overjoyed, but not naive. Everyone had warned me that he might just be scamming me. But I had read the 28 testimonials by every client he had had in his business career, and without exception, he had made a positive difference to their bottom line. Several admitted that they, the entrepreneurs, had failed to "do everything he told them to do." Taking profits out of the company was one of the most common failures, but there were many other ways to fail. It was easy. What was hard, was handing over all the decisions to someone else.

David waited for my reaction. My head was full of thoughts, mostly about what I had just learned from him. I felt, for the first time, that here was someone who knew how to market and sell. That was just what we needed.

I said "Education makes perfect sense to me," and stopped there. I was overwhelmed by his confidence.

He continued to lay out a preliminary plan for reaching and educating the market. I continued to be impressed with his knowledge and the simplicity of his delivery. It didn't take long for me to know that David was my new partner.

I listened on for a little while and then broke in with what was on my mind.

"So how much stock do you want for saving CBR?" I asked, not without a little humor in my voice. We both knew the CBR stock was worthless, because no one would buy us right now. We were $110,000 in debt with no sales in sight.

"Thirty-five percent," he said matter of factly.

Before I could respond, he continued. "But that's not all. You have to agree to do everything I say, whether your stomach feels good about it or not, or don't waste my time."

This was said very nicely, but the message was abundantly clear. Without hesitation, I put my hand across the table and said, "Done deal." His handshake was firm and confident.

He was pleased; I could see that on his face. This was a no-nonsense man. He wanted to work with someone who could make up her mind. I could do that. So we talked a little more, he asked a few more questions, and we agreed that we would put a business plan together immediately so we knew where we were trying to go, and then we'd begin.

When David dropped me off at 2121 West Club, I was still in the process of understanding what had just happened. I knew something big had happened. I knew it was good. And part of me was scared to death at the thought of succeeding. After awhile though, I began to fantasize. In my mind, I had us making $7 million dollars per year within four years. That afternoon I told Randy and Jeannie about David, and they were skeptical. They said he sounded too good to be true. I didn't tell them it was already a done deal. I knew as soon as he started working with them, they would come around.

On January 27th, Randy and I flew to Greenville, North Carolina, to present to the top executives of two hospitals. I had developed a pattern that served me well. Someone from the hospital would pick me up at the airport, and on the ride back to the hospital, I'd find out how many beds, physicians, nurses, admissions, surgeries, etc., that the hospital had. That would give me a beginning point. By the time I had actually gotten all the equipment set up, I would know the hospital pretty well. In past demos, I always focused on what the software could do. Before we left Durham, David had suggested that I educate them as to the possibilities for errors in a hospital their size. I did as he suggested, and I could see the administrators were much more receptive.

WHIM OF IRON

Usually, after these kinds of meetings, I would go back to the office fired up to have our programs do everything I had just heard the people wanted it to do. This time, however, David had me discuss the changes I wanted to make with him, and he promptly put them on hold. Randy and Jeanne had been given the assignment of making the reporting module bug-free, no easy job on a large, undocumented program. He didn't want me interrupting their mission.

My life had changed. I knew that the first day I met David. But as we started working together, there were dramatic differences I hadn't anticipated. For one thing, there was always someone around with whom to talk business. He *wanted* to hear everything I said about programming, reports, planning, etc. He *wanted* me to reach my goals, and he *wanted* me to have a good life. He kept asking me questions about who I was and where I came from, as he drove me around Durham. There was never any down time. David was filling up his well on CBR, and though I could see what he was doing, I had no idea where it would lead.

All his good energy was producing other results. I started swimming at MetroSport again and was soon doing 80 lengths of an Olympic-sized pool. I tried to get David interested in shooting pool, and the few times we played, he did very well, but he had only one thing on his mind—making a success of CBR. So, we spent most of our time talking about strategies and how we could get our message across to administrators. I was relieved, finally, to know who to sell to. The administrator first; everyone else on the quality management team, second. The mysteries began to disappear.

It didn't take David long to get into gear. Within two weeks of our meeting, he had put together an implementation plan. The first part involved relieving me of the bookkeeping (it would be sent out); Jeanne would do documentation and report design. From now on I would focus my energies on writing to hospital administrators and doing presentations; and I would continue to test the software, because I had a sixth sense about finding bugs.

I never had a plan for my life before, and it felt wonderful to know what I was supposed to do. But it turned out to be a lot harder than I thought. The first official day David came to the office, he told me about his plan for CBR. We went over each piece, me asking questions, David giving me very clear answers. When he was sure I understood the first steps, he went with me to meet Randy and Jeanne. With little ado, he explained to them what his background was, what he had been engaged by me to do, and that he would involve them in the process as needed. We all asked questions, which he answered clearly and concisely. David was not one to confuse us with words.

After a week of observing us at work, David moved Randy into the front room with Jeanne. Then he moved into my office and set up his desk right next to mine, so he could listen to every phone conversation I had. For several weeks, he sat next to me as I made my calls. He would madly make notes on his yellow pad. For the first few days, he didn't say much. He started, however, bringing the notepad with him whenever we went to breakfast, lunch or dinner. He began the process of teaching me how to sell.

At the end of every day he would announce that the next day we would go to breakfast, or lunch or have a day away from the office. In the latter cases, he would drive me to a nearby hotel or resort. We would either sit by a pool or over lunch and go through his list for the day.

"Remember when you said on the phone, 'MedstaffPLUS can create any report you want?" he said to me early one morning after breakfast had been ordered.

"Yes," I said, remembering vaguely what he was talking about.

"That was a lie," he stated flatly.

"What do you mean?" I asked, taken aback.

"MedstaffPLUS *cannot* create any report the administrator wants." David's eyes were clear and open, he was looking directly at me and he was stating the truth, so I couldn't take offense.

"Well, we don't know that it can't," I said defensively.

"Cleo, every customer *needs* to hear you say "No" at least once, or they simply will not believe you." An administrator of a hospital knows no product can do everything. Besides, I'll bet I could design a report you could not create." He sat back and waited for me to process what he had said.

This was news to me. I didn't know there was a strategy about what you say and don't say when talking on the phone. I didn't know there was a science about it all.

"You're right, I don't like to admit that there's anything that we can't do," I said lamely.

"Correct. But you must, if you want them to believe you. Even if you can do everything, you have to *tell them you can't* at least once during your presentation. Then they will believe you."

I thought about a recent experience I had when I had bought a new printer. The sales person had said the printer could do everything, yet when I got it home, I found it couldn't do envelopes. Bummer. Would I have not bought if I had known that? I probably wouldn't have bought *that* printer, but I would have bought another one. If the sales person had told me the truth, I would have been a happy customer instead of one who felt deceived. David was right.

"So you're saying that every time I do a presentation, you want me to say No at least once?" I asked hesitantly.

"Yes, at least once," he added.

"Okay, I can do that," I said confidently

"Good," he said matter-of-factly, and then looked at his yellow list again.

"Remember when you were discussing the price, and they must have asked a question about paying for it in installments?" he asked.

"Yes," I said softly.

"There is nothing wrong with saying No. No, we don't do installments. When we get your full check, we will give you full service. Until then, we don't have a sale." He looked at me with his clear, bright eyes to see if I understood what he was saying.

"In other words, if they won't buy from us because we don't do payments, no problem. Let them go to someone else," I said crisply.

"Correct. You started a policy, out of ignorance I know, but nonetheless, it's a good policy. Cash up front. You can't change that policy now because you need *cash*. Once you put one hospital on payments, next you'll have twenty, and then you'll be into collections and a nightmare. The answer is 'No, we do not do payments.'"

In my heart I knew he was right. I had developed the policy about cash up front because Mitch told me once that hospitals don't like to pay their bills. I knew if I didn't get cash, we couldn't live, so I just set the policy, and slowly everyone understood and complied. I got a few arguments over the years, but I'd just tell them to go buy from someone else. That always got them to write a check.

He was waiting again so I said, "Okay, we don't do payments. What's next?"

He laughed and said, "That's enough for today. Tomorrow we'll go over more, but I want to hear you make some calls to administrators first." When I didn't say anything, he said, "I know this is a lot for you. You love doing the books, you love developing, you love writing documentation, but you just can't. You're only one person. In fact, *because* you are only one person, I've decided that we're going to only market *one* product in *one* state."

"But what about California? I said with disbelief in my voice. "I have a hospital there who is so close to buying," I added desperately.

"Tell them to buy from one of your competitors. You can't *afford* to sell to them. The time difference will be a killer when you're trying to support them, and if you or Randy need to go look at what is happening, you can't afford to fly there. It's a bad sale."

His definitive answer, and the finality of the logic reassured me, but I was still feeling doom and gloom.

"Which product?" I asked. We had six ready to go, or so I thought. Which did he feel we could sell now?

"Credentialing," he answered immediately. "Credentialing has the federal laws behind it, the JCAHO (Joint Commission on Accreditation of Health Organizations) wants to see it done, or the hospitals won't get certification, and it's the program that you have developed the most."

Whew, I thought to myself, at least my favorite program was targeted. That would make it easier. "And stick to North Carolina?" I asked, as he started to put his papers away.

"Yes. I can fly you wherever you need to go." Not only did David have his own plane, but he was a flight instructor to boot, which gave me a lot more confidence in his skills.

He continued, "You can do several demos in one day, and you want to have 80 percent of all North Carolina hospitals within two years. When you've done that, you'll have a marketing tool that can't be beat. Then you go to other states and do it all over again." He made it sound so easy and logical.

David drove me home, gave each of us our assignments for the next day, and then was gone. His assignments would range from "give me a list of all the hospitals you have contacted to date," to "tell me which reports in your programs are used most often." As we came to know David, we knew that these were not idle questions. Based on our answers, he might have me write to all those I've already contacted, or eliminate some of the reports because no one was using them.

David knew he had a lot on his plate re-training us. He wanted us to think about what the impact of our actions were with our limited people power. He took the accounting books away from me, even though I felt important doing them each month, because he couldn't afford to have me adding up numbers. He wanted me calling numbers instead. Administrators' numbers. I absolutely hated making the phone calls but I now knew that if we didn't want to go bankrupt, I had to do what he told me to do.

He also had to teach us the basics of cash management.

At one weekly meeting, he patiently taught us:

"You have to bring in more money than you spend."

"You have to reduce expenses, rather than increase sales, first."

"If you make 100 calls a day, 10 will be follow-ups, and one will buy."

This final rule was one of the hardest for me to believe, but once I saw he was right, we were on a roll.

Randy had a hard time with David's rules. He was used to doing what he felt needed to be done, which was programming. Now David began to ask Randy to carry some of the administrative burdens so I was free to sell. He did not take kindly to David's suggestions. But in all fairness, Randy wasn't with David eight hours a day to learn the "why" to all David's requests.

David started going with me to presentations. When we went to Craven County Hospital, it was the first presentation I did using his new principles (say No once, don't oversell, listen, give simple answers). I did okay, but was a little awkward because using his style was so different. I had always focused on the products. He had me focusing on the hospital's potential cost savings by credentialing correctly. "Make them want it," he had told me just as I went into the conference room. I used the reports and other overheads I had developed the previous year.

The moment we were back in David's car, he set up his yellow pad and began asking me questions. It was clear we would not be leaving until all the items on his pad had been addressed.

"When the CEO asked you if the software could guarantee that they would pass a JCAHO inspection, you said no. But it could. What he wanted to hear was that if he bought CBR software, failing credentialing under the new JCAHO rules would not be an issue, and that is true. CBR's software *exceeds* the requirements," he said with emphasis.

"I understand," I said evenly. He was making good sense to me.

"When the medical staff director asked what data would be collected on him, you said 'Everything the hospital and JCAHO require.' He did not want to hear that. You could have alleviated his apprehensions simply by saying CBR software would collect the *public* data for accreditation, and that was all. In his mind, administration and all regulatory bodies wanted too much data on him. Putting it in the context of public data would have relieved his anxiety. He knows what public data is collected and feels comfortable with that." David sat back to let this sink in.

"You are correct," I said positively. I was beginning to like having an understanding of how to present.

"When a nurse asked you if you had a profile report on health care workers, you said yes, and then proceeded to show them the report in the software. They didn't want so much. They just wanted you to say yes. Period. As soon as you give them too much information, they lose interest. Yes. No. Keep it simple." He made a check mark, and went to the next item. Sometimes it would take an hour before we could begin our trip home.

Before David had been with us three weeks, he had raised the price of MedstaffPLUS from $6,000 to $9,000. I was getting better at presentations, and at the next hospital we went to, I got a commitment for an order in 12 minutes at $9,000. I was thrilled. I was beginning to see that his rules worked. I was very happy and feeling a little bit in control for the first time in years.

David had fired my imagination, and he was showing me how to reach my goal. For the first time since starting the business, I felt I was steering and CBR was going where I wanted.

By the end of January, we had reached a lot of people. David had designed a letter-writing campaign based on the principle that anyone had to hear our name three times before we would make an impression. I did a mail merge that allowed me to put in a personal leading paragraph and then a standard finish. Jeannie and I input hundreds of addresses, one for each administrator in the state (185), plus four other individuals such as the medical director, credentialing coordinator, head of nursing at each hospital (740).

At first we went for any sized hospital, but later on, we narrowed in on those under 250 beds. The larger hospitals had complicated information systems, and few had people who knew how to run the new personal computers (PCs). We found we spent way too much time supporting their network, instead of our software.

As I went out and did presentations, Jeannie and Randy stayed focused on getting the software "done." In truth, software is never "done," but David felt we were <u>over</u> developed and wanted a bug-free program to reduce the support needed. He gave that mission to them and they dove right in.

I was still involved in development in one important aspect. One night after a long day at the State, I came home and realized we had to write 25 verification letters for our credentialing program so I could demonstrate it the next afternoon. We finished with little time to spare. It was important that I focus on the day-to-day tasks, as David tackled the long haul of making us a real business.

From the very beginning of David's relationship with CBR, getting us financially stable was his major preoccupation. I had no credit. I hadn't had a credit card in years because I got behind in the SBA loan payments. If my daughter hadn't loaned me one, I wouldn't have even been able to rent a car when I was out of town. I also had no health insurance, nor did Randy. Jeannie got hers through her husband's work.

From day one, David started talking with the SBA (Small Business Administration) about my loan. He told them that 16 percent interest was highway robbery, and they finally negotiated with him down to 8 percent (Oh my God, I'd been paying 16 percent for eight years! I didn't know you could negotiate something like that).

He also met with the man at the State who was in charge of my $50,000 loan. David was pretty hard on him about 50 percent interest on a loan to a start-up business. He finally agreed that when we were ready to pay it off, they would negotiate the balance. David was not happy, but it was the best we could do.

Finding a bank to do business with CBR was not easy. David sent me off with a balance sheet, business plan, and lots of hope, but after I had talked with three banks, David realized it wasn't going to happen that way. He finally heard about a vice president at Planter's Bank in Durham who was friendly towards new businesses. I'll never forget our first meeting. Here we were, greatly in debt, and David acted as though we were the hottest business on the market. The bank VP agreed that if we made six sales at $9,000 each over the next three months, he would give us a line of credit.

On January 31st, I signed papers from SBA lowering my interest rate from 16 to 8 percent. On the same day, Union Hospital sent in a check for $9,000 and Cape Fear Hospital decided to keep our software, instead of going with a competitor. David and I were proving to be a good team.

Now that we were focusing on the MedstaffPLUS software, Randy and Jeannie were really making progress. Randy spent a good deal of time, to David's frustration, on the design and color for the Main Menu. I felt like Randy felt…that how the screen looked made a difference. David said it didn't—and in the end he was probably right—but we needed it to look great for our inventive souls.

So the software was emerging under Randy and Jeannie's hard work as I made my hundreds of calls daily and started churning up leads. David continued to teach me how to talk on the phone and how to present. He never missed a chance to compliment me on how I was doing or to encourage me to relax and have fun.

Boude, my beloved dog, developed degenerative hip disease, so I started him on a round of shots. What would I do without my friend to walk around the golf course and talk everything over with? My mind couldn't even comprehend the idea.

By February, David and I were working long and hard to make basic changes in CBR. If Randy wanted equipment or new software, David asked, "Why?" Speed, convenience, more productivity wouldn't cut it. In David's mind, we didn't have the money to pay for what we already had, what's more buy more. So he tightened our belt and started teaching us fiscal responsibility. Here were some of his major themes:

- You have to have more money coming in than going out.
- No debt allowed; pay off what you owe, don't incur any more.
- Cash is king.

It was exciting having someone teaching me one on one every day. One day David started a practice that really worked for me. He said, "Tomorrow we are going to do some planning. Come dressed casually, bring a bathing suit, and we'll be gone the whole day."

The next morning he met me at the house, told Randy and Jeanne we were going to go plan for the day, and off we went. I loved that I didn't have to make any of the plans...just get in the car and go. David drove out to the Research Triangle Park, found a large hotel, parked and said, "Okay, here we are."

I didn't ask any questions, I just followed. He went into the lobby, looked around, wandered into the back and found a pool and hot tub with dressing rooms. He pointed to the ladies room and said, "Go ahead and change. I'll meet you back here in a few minutes."

When I came out, David was already in the hot tub. I got in and we talked small talk awhile and then he got into the subject of the day. "So, Cleo, where is CBR going? Where do you want it to go? And how do we get there? That's the topic today."

For the next few hours we alternated between the hot tub and pool, throwing ideas back and forth, slowly resolving differences, and coming up with a plan. It was great fun. He never let me make a statement I couldn't back up. I couldn't dream unrealistic dreams. "What's the first step we have to take to get there?" was always a question he would ask. By lunchtime, I was exhausted, so we got dressed and went into the elegant restaurant by some fountains and ate a terrific meal. All the while talking, agreeing, disagreeing, and finally coming together on an overall business plan.

One of the major decisions we made was to rename our product from MEDSTAFFplus to PRIVplus. MEDSTAFFplus was too close to the name of a competitor's software, and it sounded like we wanted to manage the medical staff, instead of their privileges. We refined our new business plan many times over many months. What finally evolved was a working understanding between David and me, as to our goals. It was time well spent because he was teaching me to think correctly (focused), so when he was away, I still knew how to make decisions. I felt very fortunate for the training I was getting.

David had other projects on his personal list, so he went away for a week or so. I buckled down and wrote 30 letters a day to administrators or other interested people plus made many calls every day, trying to catch up.

David wanted the program debugged and ready to send out with as little support needed as possible. That meant no *new* development. This was a new way of thinking for Randy and me. We had always listened to what the customer wanted (coordinators, administrators, medical directors) and tried to give them *everything*. What David was saying was they don't *use* everything, so get back to the basics and make sure they work perfectly. Software developers, by and large, like to invent, so what he was saying didn't sound like much fun to either of us.

Randy tried, but when a coordinator would say something like, "Gosh, if I could go directly from privileges to letters it would be great," the next thing we'd know Randy would do it. I loved his responsiveness. David said we couldn't afford it. Neither Randy nor I understood...yet.

By this time, the weather had changed. It went from 70 degrees to 58 in one week, which didn't help my mood. While David was pumping up, I was losing air. I was feeling tired of learning, tired of trying, tired of having to change the way I worked. I never, however, lost faith or questioned David. Our cash flow was improving a little, and we had a plan. I just had to push myself a little harder to do everything.

February 15th, 1989, I drove over 300 miles to Catawba Memorial Hospital to help them with their system, and then to Fry Memorial to set up their system. David had loaned me his car. On the way back, I stopped at Iredell Memorial to talk with them (they were thinking of buying), but I was really too tired to sell.

The North Carolina Hospital Association held its winter meeting in the Research Triangle Park outside of Durham. David went with me. Even in a room full of people, he was teaching me. He told me not to talk for more than five minutes with any one person, to get around the room and touch as many people as I could, and not to sell, not to even *sound* like I was selling. I tried his style and understood his reasoning, but habits are hard to change. Slowly over the years, I can say I got good at entering a room and "working it."

By the end of February we had entered a new phase. The year before I had done a business plan presentation at the Fuqua School of Business for some 80 investors and the CED videotaped me. The video was okay, but after a month of David's coaching me on how to present, he felt we needed another video. What the CED decided to do was re-video me, put the two together, and use it as an example of a good business plan presentation and a great one. The new one was shot and when they were put together, it was a good lesson on what to do and not to do. The CED used the video for years for aspiring presenters. David's only goal was for me to "see" how I had changed, and he certainly accomplished that.

While I had my good moments, I now began a period of uncertainty. Every time things started to go well, I would get apprehensive. Based on my life story, this made sense. The little girl in me was used to chaos and having to figure things out. She was not used to success, and I believe I sabotaged my success many times because I just didn't know how to handle it. David's confidence helped me through many a doubtful day.

I hate selling even more today than yesterday! I always feel we won't make the next sale. That kind of thinking means we won't! Positive Cleo, think positive. Two hospitals called wanting demos. David wants two sales before the end of the month. Oh God!

I try to treat each day like a new day. My hopes are high. Bill (from the Hospital Association) is developing a public relations plan; David is developing a marketing and sales strategy, and me? Just sell! Randy and Jeanne doing terrific, high-quality work.

The pressure to sell was intense. In the past, selling was something I knew I had to do, but I had avoided setting any goals. As David soon learned, I didn't know *how* to set goals. I had lived my life acting on whims. Setting goals was scary and new. David suggested we set a goal of two sales before the end of the month, which sent me into a panic. I made calls, but never seemed to be able to get through to the right people. Some days when David wasn't around, I would crawl in my bed and just try to sleep off my sick stomach. The fact that phones were ringing and Jeanne and Randy were right in the next room didn't help.

Things were getting stirred up though, and we weren't as badly off as we had been. Toward the end of February, I was asked to fly to Buffalo and present to 13 hospitals in a consortium. We agreed to do so because there were so many of them, even though we had to pay our own fare. David's stand was that if they would pay for my expenses, I would go. I argued that they never would, because none of the other software companies did it that way, and we might lose the sales. David said, "Who cares? We can't afford to sell to them in that case." I won the argument, we spent the money for me to go, I did a good job, and we never saw one sale out of it. After that he began winning the logic wars more regularly.

David's lessons were very logical. He taught me that if a hospital decides to buy, they usually do so right away. But, if the medical staff coordinator (MSC) loses enthusiasm because we don't get back to her soon enough, or she can't see the system, or she can't get anyone at the hospital interested in buying, then her positive energy turns into frustration, which is a poor investment of her energy and ours. The trick was to get to the top person who could buy, and get a commitment. After making hundreds and hundreds of phone calls, I knew how hard that could be.

Bill and I drove to Morganton, North Carolina, to make a presentation, and it went very well but no commitment. In fact, for the first time I was aware that *no* buyer was in the room. That was a very big learning experience for me. If a person who can write a check is not present, then the sale is dependent on someone else in the room being able to sell the product to the decision-maker. "Won't happen," David said, and he turned out to be absolutely right.

In March, money came in for the first time in quite awhile. Craven County had owed us $650, and Saddleback Hospital paid $8,000 for PRIVplus. Our financial situation was still precarious. David was paying all my traveling expenses and for his plane, etc., but he still seemed confident. I tried to go with the flow. He was not taking any money out of CBR, which amazed me.

Good, long day. Swam 80 lengths at 6:30 a.m. then a non-stop day – training, working with David on marketing.

It was David who urged me to swim, and so I kept at it because he was right, it did help me keep mentally stable. Not that I was a basket case, but sometimes I got close. The pressure of no money and no sales was getting to me.

As hard as it was for me to make the calls, they were bringing forth prospects. I flew to Miami, then rented a car and drove to Jupiter Hospital in West Palm Beach and did a demo. It was clear to me that the coordinator wanted our software and that the administrator could not care less. I then drove to Indian River Hospital, who had our software, but were having problems. I hated these kinds of calls because I only knew enough to get in trouble. With considerable phone support from Randy, I soon had them up and running.

I went home, turned around the next day and flew to Atlanta to fix Scottish Rite's system. This was before the days of telephone-modem hookups—before we could see what was happening from our computer in Durham. I understood now why David didn't want out-of-state sales…we couldn't afford them in time or money.

When I got back, David and I drove to a hospital several hours away. At first, they seemed quite interested but money, as always, was an issue. A hospital would spend hundreds of thousands of dollars to ensure the bills are sent out regularly, but they were having a hard time allocating funds to ensure the quality of care. I didn't understand their thinking and still don't. On the way home, David tried to teach me a whole new approach to sales, one that was more educational rather than sales oriented. He knew it would take time, and that I would try. That's all we could ask of me.

When the South Carolina Hospital Association called and asked for a presentation, David gave it considerable thought. North Carolina and South

Carolina were one community in the eyes of the Duke and Fullerton Foundations, who had helped out with funding for the Small Hospital Project. It would be real good if we could get South Carolina sponsoring CBR software. He decided it was worth the trip.

Traveling with David was a totally different experience. All I had to do was show up at the airport with one light bag for what I needed personally. David had loaded all the equipment into his plane. When we drove up to the waiting plane, I just had to get onboard. I was fascinated with his checklist and careful attention to detail.

He would always say, "You can't be *too* careful."

Which reminded me of an old mushroom hunter's saying: "There are old mushroom hunters and there are careless mushroom hunters, but there are no old, careless mushroom hunters." I assume the same would apply to pilots.

We arrived at the Charleston Airport at 10 a.m. David checked our presentation equipment into a baggage check, which I didn't even know existed at airports, and hailed a cab. He took me off on a wonderful tour of Charleston. Our association meeting was not until 3 p.m., so we had plenty of time. I soon realized he planned it that way. David was enjoying making me happy while he turned the company around. A remarkable man.

WHIM OF IRON

We took a carriage ride, and that just impressed the heck out of this little beach girl. I was in awe of the buildings and the setting. Charleston is a wonderfully restored and maintained old-line town. Lunch was a lobster for me and something equally delicious for David. We talked about the presentation, and we talked about what makes me happy. He noticed that I *loved* to make people happy, and he thought that was my main motivating reason for doing all that I did. I agreed.

When we finally showed up at the association and all the introductions had been done, it was clear we were there because they had to do their duty and see more than one vendor. David and I both knew they were not buyers. We gave them a good, though brief, review and they thanked us and we left. David blamed himself for not qualifying the people enough. It was natural for him to think they were receptive, because I was always sure they would be. We were learning. There are no mistakes though…I got to see Charleston, and that was a real treat.

While I was making phone calls and testing the software, I also was educating myself more and more in information technology because most of the mainframe managers weren't up to date. I had to answer my own questions about how to interface with a mainframe. It was an exhausting subject to learn at this time, but I needed to be really current in how to get things done.

Life was hectic with David training me every day, lots of phone calls and managing Randy and

Jeanne who had lots of questions for me. My main personal diversion was playing pool and going to Under the Street to dance.

April rolled around and things were moving along at a snail's pace. I would get so impatient, but David would stay steady and keep teaching me what I needed to know. Money was tight. I owed the State of North Carolina $2,000 on taxes, and that was certainly going to hurt. While David didn't take any money *out* of CBR in salary or bonuses, he also wasn't willing to put any *in*. He felt if he was doing his job, then we could pull out on our own.

Many hospitals were now calling and wanting a presentation. David made me qualify each one. Who can write a check (though I didn't ask it that brusquely)? Who is a decision maker? Will that person be at the meeting? Are there funds? Lots of hospitals wanted the software, but few were prepared for the costs, not of just the software, but of hardware, training, supplies, etc. On top of all that, they had to fly the coordinator to Durham to be trained.

David and I had discussed training, and I had said how disruptive and non-productive training at the hospital site could be. We decided to train in Durham and let the hospital bear the cost. We knew some would balk, but in the end it was a good plan for everyone. The coordinators could focus more on what they were learning, so the hospital got more out of their investment, and CBR could focus on giving them the best training.

WHIM OF IRON

In mid-April David and I drove six hours to a hospital, only to be shot down by the purchasing agent who didn't understand what the software could do, or that they couldn't do it all manually. We were also learning that data processing people were likely to shoot us down. They didn't want the competition, they didn't want to spend the money from their budgets, they didn't want to lose control, and they didn't want to complicate their lives. We added data processing people to our list of people who should be at our presentation. Most often they didn't come, but we tried.

By the end of April, David had our strategic plan ready. He took over the living room, turned off the phones, and using a flipchart, gave us all a picture of where CBR was going. He inspired all of us. (As a quick footnote, the strategic plan was backed up with a business plan, which fourteen years later was still being followed.) All it would take would be sales, lots of them, for us to reach our goals.

About this time, David suggested that he was going to have to ask everyone to take a 50 percent cut in pay in order for us to survive. There just was not enough cash coming in. I felt I had failed everyone, but David insisted. We met with the team and told them the bad news. To everyone's credit, they agreed to hang on for a while longer.

April 15th arrived and I was $1,000 short on tax money. David loaned it to me.

Talked to Lisa and lied to her about Visa card. I lost my wallet, but didn't want to cancel, because I'll never get it again. Anyway, she's worried she and Andy will have trouble getting credit cause I have $4000 on it. I cried, reported it as lost, and will not go to Paris to see her. I'll use that money to pay off Visa. It's awful to be 50 years old without credit. And I've always paid my bills. Well, I owe a lot, time to pull back. Tears.

9:30 pm Hazel called, bless her. She gives me faith in myself. I'm glad she's at least all right. I'm in a depression. Need to pull out but not sure how.

The fear of having no credit card was not easy to live with. I was obsessive about knowing where the card was at all times; it was like my last lifeline. When I lost my wallet, all I could think was they wouldn't give me another one, or if Visa would, then my daughter wouldn't, because she was afraid I couldn't pay. This added to my feelings of not being good enough in sales, not being good enough to keep everything in control, and I felt like I was three years old and not good enough for Daddy all over again.

But I would rebound. A night's rest, some phone calls, seeing something new the software could do, and boom, my energy went up and I was invincible again! David was teaching me patience, but I was a very, very slow learner.

Randy was working hard to put in all the requests he got from clients. What always impressed me about Randy was that he cared as much as I did that the clients have everything they wanted. Working hard was fun for both of us when we were accomplishing something. To David, however, we were just putting the software more at risk—more programming code to test, more bugs to check, more documentation. Neither Randy nor I understood what he was talking about.

The week was incredibly busy and exciting. Randy and I did an overview of all reports, and they are excellent! We do work so well together; we both have the same values and stamina.

Met with Head of the Dept. of Medicine at Durham. He is a very tough, very bright, very good man, who wants to see QA done right.

We are doing it. Every day I walk in the door, hospitals have called. One called today, and he gave me a date and time for a demo.

But by May first we were really out of money. David suggested I call the North Carolina Hospital Association and see if they would co-sign a bank loan. I was horrified. As a child, taking charity was not something Mom let us do. It felt the same now. David finally suggested that the worst thing Ed, the president, could say was no. Without giving it much thought, I quickly picked up the phone and called Ed. He took my call immediately. I told him about David, our plans, our strategy and the fact that we were out of money. I asked, with hope in my heart, "Would the Hospital Association co-sign for a $25,000 loan for CBR?" Instead of the no I expected, Ed said, "Give me a few days, and I'll get back to you." It sounded like a delayed no, but I had hope nonetheless.

I don't have next week's payroll or rent. Catawba may come through, or Alamance, or the loan from the Bank consigned with the Hospital Assoc. The money will come from somewhere. We are doing it. We will succeed. We are succeeding.

David was working hard with me and Randy and Jeanne, but sales were slow. We talked about lack of sales constantly and David was concerned, but we both had confidence.

All right. What is <u>this</u> all about? I go to walk up Sunrise's steps and pull a calf muscle <u>so</u> badly, I cannot walk. Bob loaned me crutches, and David loaned me his arm and support. For the first time I can remember in many years, I let someone take care of me. Randy too. He went and got the crutches. Don't know why this happened, <u>and</u> there are no mistakes. Such pain though!

Actually this was following a pattern. Whenever things got exciting or good in my life, or very scary, I would get either sick or hurt. This time I hurt what I stand on! Injuries, however, never slowed me down, so I drove the next day to Rowan Hospital and did a presentation.

Through a series of events I met a younger man named Jeff. He was an outdoors person with a great sense of humor, and no aspirations to "be" something.

We started hanging around together on the weekends, playing pool, dancing and having a lot of fun. He was a great balance to my daytime life of phone calls and working hard. All we did was have fun together and he gave me a lot of support during the hard times.

David encouraged me to go visit my daughter in Paris. He could see I was starting to fall apart and needed a break. Two days after booking my ticket, I heard back from Ed at the Hospital Association. He had called the Board members, and they had all agreed to co-sign, a first for them. I was ecstatic! I was always surprised when people valued the work we were doing, and it meant we were alive for another few months. I believed David's sales plan. The money would come.

One weekend in May, an event happened that really made me happy. I was taking a walk along the Eno with Jeff and his girlfriend, when we came upon a young man, all wet and quite upset. The weather had just turned cloudy and cold. "Which way is the bridge?" he asked in a daze.

As Jeff explained that there was a bridge a few miles down river, I realized from his reactions that the man was in shock, and I asked him what had happened. He pointed toward the river, but could say no more. Just then his two friends showed up (all in their early 20s), and they, too, were soaked. They had left their truck by a bridge to go canoeing and obviously had run into trouble. They were exhausted, that was clear.

I finally said, "Look, Jeff, you and Sara continue to walk. I'm going to drive this young man to his truck so he can drive back here, and they can load the canoe onto it." As soon as we got in the car, I turned on the heat, high. The man sat in the seat next to me in a catatonic state. I left him alone and concentrated on getting to the bridge. When the car was finally warmed up, he said, "We all thought we were going to die."

I looked over at him as he was trying to rouse himself and said, "Why?" and tried to look in his face, but he was still in shock.

"We just did this on the spur of the moment. It was sunny out, Larry had a canoe, he said let's go, and we all jumped in and started off."

I could see it was an effort for him to talk, but the car was really warm and he was sitting up straighter. He continued.

"As soon as we got out into the main part of the river, the canoe capsized. It was a real struggle to get all three of us back in. But the rapids were quite strong and the water cold, and we tipped over three more times finally losing the paddle. We couldn't land because the water was going so fast, and all of our energy was spent just trying to stay with the canoe. At last we were able to grab hold of some rocks and pull ourselves ashore. That's when we ran into you."

I could see he was coming out of his shock. Color was coming into his face, and he was more animated. When I pulled up in front of his truck, his relief and greatfulness was obvious. He followed me back to his friends in his truck. They too had thawed out and could now talk coherently. They thanked me profusely, and I told them about the man in California airport six years before, who had helped me in my time of need. I said to them before they left, "Now remember, you have to help someone else out *to the same degree* as I helped you." As they trudged off, canoe raised on their shoulders, they all three said, "We will!!!"

It had taken me six years to pay back my debt of thankfulness, and, as always when you help someone else, I felt like a hero and not quite so stuck on my own problems.

One day David came up with the idea to give out stock options to everyone at CBR. He had asked for 35 percent of the stock when we had first negotiated working together. Now he felt that since everyone had taken a pay cut and was hanging in, that they deserved some stock, too. He suggested 51 percent for me, 30 percent for him, 14 percent to Randy and 5 percent to Jeannie. Jeannie was very happy with the arrangement. Randy felt he deserved more. He wasn't spending as much time with David understanding stocks and bank negotiations, so he didn't see that without sales, the software was nothing. David and I had to make the sales.

As time went on, David continued to try to get Randy to assume some of the management responsibilities of the business. His contention was that we were too small to have any one person doing only what they liked...everyone had to cross train to help others, even if they didn't like doing the other work. It was hard on Randy because he was a very hard worker, and he just didn't understand why it would be better for him to answer the phone than program.

Even though there was some underlying stress, Randy still managed to make my holidays. For Mother's Day, he always went all out.

Gary called to wish me happy Mother's Day and we talked. He's doing so well. At two p.m. Randy showed up with flowers, a full set of dishes and a full set of glasses for our kitchen, plus oysters, salmon and swordfish steaks! Had a great grill out—lovely.

Randy loved to give gifts and he did it so well, always choosing things I would love. Both Randy and I were struggling with the changes we needed to make to survive. We had been in the software-development business together for six years. Changes were coming fast and at great cost, as success always does. Since David was the designer of the changes, he was not always the most popular person around.

David and I walked to Lookout Point on the Eno and talked business. A very good time. I'm just beginning to feel who I am. I am a lot to others—why not to me? Ah, well, David works on me to improve my self-image.

Many of the things that weren't going well in the business had to do with my immaturity. Having grown up without any father in the house and no boundaries from Mom, I tended to revert to acting like a child when things got difficult. David recognized what I was doing, and he gave me tools to help me grow. It was not easy. When I was doing a presentation, I was terrific and very adult. When arguing with Randy, I immediately turned three years old and whined. I'm not sure he knew what a big job he was taking on, but he seemed up for it, so I worked with him every day on these issues.

> *Tuesday. 7 pm. Forgot to deposit taxes! Up at 5:15, to club to work out, stretch, and then home to my room to meditate and relax. Having only one room in the house that is mine feels okay most of the time, but not now. I would love a little more privacy.*

> *Albemarle bought! HCA here all day to look at credentialing, and QA demo went well.*

> *Very good day with David. He is very articulate, organized and kind. We work well together. We are together a lot talking strategy and making things happen. He treats me as an equal working partner, and though he is a very tough no-hands-barred type of teacher, I'm learning quickly. He is very encouraging to me and accepts that it's really okay if I'm not perfect! That's my standard, not his.*

> *I've never had a teammate before in business, or in life, for that matter. David is leading us gallantly into the race, so we can eventually be in the winner's circle. I can't believe I make my living making good things happen. We can pull this off, David, Randy,*

Jeanne, and I. We can make this CBR balloon go into the air and soar. We will be a success story.

David was the most patient person I had ever met. He wanted me to understand why we were doing the things we were doing, so I could keep doing them even when he wasn't around. It was not an easy job for him, because both Randy and I were headstrong and sure we knew what was right most of the time. His biggest campaign was to get me to zip my lip and listen to what the administrators, etc., were saying. It was a difficult thing for me to do. I wanted to tell them what a wonderful product we had. Poor David, he wanted a sale and I kept putting my mouth in the way. I did make progress, however, and I could see I learned more by listening, but it was a hard habit to break.

One of the joys of working with David was he made it fun. He would often pick me up at 7:30 and we'd go for breakfast somewhere. Sometimes he would even order for me, letting me continue to try to absorb what he would be telling me about calls, strategy, direction, or whatever. He would have a list of things he wanted to discuss, and we would go through them until he was sure I understood what we were trying to accomplish; then he'd drop me off, and I'd go accomplish it. He had no idea how nice it was for me to be listened to and taken care of...not something I had experienced much in the past.

We were flying quite often now, going to hospitals all over North and South Carolina. We knew that the North Carolina Hospital Association was going to the Duke Endowment to ask for funds to support the purchase of hardware for smaller hospitals. All of them had an interest in using software, but none of them had the money. We had great hopes that having free hardware would remove all barriers. It took us awhile to find out that *nothing* could remove all barriers.

By the end of May, Catawba had sent their money in, so the pressure was off a little.

By this time David realized I worked best if I had a system. So he started working with me on a sales system that was starting to make a difference. I had put a system into place in the early years of selling, where I filled out a contact sheet I had designed for every hospital I contacted. The header would have all the demographics about the hospital—number of beds, number of employees, etc. Then the contact section would list chronologically every contact I talked to and any follow up action. That way, I always knew everyone I had talked with at a hospital and what had been said.

Because sales were not coming in quickly enough, David added a series of red and green dots to my system. He took me to lunch one day and explained how he saw it working. First, however, he discussed monthly goals. In order to survive, we needed two sales per month. In order to breathe easier, we needed three sales per month. In order to thrive, we needed four sales per month. I panicked. I knew I could not do four sales a month. It was impossible, and I told him that.

We finally agreed on three sales per month. I would use the red and green dots to let me know at all times how I was doing. If I knew a hospital would be sending in money within 30 days, it got a red dot at the top of the contact sheet. If I felt they would send money in within 60 days, it got a green dot. My job was to create green dots, turn them into red dots, and we would succeed. The system also helped me relax a little. I could "see" at any point of time how I was doing. Red dots, green dots.

The next day after setting our goal of three sales per month, David took me to lunch and said, "I am putting too much pressure on you. All I ask is that you make two sales a month. That's it. Two."

I smiled and said, "You must have heard me worrying last night." He laughed and I continued, "Thanks, David. Three is too much, but I do think I can make two. I'll do my best."

He never asked me to do anything more than my best, but David had learned a key to my personality. Give me a challenge (three sales), let me say it was too much, reduce the challenge (two sales) and I would make the three, because I loved a challenge. Somehow doing it this way removed the pressure and left me open to do as many as I could, knowing it would be difficult to fail. There is a rule somewhere out there that says, "Never set goals higher than you can reach, so you can't fail. Reach the lower goal, and then the higher goal will follow."

A computer clerk at Raleigh Community Hospital ruined the main database in their PRIVplus software. Randy went over on a Saturday and fixed it, and then again today he updated their system. I called to check on them because Randy had left for Paris to visit his sister, and I wanted to know if their problem was resolved. It was. Randy completely updated them.

The clerk said to me, "Cleo, I want to thank you and Randy for the wonderful support you have given us. I hope you can keep it up and whoever you hire is as nice." Good to hear.

My dream was to have CBR known as a service organization, not a software company. A dream David put into reality by always giving priority to solving customers' problems, even when it cost us money to do so.

At the end of May, I drove to a hospital in the western part of the state, but I didn't feel good about the contact. They were doing what they were told to do—look at software—and that's all they were doing. There wasn't a buyer among the group. I drove home going over in my mind how I could have qualified them better.

David had agreed to fly to Cape Fear Hospital and present to them himself, since I was out of town and they wanted to meet immediately. He sold PRIVplus in one meeting, which pleased us both very much. He never offered to go again, however, I think he wanted us to survive without him someday, and we wouldn't if he became our salesman. He continued, however, to refine my sales skills.

David flew me to Banner Elk, North Carolina to meet with everyone at the local hospital. What a great thrill flying is—I even steered the plane a little. He took care of everything, and we got the sale! Flying home, we both knew we are on a roll. I don't know how the Duke Endowment meeting went on giving the hospitals free hardware. We'll know tomorrow. Randy is in Paris with Lisa!

The first week in June, Rowan and Cannon Hospitals bought, which took care of my quota, followed by Albemarle, Davie County and Wayne, all in June. David was ecstatic, as were the rest of us. Money was flowing in, and I could breathe easy again. I still had to make my two sales in July... David would not allow me to throw the extra three from June into July's quotas. He was a tough teacher.

Luckily I had wonderful friends who brought me great diversions. Peter and Annette invited me to go white water rafting, and I gladly accepted. They were friends of mine I had met through the CED. Peter owned his own company and was a very dynamic, savvy businessman. His wife had just as much smarts and helped run their business.

We drove to the New River, and what a time we had. The water was still cold, but I had on a wool sweater and socks, so I rolled over into the water and floated around just for fun. Suddenly a kayak pulled up with a photographer sitting in the seat, camera in hand. He saw the fun I was having, so he said, "Hey, want to get rolled?" He assumed I knew what he meant, but I didn't. I said, "Sure" anyway because he seemed so happy to "roll me." He motioned for me to jump on the back of his kayak, which I did immediately, sitting up behind him, holding on just like we were on a motorcycle.

He looked back and said, "You're not supposed to be able to sit like that! Lie down on your stomach and put your feet and arms around the kayak and hold on."

I did as I was told and suddenly found myself upside down, just hanging in the water. I wondered if I was supposed to do anything other than hold my breath, but suddenly we were right side up again.

I heard him say, "Here we go again," and sure enough, I was upside down again, but this time I just relaxed and hung out. When he brought us up again we both laughed, I thanked him and swam back to my raft and joined my group. Peter said as I got in the boat, "Cleo, you're the only person I know who's been rolled on the New River." He even got a picture of just my hands and feet showing.

Because cash was flowing, David had decided it was okay for me to go visit with my daughter. I was scheduled to fly to Paris June 13th. They lived in a lovely apartment in downtown Paris, and I could hardly wait to go. The day before I left, we got the check from Cannon Hospital, which made it even easier to leave.

Cleo B. Robertson

David drove me to the Eno River, where we sat on the bank and reviewed where we were and where we wanted to go. I had no doubt he could handle everything while I was gone.

The next day I flew to Paris. Before going to my gate, I stopped in the ladies room, which was empty. I did my thing and just as I opened the stall door, the door to the next stall opened, and there we both stood looking at the other in the long mirror directly across from the stalls. I said, "I believe one of us has made a mistake," to which the man in full business suit said, "Yes, and I believe it is you."

I laughed, and we both walked out to look at the WOMEN sign posted on the door. Some women were just going in and I said to him, "You know, we really must stop meeting like this." He turned beet red and stomped off, and I just laughed all the way to Paris.

It was a magical trip. I had been to Paris in 1980 on a fluke, so this was, in a sense, a return trip. But this time I was with my daughter, who spoke French and could help me get around. Many years later I realized that I went to Paris as a child; I wanted Mommy (my daughter) to take care of me and show me around because I didn't speak any French, and it was all so new and overwhelming. It had never entered my mind that I would not be able to read street signs, or store signs. The money was different, the people less than friendly, and we had a wonderful time anyway. I was glad I went, and I was glad to go back home. Things were heating up and getting very exciting.

WHIM OF IRON

By the end of June, Davie County, Rowan Memorial and Wayne Hospitals had sent their money in making total sales for the month 9. We now had $67,000 in the bank—I shall always be eternally grateful that David was with us to help us manage this amount of money. It was more than I had ever thought of, and I didn't really know how to manage even small amounts of money—I hate to think what would have happened with just me in charge.

David and I spent much time discussing how to use the money, dreaming up new sales strategies and covering once again my personal challenges. Weight had always been an issue for me since the first month of my first marriage, when I put on ten pounds. I just wasn't used to having three meals a day and being able to buy meat. I also think marriage was more confining to my free spirit than I had ever imagined it would be, and weight gave me a little distance and space. But now, with things going well, I wanted to look good, too. I weighed about 185 pounds, and my best weight was around 150…I went on a fast after Paris and was struggling to keep losing weight.

In my early years, Mom had given up on preparing dinners every night and left us to manage on our own. Now, years later, I was still living with the anxiety of "where's the food?" It was David who allowed me to struggle openly with my challenge. There were no miracles, but I had someone who would listen to me, and that was almost as rare as having food. He was a great listener because he never judged me.

One day I took David over to meet Sunrise, since he was hearing so much about her. Sunrise was quickly charmed with David's good looks and was delighted he asked questions about things on her walls, so she more than willingly told him the stories behind each. As she did, I was looking around, too, and I saw an animal fetish I had never seen before. I put my hand close and said, "Oh, Sunrise, I never saw this before." She suddenly became very angry and said, "Don't touch that! You can't just touch anything you want you know." I said, "I didn't touch it, Sunrise, I was just pointing to it." She certainly seemed to overreact to the situation. I could feel myself tightening up inside. It seemed that impressing David was more important to her than being friendly to me. We left soon after, and I didn't call her again for some time.

Mid-July Sunrise called me and I didn't soften inside, so I knew I was still angry. I felt that she had not been loyal to our friendship by belittling me in front of David, so I just cut her out of my life—a pattern I had maintained in relationships all my life. The fact was I had little time to visit.

The CBR team was moving right along. Jeannie trained three hospitals at one time and did a great job. We had set up a training center in the living room of the house. The coordinators loved being able to leave their hospitals and come to Durham to be trained. It was a small perk with big rewards. We would give them two concentrated days of hands-on training. It worked like a charm—it reduced our follow-up support and got us more referrals.

WHIM OF IRON

David had started me on a letter-writing campaign to hospitals, which I attacked with vigor. I loved to type and compose, so I quickly had 50 letters or more going out daily. Randy tried to get me to stop spending my time writing letters because he thought it a waste of time…he didn't understand David's law that a person had to see our name three times to begin to relate to us.

A new opportunity presented itself in the form of the North Carolina Hospital Trust. This was a group that managed the risks experienced in hospitals. It was a daunting task to do manually, so they began talks with us about developing a risk management package. David thought risk management was the biggest issue hospitals would be concerned with. Wouldn't every hospital want to lower their risks and increase their bottom line? We thought so. Randy and I went to Winston Salem to Baptist Memorial to talk with professionals and begin the design process. It was fascinating to see the many variables that had to be tracked, from type of incident (incorrect medication, surgical errors, incorrect diagnosis and hundreds more), to where it occurred, who was involved, time of day, etc.

I *loved* developing software. It required good listening, good analytical skills, and immense organization. When we started to go back to the hospitals with software that was evolving, it was very exciting to see what worked, what didn't work, and what more they needed to be efficient. The reports that Jeanne designed were awesome. A hospital using this software would be able to spot problems immediately, *before they became a lawsuit*, and intervention was still possible. The system tracked all actions with the patient, insurance companies, physicians, and family. It was a very exciting project.

When the North Carolina Hospital Association had its summer meeting, I went to Myrtle Beach to talk to people about risk as well as our other products. I went to meet people more than anything, and meet people I did! Unfortunately, I still hadn't learned not to sell at every opportunity, so I wasn't as popular as I could have been if I'd stayed strictly social.

When I got home, Randy and David had rearranged the offices to allow for better training. David had set up his office permanently in with mine so he could supervise my calls. I was getting better, but I still hadn't made *any* sales in July, and we were both very anxious.

As Randy and I designed RISKplus, Jeanne was busy at work designing reports for QUALCAREplus, our quality assurance software. How we all kept it straight, I don't know. The plus stood for "plus lots of reports ready to use the minute you get your data in." Credentialing staffs loved it.

David had to go out of town for a week, and I had thought I was doing fine. When he called, I fell apart. Slowly, with exercise, David's encouragement, and talking to myself, I came around. The pressure of selling was getting to me, and we both knew it.

WHIM OF IRON

The CED asked David and me to put on a program for the CED on Marketing 101. It went very well. David was a great presenter. He kept things simple and direct. A man came up to me after and said, "I've watched your video on doing a winning business plan presentation 12 times, and it helped. Do you know you wore your glasses in the first half, but not in the second?" We both laughed, and I felt personally very happy that I had helped someone. I wasn't doing so well taking care of me.

Trying to sell, keep the books up to date (we couldn't afford to send them out yet), writing all the correspondence and always worrying about how everyone was doing, was taking a toll on me. Luckily just toward the end of the month, I got my two sales: SE Specialty Hospital and Richmond Memorial in Virginia. With some cash in the till, David agreed to hire a secretary. Jenny started the last week in August. She was fast and seemed on the ball and willing to work hard. Relief for me was in sight.

David was concerned that CBR had no credit, so he approached Larry Clark at Planters Bank and asked for a $70,000 loan. Larry agreed to try to get approval because he liked my commitment to fight for what we were doing. If we got it, relief. If not, stress. David pointed out to him that our sales goal was three units per month, and I had done nine in June, six in July, eight in August, and working on three in September. That helped us a whole lot in his eyes.

By this time, I was driving to hospitals in North and South Carolina a lot, because David was on a project and not available to fly me. The long road trips were killing my back and hips, and I felt lonely and disassociated from everyone, but I kept on slugging. Every few days, David would help me make sense of my feelings and I would feel better.

The first week in September, Jay entered my life. Jay was a 38-year-old man who was as kind and nice as they come. For reasons we never understood, Jay and I never wanted to get involved with each other. I think we valued our friendship more. We started cooking together on Friday nights because he wanted to learn how to cook after being divorced. These were wonderful breaks in my life, which allowed me to laugh and relax a lot. Jay had two children, and I enjoyed relating with them. He had them every other weekend and several times during the week, so they became part of my extended family.

Lisa called to let me know that she and Andy were moving back to Boston and would be living in Beacon Hill. They decided that the tradeoff between commuting and living in town weighed heavily towards living in town, because they could spend more time together. I was happy they were happy, and I was ecstatic they would be back in the US.

My friends, Diane, Jay, and David, as well as my family, all helped me out during this time. The driving was giving me too much time to think, and depression was always lurking around in my mind. Their company, when I was in town, helped keep me centered.

The road trips were not all work. Playing pool helped me keep a perspective.

Just got back from Cape Fear and Veterans Administration Hospitals' demo in Fayetteville. Played some great pool and made a 3-bank on the 8 ball! The guy I beat was so pissed he walked out!

I remember one trip after a presentation in South Carolina, when I was traveling north on I-95 and needed to stop for the night. After finding a motel, I wandered over to the fireworks booth and asked a local man, the location of the nearest pool hall. He gave me a funny look, then said, "Well, there is one about a mile from here but it's…well, it's not really for ladies."

I laughed and said, "I'm not always a lady. Tell me where it is."

I drove the mile to a small, southern town that looked like it was a setting in a movie about the '20s. Dogs asleep on the steps, old, worn buildings that didn't look occupied, rotting wooden doors, and a silence that only can be heard in a deserted town. I walked into the front foyer of the pool hall and looked around. It was very dark, and I couldn't see much at first. Slowly I saw a man behind a bar, drying glasses. I walked up and said, "Hi, I'd like to play pool and have a beer."

The man looked at me thoughtfully for a few seconds. "Not from around here are ya?"

"No," I admitted and then waited.

He served me a beer and asked where I was from. I told him Durham, and we chatted a little. He finally told me he was from New York but had moved down to take over his wife's family bar, and here he was. When I finished the beer he said, "Now about playing pool. It's in the back room there, behind that wall. Uh, the boys aren't used to having a woman come in, so just ask if anyone wants to play a game and see what happens."

I walked into the poolroom and stood for a few minutes, taking it all in. There were probably ten or twelve tables set up in a dim, warehouse-like room. Some lights were on, but not too many, so it was very dark and dingy. As my eyes adjusted, I saw that against the wall sat eight rednecks. How could I tell? Each had on a dirty hat turned backwards, tattoos on one or both arms, dirty jeans, a big belt buckle, and a Budweiser in one hand.

No one said a word to me as I stood in front of them, taking them all in. Finally I said, "Anyone want to play pool?" Still not a word. I shrugged, turned, and walked over to a table that had some light and was about halfway across the room from the men. I understood the game they were playing, and I was having fun luring them in.

A game was fifty cents so I put my quarters in, racked up the balls and chalked my stick tip really well. Pool was a game I came to late in life, but which I took seriously. Practice consisted mostly of placing a shot and then trying to make it two times in a row, which would indicate that I had an "eye" for that shot and could move on to another. Now as the beer-drinking men watched, I took my time. I broke the balls with a powerful WHACK and spread them very evenly over the table, a good beginning. Slowly I put each striped ball into a pocket until they were all off the table. Then I started in on the solid balls. Before I had finished the table, a young man walked up and said, "Mind if I play the next game?"

Of course I accepted. I knew the "big" men had sent the young man over to test me at a game, and I was up to the challenge. I did not, however, underestimate the young man's skill...I had no doubt he had played a whole lot more pool than I had. He let me break the balls, and then I ran three balls, before missing on the fourth. He got two in, and then I put two more in. Slowly the table cleared; I was down to the eight ball, and he had one other, before he went for the eight. My final shot was a long one, and I could have easily scratched, but I took my time, looked it over carefully and then shot firmly, but gently. The eight ball sank solidly in the pocket, and I smiled and shook his hand.

He went to buy me a beer (the local tradition for the loser), and I racked up another set of balls. The next game was not as easy. He realized I knew how to play and focused in on winning. He did, and when I went to buy him a beer, I found the $20 I had come in with was not in my pocket. I searched my body; no money. I went back to the table and looked around; no money. I said something to the young man about my losing $20, but he didn't say a thing. I went back to the bar and told the NY bartender, and he waved the cost and said, "Go ahead, it's on the house."

As we played the third game, the men along the wall slowly broke up their meeting and went back to playing pool. No one played close to us, however. When I was at the far end of the table, the young man came over as he put chalk on his cue tip and said in a very low voice, "You dropped the $20 at the end of the table, and I picked it up. If I just give it to you, my friends will beat the shit out of me. So, when I can, I'll pass it to you, and you pretend nothing happened, okay?"

He was looking around as he said this to me, and I quickly said, "No problem." Within a few minutes I could feel his hand go in my pocket, I checked, and sure enough, there was the money, and we continued to play as though nothing had happened. After I won the third game, others came over and challenged me, and I didn't have to buy another beer all night. When I drove back to the motel about midnight, I was chuckling to myself—the bartender had told me as I left that they had never had a woman walk into the bar before. Good. Now they had.

My new friend, Jay, brought much needed relief into my life in the form of music. He loved music and was always going to concerts. On September 23rd, he took me to see Elton John. What a concert! We saw it in the Smith Dome, North Carolina University's sport complex, and the rules were very strict. No dancing, no leaning against the upstairs railings to see better, no blocking of other people's views, etc.

Jay and I didn't like our seats high up in the stands, so we went on the floor and walked up to the next level. There we could see much better standing in the wings, so to speak, and we were having a grand time along with about 50 others, who had gathered for the same sight. Suddenly an older University security guard strolled by us casually, climbed over the railing that was intended to keep everyone back, and blocked all of our views, as he sat and watched Elton perform.

Now, one thing I can't stand is when someone in authority takes advantage of his/her position. I seethed awhile, Jay tried to calm me down, I continued to seethe, and finally I went over to a young attendant nearby and said, "Miss, would you please tell that gentleman that he is standing where he is not allowed to stand, and he is blocking all our views, and we'd appreciate if he'd move?"

She looked at me skeptically, saw the man, and decided I was right. She went over and told him what I had said. I saw him turn to look at me, and then she returned to me and said, "He said he can stand any damn place he wants." I laughed. I have a loud laugh and he heard me. He knew I was laughing at him. Within a minute, he turned and came over towards me. I could see other police-types in dark suits come in closer to me as if getting prepared for trouble. I waited. The man came right up next to me, put his face close to mine and said, "Lady, you got a problem?"

"No sir," I said lightly with a song in my voice. "I have no problems at all. It's you that has the problem, because you are using your authority to break the rules. But hey, if you want to do that, be my guest."

Quite a crowd was listening now, and the other security people had moved in even closer. I could feel my heart pounding. I refused to look intimidated and I waited for his reaction.

He blurted out at me, "I can stand anywhere I want."

I said, again cheerfully, "Of course you can. I just thought you might not want to set a bad example for all these young people."

With that I thought he was going to erupt, because clearly I was embarrassing him. He just turned and walked right back to where he had been sitting, blocking our view. I let it go and went back to listening to Elton. I needed to calm down. Jay had disappeared during all this (he said he didn't want to get locked up with me because I'd need him to put up bail), but when the officer returned to his place, Jay came up and said, "Whew, that was close."

Just then someone nearby said, "Look," and we saw the officer climb back over the guardrail and disappear down the hall. "Good job," someone said to me, as everyone started to relax and have fun again. Jay said, "Cleo, do you think we can just listen now?" I laughed and said, "Of course Jay," and we did. Elton

John put on one of the most powerful performances I have ever seen.

Several days later, David was scheduled to fly me to Charlotte so I could put on a demo to a large hospital there. We had been told the purchase order was filled out and ready to go, so we were excited. At that time, we thought that having larger hospitals using our products would add to our prestige. This was soon after Hurricane Hugo had ripped through Charlotte, so immediately after taking off from Raleigh/Durham Airport, we were in a dense cloud cover. David went into autopilot and was very tense, so I just lay down in the back and went to sleep.

The next thing I knew, we were landing. There was still a dense cloud cover and we were all a little nervous, but when we broke the clouds at 200' we could see again. Those two black centerline strips on the airport runway were lined up directly under our wheels—it was a sight for sore eyes. Personnel met us at the ramp with candles; electricity was limited. As we drove toward the hospital, we saw huge trees sawn in half to clear the road, lining both sides of the road for many blocks. It was a weird experience. The demo, however, went well and we got the sale, although it took several more months for us to receive the check. We were learning that what the person purchasing said, and what the finance people actually did, were two different things.

Over the months, David had spent a lot of time with me putting together a new presentation. I asked my ex-husband if he would do some cartoons for us, which would help me educate the hospitals, with humor. He agreed, and after a nice dinner and discussing the project, we fell into talking about old times. We had divorced more than ten years before and thankfully, had remained friends. I asked him how he could have married me with three children, 4, 5 and 6 years old, when he had three sons of his own. He said he wanted me and knew the kids came with me. Thank God he was willing, because I think we did a good job of raising all six. We had a great visit.

Randy had been working feverishly on the risk management program. Each time I tested it, I was more and more impressed. He had listened well, but he had also added things that only he knew they would need at some point. When we took it back to Baptist to have their people take a look at how it was progressing, they couldn't stop raving. Randy had come a long way as a programmer, and I was very proud of him.

Moore Regional finally purchased after a year and a half of consideration, so money was finally coming in, but it seemed to just go out the back door.

Early in the summer I talked to the Texas Hospital Association to see if they would sponsor our software to their members. My friend Ed did some groundwork, and early in October I flew to Austin to talk to the top people at the association. They were very impressed with what we were doing, felt they had a need, and said they'd look for five hospitals to do a pilot project. I was so excited. It was one thing to stumble into the North Carolina Hospital Association sponsorship, which I always attributed to my association with Duke. This was different. I had sold them, and I could hardly contain my excitement or pride.

In the end it was David who put the deal together. He wanted it clean and neat. Easy to manage. Easy to package. Non-political. That's what we finally ended up with, but without David's tough negotiation and clear vision, it would never have happened. I flew home feeling like we truly were on our way to success.

Meanwhile, over at Duke, there were some rumblings about the source code for the credentialing software we had developed with the Duke programmers. They wanted access to the code so they could change it to meet their specific needs. David said absolutely not, because then we could not update them with our changes. They said their needs were different, and they didn't need our updates. David said they would want them, and that they could not have the code.

In the end, David won, and he found a way for Duke to win, too. This was so typical for David. He had Randy design custom reports that were specific to Duke and bundled them into the regular program. That way Duke could get the information they needed in their format, and they could also get our updates. Everyone was happy.

Hazel's birthday was October 13th, so I decided to fly to Princeton and visit all my old haunts and friends. Hazel was so glad to see me. She was full of wisdom and love as always. I stayed in her little apartment for three days, and we ate, laughed, visited with friends and had a good old time. She surely missed me, as I missed her.

I also missed my daughter, who had always been able to cheer me up. I wrote her a poem:

Lisa, I see you wrapped in love
as I look back at times we spent together.
Walking beaches or campuses,
we always walked as one.
I've always known you love me.
Never had a doubt.
And I love you the same way too,
with me you've always carried clout.
You are so strong, I stand in awe!
So beautiful, I cry.
And all I ever wish,
my child, is with your wings
      you fly.

From what I could see, she was surely flying and having a good life.

By the end of October, David was not a happy camper. One day he came into our office, closed the door and said, "Cleo, we have a problem."

Even though I had made many presentations in September and gotten four sales in, only one had come in for October. It was David's opinion that if I allowed myself to not make goals *every* month, then soon I wouldn't be making goals at all.

He started out very direct. "You are not getting through to the administrators. I've looked over your contact sheets, and you're talking to secretaries and coordinators, but not administrators."

He wasn't angry, just matter of fact, but I could see he was unhappy. What David didn't know was how tired I was in my soul of living with sell, sell, sell. I didn't question what I had to do; my body was just tired from doing it.

I denied what he said, telling him it was just hard to get through, secretaries wouldn't let me get through, etc., etc., etc.

"Excuses," he said.

"Bullshit," I said.

At some point, we were raising our voices so loudly, that he suggested we go for a walk outside and talk about it. We barely got down the steps and onto the front lawn, when I said, "David, I can't do any better. I'm doing the best I can. If you think you can get through to them, you try."

"That's not the solution, Cleo, and you know it. We have to find out why you don't want to talk to the administrators."

He was questioning my ability, my character, my passions, and I was furious.

Suddenly in the midst of our yelling, David said, "You know what I think? I think you need to go see a shrink and find out why you're avoiding talking to them."

I shot back, "Okay, I will," and stomped off into the house. No one said a word as we resumed our day, but of course everyone had heard every word.

The next morning I called the head of Psychiatry at Durham General Hospital, where I had done a lot of work, and made an appointment. That started a year-long process, but within a month, my selling style had changed. David had been right. I was afraid to talk with the administrators because I saw them as Daddy, and I was afraid he was going to say no. Once I understood what was happening, I changed. On a dime. I got through to administrators. And I got sales. Five for November, three for December. David was happy and so was I.

Early in November I drove to Washington, D.C. to see a hospital and to visit with my brother and his wife. We always had a good time together, and this time was no different. They took me to a mountainside retreat, where Tommy fixed the freshest, best fish I had ever had. It was great talking with Sandra, because she was a businesswoman and I valued her comments.

At one point, when Tommy and I were alone, I told him about my visits to the psychiatrist. I also told him that I still didn't know in my heart who my dad was, since both Mom and Dad had always maintained that neither of them knew. Tommy said, "I don't know who your father was, but whoever it was, he was the father of us all!" Tom had no idea how much his comment meant to me.

The next week David flew Randy and me to St. Petersburg where my sister, niece and her husband met us. It was so good to see everyone. We went to my niece's river property and had a fire and barbeque, which was quite a treat. I was beginning to feel closer to my family.

These little trips were good for me. They gave me a much needed break from the pressure of selling. David was really trying to reach certain performance numbers for the bank and for him. I could feel the pressure as I woke in the morning and as I went to bed at night.

As soon as I got back home, I dug in. I woke at 4:30 a.m. with my feet running. It took me until 7:00 a.m. most days to get caught up on all the correspondence. Mid-November I presented to Wilkes Hospital and they bought; then Cape Fear Valley and Hendrix, Texas, bought...we were on a roll, or so I hoped.

Randy was sent to Chicago to get intensive training in KMAN (Knowledgeman), the software we used for development. Jeanne was busy testing software and writing documentation. Jenny wasn't proving to be as valuable as we had hoped she would be, but we kept her busy. To give me a break one day, David took me out flying just for the fun of it. He taught me more about the instruments, direction, compass readings, etc. At one point he said, "Ready to fly it?"

I didn't hesitate a moment before saying, "Of course."

It turned out to be hard, and easy. The hard part was keeping the horizon level; the easy part was doing what David told me to do. He said he wanted me to be able to take off, fly and land the plane in case anything ever happened to him. I agreed, but didn't realize he meant *today*.

David was an excellent teacher, and later on during this trip I actually flew the plane, taking off and landing without a problem. Though I didn't develop a passion, I did discover that I could do such *manly* things as fly a plane.

Got nine hospitals signed up for demo in Tampa and nine for Austin! Wow. I have a new slide show thanks to David, Jeanne and my ex-husband. They did a <u>great</u> job.

Organization is my strong suit, and lining up hospitals for demonstrations was right up my alley. Since I was feeling less and less needed in the office, I dove into organizing demos. The cost on my body was heavy (no pun intended), yet it helped me a lot, psychologically. My weight continued to be my main criticism of myself; in all other areas of my life I was doing quite well. Or so I thought!

A routine checkup revealed a fibroid in my abdomen about the size of a grapefruit, which may have been what was causing all my back pain. At first I was terrified, visions of cancer looming in my mind.

WHIM OF IRON

The woman doctor I went to recommended surgery immediately. Having been around hospitals long enough to know, I called another specialist for a second opinion, one connected with Planned Parenthood, whom I had always found to have a level head when dealing with women's problems.

The second doctor told me fibroids were common in women; I could have it removed, or I could wait. Chances were real good it would go away on its own. I decided to wait, and I was glad I did. It eventually did go away. I promised myself I would relax and play more.

One of my first major road trips selling was to Florida. There was a lot of interest from hospitals in all parts of the state. Instead of qualifying each one carefully and doing all my homework, I relied on selling them by "show and tell." This is a very exhausting approach, I can tell you, and not one that is very productive. I was still green, and hands-on made me feel more needed and important, I think.

In Tampa, my demo went well in technical terms, but in selling terms it was a disappointment. Most of the people had been *sent* to the demo; they didn't come because they wanted a solution. Several people who expressed the most interest had actually already contracted with a competitor to buy software, and were just shopping around to make sure they had the best. It was a difficult thing to do, because how do novices at computers understand which program is going to help them the most? The biggest difference between CBR and our competitors were the reports.

We gave them hundreds of formatted, meaningful reports immediately, while everyone else required each hospital to have their inexperienced coordinators come up with what questions they were trying to answer, and then use complicated software to design the reports. Novices, however, do not know the impact of such differences, so I watched sadly as they left the room.

I was still in therapy and learning more each visit. Therapy helped me understand why I did the things I did (like cry at the drop of a hat, etc.) and it helped me cry a lot!

I cry all the time. I want to climb up in Daddy's lap and have everything feel safe and all right for just a little while. Not too long— maybe an hour. Time to know I don't have to do it all. Someone to talk things over with. Talked to shrink and he said because I had to be an adult child, I've never allowed myself to feel sad or scared as a child. Too overwhelming.

The psychiatrist I was seeing was trying to get me to grow up, stop reverting to a child when things got tough. One day he said to me three different times, "Cleo, your daddy is dead." I didn't hear him. It would be many years later, before the message sank in. When it came to business, though, my competitive adult came out in full form.

Randy was growing as a programmer. He showed me a new routine he'd developed for doing searches (searching for a name, department, type of incident, etc.). I gave him my input, and when I came back hours later, he had done amazing things! He was building positive psychology into every interaction with the client in our software.

My conversations with the Texas Hospital Association were very encouraging, and they seemed confident they could get hospitals to purchase. I often had to call David to see how I should handle one more of their requests, and his response was always pointed—will it help us sell software? If no, then no.

When I got home, Jeannie was very excited to tell me we had received $24,000 in one day—definitely a record—and I was glad, but I needed *more*!

The next day I told David I wanted to make more than $20,000 per year. I had had conversations with salespeople over the years and knew that they got a healthy commission. I wanted more than $20K.

David asked, "How much more do you want?"

Without hesitation, I said, "I want 5 percent of every sale."

"Absolutely not," he replied firmly. "We simply cannot afford that."

"I don't care," I said firmly. "I'm not going to keep traveling and being away by myself all the time, if it's not worth my while. And $20,000 is not worth my while." Since 1980, I had been struggling by on any cash that was left over after everyone else was paid. I wanted to be paid for my contributions.

We started arguing, David pointed out that humans tend to spend what they have, and I had a history of not knowing how to save. I countered that all salesman get paid a commission, and usually in the 25 to 40 percent bracket!

All of a sudden, as he had done on one other occasion, he said, "Let's go outside to finish this conversation."

We walked out onto the lawn, while Randy and Jeanne watched from inside. I was not going to give in. I had no long-term vision, only short-term, and I wanted some of the pleasures NOW.

We screamed and yelled and I held my ground and finally, all of a sudden, David said, "Done. You're the boss." He saluted me and motioned his hand towards the house.

He turned out to be right—I spent every penny I made. But I also was right. I needed to *feel* like I was making money… I had been poor too long. In retrospect, I saw that David wanted to save more money before he started giving it to me in cash, but when he saw I couldn't wait, he backed me 100 percent.

A Boston hospital was interested in our credentialing software, and since my daughter had moved from Paris to Boston, I didn't mind flying there to do a presentation. Lisa was an inspiration to me.

She was working in the big corporate world and more than holding her own. I was so proud of her and often felt in awe of what *she* had accomplished so far.

When I got back to Durham, work was piled high and I dug in…again. Where I got my energy, I do not know. If things were going well, I could do the work of four people in a day. If things were going badly, I had a hard time getting out of bed. But I did.

We had to let Jenny go. She did what she was told, but she never *saw* what needed to be done. We were all too busy to do it ourselves, and we needed a self-starter. We hired Julie and hit the jackpot. Julie was young, new to computers; eager, aware, bright… in short, she was just what we needed.

As the year wound down, David arranged an end-of-year review at a local restaurant and put on quite a show. He wanted us to see how far we'd come and where we were going, and he did a great job. I always appreciated that he treated us as professionals, raggedy as we were, in a small house on West Club in Durham, North Carolina.

It had ended up a good year: Lots of sales, lots more in the hopper, and the programs were all getting in great shape. We now had PRIVplus, QUALCAREplus and RISKplus, and our outlook for 1990 was very good.

David was constantly trying to get us to see ourselves as a professional business, instead of a Mom and Son shop, and to that end, he had us write an Annual Report for 1989. It was the first of many, and for me, it was the most exciting. We had survived. We had succeeded in meeting goals. Heck, we even *set some goals*! We still existed! Our year-end financials showed we sold 33 units for a total of $270,865 in income. I kept saying to myself during the holidays, "Oh my God, we're doing it!"

David had turned us around, and we knew where we wanted to go. All I had to do was to keep doing what I was doing, and we would get there. A small miracle!

1990 — Separation of Church and State

New Year's Eve had been quiet. I had a lot to think about. David had turned a soon-to-be disaster into a miracle story, and I knew in order to continue the miracle, I had to continue to sell. Instead of taking a few weeks off and resting, I started to make calls soon after the New Year. I was also listening to a tape by a woman doctor who had me imagining that I was thin, healthy, and happy. I listened to it every night before sleep, and I started to lose weight. She sounded like a caring mom, and it was pleasant having her talk to me. So, here I was with a business that was going well, lots of friends, *and* I'm getting thin and more beautiful in my eyes.

Consistent with my history, I proceeded to get a cold, which turned into bronchitis, which brought on a terrible hacking cough. I was so disappointed because I knew that this was what I did every time things started to get too good. I'd get sick or I'd get hurt. I decided to ignore the cough, of course, and dig right into work, which too, was consistent with my history.

I've been busy, reorganizing files, sorting through years of correspondence, both business and personal, and feeling good. Our lives are made up of snapshots—wonderful stories. House is getting real cleaned and organized—I'm ready for a move.

David had begun talking about moving the business. He felt I needed to have a place to live by myself, and he also felt CBR needed more room. I agreed with both, and the need for both became quite evident the next day.

Went to do presentation at Lexington Hospital and then home. Was going to walk, but got involved in business and never left. About 4:30 p.m. I stood up to go get water, and when I felt a cough coming on, I leaned forward, and as I coughed hard, I heard a rib crack in two! The pain almost overwhelmed me. I called a doctor I knew at Durham General, but he wouldn't be in until the next day.

I called a friend who immediately came and took care of me. She got me into my bed, propped me with pillows, and fed me. Once in bed, I realized I couldn't get up to go to the bathroom. Panic. Scooted around and got to the phone. Help, Randy! He brought Unisom for sleeping, a bedpan and aspirin. I slept fitfully. Why did I break my rib? Maybe I'm breaking inside from trying to follow David's routine—it's not mine. I have to listen to and heed mine.

Still, life goes on. Halifax Hospital bought a competitor's program. Too bad for them. Sometimes I get convinced I'll never sell another package, and I make four calls and get all No's and then on the fifth, <u>Yes!</u> Yeah! So I think I'm going through a phase of feeling the power and joy of being able to help get hospitals organized. It makes it easier to sell. A friend sits in on a board meeting at Boston City Hospital, and he sees why we're losing our health-care system or the hospital portion. There is no accountability. Our software is their accountability system.

What I didn't understand was the pressure David was under. He had set some goals with the bank and in order to meet them, we had to have financial security. He also wanted us to look and feel a little more like a business. Not a lot, but some. When we talked about moving the business, I said I wanted it to stay in a house because 100 percent of the people who came to training to date were women, and they could relax more in a house than a sterile office building. He agreed and began looking for such a place, unknown to me.

David says he is a "tough-time, turnaround specialist," not the "long haul" manager. That's fine—he's preparing us all to move forward securely.

There was only one issue that came up between David and me that was of a delicate nature. David was used to working with men primarily, and he had developed a pattern of quips and jokes he used to break the ice when things got tense. He was now working with three women, and the jokes, which men had always responded to with a laugh, only brought a frown from us. It never occurred to him that he was making us angry. We didn't want to hear the jokes, and none of us knew quite how to tell him. I finally decided I had to speak for all three of us.

I told David about my upset with his use of sexual jokes and remarks. It was very hard for me to do because I didn't want to push him away. He took it well. He recognized I was telling him as a friend and asked me to help remind him for a while so he could stop. I could have had this conversation last year—no, no, I could not. I had to go through this year with David to know I could trust him.

David did stop eventually, and all of us just admired the blazes out of the man.

David says I have changed a lot this year. I appreciate his patience—it is paying off. David also said I should keep a diary so I can write a book. I told him it was already being written.

David's influence on me was changing my life. He had become my dad, mom, friend, confidant, financier, planner, and personal support group all in one. It was not, as some thought, that I gave control to David without any sense of retaining some myself.

WHIM OF IRON

He always let me know, and I always knew, that I was president. It was my company, and I *could* challenge any decisions he made. He just made such good ones, I didn't feel the need to argue often.

The CED had turned into a resource for David as well as myself. They asked us to do a monthly meeting on how David structured the turnaround of CBR. We had a great time doing the program and using CBR as an example of marketing and sales principals. The more we worked together, the more we respected and liked each other.

I was spending my time selling, and David was spending his time planning. He could see that I needed to have my own living space. One day while we were out for a drive, David asked me, "What do you think of that house?" I looked and saw a small (good), very old (acceptable) house, in a bad location of Durham. After a little discussion, I said I could live with it, and it was within the price range he had set. He left it at that, and I didn't ask anything more.

Went to see Sunrise after hearing from a friend that she had cancer. What a change in six months. From vibrant and alive to small, filled with cancer—all her long hair gone. Spent a lot of time with her. She could come back. I'm going to do what I can to help her.

Even though I had not seen her since our falling out, I could not imagine this active lady in the condition I found her. She didn't come back; in fact, I think she gave up very early in the disease's progress because she knew it was the end of her freedom.

I feel so humble—for friends, for opportunity. Tonight at midnight the Gulf War may start. And while I sit in my cute "sitting" chair, there are men and women sitting in hot sand wondering if they'll see the sun rise tomorrow. All I can do is pray for them.

I was lucky that my major problem was weight. I realized the extra weight diminished my self-image and kept me from feeling 100 percent great. Since I was seeing a psychiatrist, I felt I had the support to take the pounds off and keep them off. I began the New Year weighing 164 and wanted to get down to 138, which was what I weighed at the end of high school. I was determined to stay with it this time, and David was very supportive.

I am the thinnest David has ever seen me. By April 9th I will weigh 138 pounds. The audiotape on visualizing myself thin has been a big help. I have been a big help. Therapist, David, and friends have all been big helpers.

138—I can't wait. I'm going to buy one dress per month till I have a versatile travel wardrobe—a few very good, interchangeable pieces, and two dresses.

Bought new Polka Dot dress. Nice, want to get shoes and belt to go with it.

Dieting was not new to me. I'd weighed 225 back in the '70s, and when I lost 90 pounds over three years, I looked terrific, but didn't stay slim long. My feeling was that to be thin was dangerous…sexy, attractive, luring…all associations with growing up that were scary, and I wasn't over those feelings yet. But with David's belief in me, I was hopeful that this time I could really do it.

Spent time with accountant, looked at houses, and got a lot done. Took walk in Duke Forest with David and talked about computer networks the whole time. It takes a lot of conversation to come to an understanding of some concepts and inventing ways to control them. Multi-user environments, for example.

These sessions with David were the highlight of every day. I loved hearing him make a complicated subject, simple. He would never move on to the next topic until he was sure I understood, and agreed to, whatever was on the table. He also was learning that if he told me I couldn't do something, by God I would do it. He was no dummy.

In the evening, we went to look at the Knox Street house. Owning a house had never been a priority in my life, but living in one room, which was crowded to the gills, was getting old. I wanted some privacy and was about ready to move anywhere to get it. The next day David learned that the house had already been sold.

Unbeknownst to me, he kept looking for a house in his spare time. One day he drove me by a house on Alabama Avenue in Durham. It was a small

Spanish stucco house, badly in need of repair. The price, $50,000, was what we could afford, and the location was great. I said yes.

At the same time, David also found an old house on Broad Street, and the office was moving there! Time for a separation of church and state. Yeah! CBR would have their own offices, and I would have my own home. Such miracles David created!

Sunrise was going down hill quickly, so I tried to spend as much time as possible with her. It was so sad to see the feistiness just melt right out of her. From time to time I felt guilt about her cancer. *If I hadn't gotten mad at her and left...If we had gotten help sooner...If If If.* Holding her frail hands that had once so professionally sewn beads or turned an omelet, broke my heart.

Spent Saturday morning with Sunrise getting her to eat, making out her will...Saturday afternoon I cared for Damon (5) and Crystal (8) while Jay and Jeff did lawn work. Then I fixed a barbecue dinner for all. Jeff did dishes, then I went and spent all night with Sunrise. Now it's Sunday and I want this day for myself. What would I like? I'd like my man to give me a back rub, walk the Eno, swim 50 laps and come home to relax by a fire, make love, and sleep soundly. Lacking the man, I think I'll swim, walk the Eno with Boude and rest all day. I will fix dinner for Sunrise tonight.

My swimming, along with the therapy, gave me a break from sales, and I was thoroughly enjoying both.

Swam 40 lengths, and then went to therapist. I learned I help people well because I do for them what I wanted done for me. Good session.

My time in therapy was helpful. I got a lot of positive reinforcement and found ways to change my behavior somewhat, but it was slow, and I was still holding on to my "mads," anger about what I didn't have as a child. I knew that until I got rid of them or understood them, I would continue to have a poor self-image.

I'm moving forward and feeling better being alone. Went to Duke Forest with Boude yesterday, got lost and spent 4 hours walking, which was actually good for me! There are no mistakes!

I'm resting up for a hellacious travel schedule—David says to make it <u>fun.</u>

I feel I am ready to succeed in business. Last year was the beginning. I'm getting better every time out.

9:16 p.m. I feel so isolated. From everyone. Even me. I can't stop crying. Wanted to cry in safe arms, but none available. I must pull out of this. See therapist at 8 a.m. He'll see I'm not making progress.

Cleo B. Robertson

I want to stop for a while. The pressure I feel is immense. So big. I must succeed, quickly.

From time to time, I would get so angry at me for not making sales, or doing something wrong, or making a mistake, that I would revert to an old, destructive behavior. I would stand in front of my bathroom mirror and beat myself up, literally. I would slap my face again and again and again, as hard as I could, until it was red and I was exhausted. I could feel I was really angry, but I didn't know how to express anger, so I turned it on me. Therapy was supposed to help, but it took a long time for me to stop this behavior. Just as staying thin was difficult, if not impossible.

The first week in February, I was scheduled to go to Texas to install our first two clients—HCA and Hendricks Hospital. I was scared that everything that could go wrong, would. In the past, everything from equipment not having enough memory, to a security code being needed, and the person using the computer didn't know it, had happened. Sometimes there would be conflicts with other software on the machine, and that could take hours to find. I was becoming fatalistic about how installations would go.

In the end, however, the training went very well, and the Texas Hospital Association's Healthcare Division was ready to market us to Texas hospitals. Considering there were over 500 hospitals in Texas (compared to 185 in North Carolina), we felt we had hit the jackpot.

WHIM OF IRON

While I was away, I got a contract in the mail on the Alabama house. The owner's had agreed to $49,000 and David was happy. I sent it back immediately and couldn't wait to get home and see my new, and first, home.

As soon as I got back to Durham, I went to inspect my house. Now, most people would have fainted, it looked so old and run down. But I had never owned a house, so I felt I could make it presentable. There were only 940 square feet of living space, but it was on a good lot with privacy all around. David tried to get me to see that this was an *investment only*, and that I didn't have to make it great, just livable. He was soon to find his words fell on deaf ears.

When the North Carolina Hospital Association had their winter meeting, I went to "schmooz" with everyone. David did <u>not</u> want people to perceive me as a vendor, so he would not allow me to set up a table. I fought him on this many times, but in the end he was absolutely right. People didn't buy at trade shows, they shopped. Having a table only gave my competitors a chance to see what we were doing. Mingling was something he had taught me well, so I just mingled, and that way I learned a lot.

David was tackling my private life as well as my business. High on the list was getting my body healthier. The hundreds of miles I was driving to visit hospitals was killing my back and legs. A 300- to 500-mile trip in a day was not unusual. He encouraged me to buy a mountain bike, and he took me out around Duke's campus to teach me the ropes. He was surprised at how timid I was, but with great patience he got me to adventure around a little. We both knew that the weight would come off easier with exercise, but I had a hard time doing aerobic type exercising. He was patiently trying to get me over my aversion, but I was a tough nut to crack. To me it was quite simple. I had grown up on a piece of land one block wide and 30 blocks long—I liked to stay in familiar places. Unless business called, of course!

Can hardly wait to move to Alabama Avenue. I'll learn the meaning of the word privacy once again. Six years in public view in my house/office. Anxiety about the house and what a big responsibility it is starting to numb me. Called David, he reassured me. Worst that can happen, he said, is I have to find a new house, even if we pay cash! The office move is taking a lot of energy. The office has to come first right now. I need to make more sales. I'm going to put the house out of my head for right now. Creator is using me in a wonderful play with David, my leading man, for now, in any case.

My primary male friends, Jack and Peter, were businessmen who had never been anything but professional and straightforward with me. They never once even flirted, so when I was around them, I felt comfortable. We often liked to brainstorm—each of us trying to figure out what we were doing and how to do better in our businesses. David was invited, but would not go. Not because he didn't like these men, but because he was putting together a strategy solely for CBR, and he didn't want to discuss it with anyone, or diffuse his focus one iota.

My social life in early 1990 consisted of meetings with my buddies, going walking or biking with David, taking care of Sunrise, and long walks along the Eno River.

Everyone was excited about our new offices. David had chosen an old home that was now part of a business district on Broad Street. The upstairs was rented out to a very quiet businessman. We had the downstairs, which consisted of a living room across the front (which we turned into the training room), a dining room (which we turned into the secretary's office with filing, fax and postage desk). The large room off the dining room became the training center for Jeannie and Julie, and the kitchen was the kitchen. The only bath was a mess, so David had the bathtub torn out and I did the wallpapering.

Sometimes funny things happened, and the bathroom turned out to be one of them. We were trying to keep costs down, and David knew I had some wallpapering experience. David said it should be done by the next Monday. When I went in with Jeff on Sunday to wallpaper, it never occurred to me to wait when I saw the walls were rough and unsanded. David had said to have it done by Monday, so by Monday it would be done. I went right ahead, and put up several rolls of very pretty paper. I noticed the ugly, unfinished walls and how they showed through the wallpaper, but I wouldn't stop. The next Monday when the workman came in, he was shocked. He said to

David, "I was going to smooth the walls today." In the end, no one cared, and we left the paper up for well over ten years, ripples and all. Not one person got less trained because of it!

During the office renovations, David was busy directing the work. But when it was almost done, David called a meeting with Randy and me. The main point David had been trying to make to Randy and me for a year was that our product was *overdeveloped*. We didn't share his feeling. Developing was what we both loved and wanted to do. It made David nervous. In this meeting, he again stressed that we had to stop making changes, and *all of us* focus on sales. And if we couldn't sell, at least *support* the sales (which meant give me more time to sell by doing what I did every day...writing letters, testing, etc.).

I could see what he meant. Every time we came up with a new choice on the menu, not only did lots of testing have to take place, but also all the choices were becoming too many, too confusing, to the very person we were trying to please—the client. I agreed to stop, hard as that would be. Randy was non-committal.

We had six sales in January, but only two in February. March had only one so far, and this was at a time when we were spending more cash to redo the offices and my house. David wanted to use Randy to do more of the management part of my job, so I had more time to do more selling. They clashed. Randy wanted to do what he was good at; David wanted him to do what the company needed. I was part of the problem because I loved developing, and Randy supported all my "Oh, wouldn't it be great if the program..." wishes.

David pointed out to both of us again and again that every time we made a change, we had to test, update our clients, and fix the bugs that *would* be found (all software has bugs, you just try to eliminate them). We hadn't been listening because we were having too much fun. Now I saw what he meant. The more time I spent on the phone, the more sales. Period. David kept trying to change Randy's mind, but it was hard, and it was to be an ongoing issue for some time.

Randy was a wonderful support during the move, just as he had been when we moved from Princeton to Durham. It was all part of the challenge to him. For me, it was a nightmare. I didn't know where anything was, the phones weren't working right, people in and out distracted me...I was getting very little done.

David had once had me tested with Briggs Meyers. What I learned from it was that I was a "last in, first out" type of personality. If I was in the middle of making a series of calls to a hospital, and a workman asked me where the cabinet in the training room should go, I would drop everything and go show him. Drove everyone nuts.

I also believed in my head that I could do anything that was needed to succeed. Drive long hours, set up equipment, do presentations to 1 or 200 people, take care of marketing, test software—these were all tasks David had trained me to do efficiently, and I relished the challenge, most of the time.

On March 18th, 1990, CBR Associates moved to Broad Street, less than a mile away. David had also set up the closing on the Alabama house, so I, too, would soon leave for my own place. I was awed by all the progress we had made.

David was in full swing now. He had negotiated an unbelievable deal on the new office space. We were to pay $700 a month and keep up the property, pay the utilities, and pay for any improvements ourselves. David was a home-repair-redecorating expert, having redone several large homes, so the office started to look professional. He had a man build in cabinets out of pine in the secretary's office and painted them white. I had the best office, with a large desk made out of doors Randy had made years ago. All in all, with little money, he was transforming our self-image. When he installed the very professional-looking CBR Associates, Inc. sign in the front yard, I really appreciated that we were on the move, upwards!

On March 30th I was ready to move to my house at 1110 Alabama Avenue.

House puts me in tears. This is a very emotional move. My own home. Mom and Dad (in heaven) must be very proud of me, as am I.

If someone had asked me to make a list of "wants," a home would not have been on it. Not that

I didn't want a home, but it was just not something I thought I'd ever have. To my knowledge, my parents had never owned a home, and certainly once my mom left dad and moved us to Pass-a-Grille, owning a home was out of the question. My first and second husbands had tried to buy homes, but we could never come up with the down payment. The fact that it was really happening stunned me. We had an inspector check the house, and he said the roof, electrical wiring and plumbing were all in good shape.

As much as I wanted to stay at the house everyday and work on it, I couldn't. All of the moving was disruptive. By the end of March, we still only had one sale.

Down to $16,000 in bank account, less than a month's operations! I'm failing. No, I'll come through. Sales.

Actually the saga of the Alabama house was just beginning. Over the months ahead, a story of bribery, decay and injustice unfolded. It began with mildew.

On Sunday when I walked around I saw mildew on the walls, rotten wood in the kitchen, and tons of work, I felt depressed. On Monday, Steve (a friend of Randy's) joined me and Randy, and we have a team!

Tonight, after driving to Charlotte at 7 a.m. to do demo at Orthopedic Hospital, I drove home in 6 hours, changed my clothes and started scrubbing mildew off the bathroom walls with a diluted mixture of Clorox and water.

Steve and Randy came, then Jeff with the sheetrock and supplies he got on his account at Lowe's. Jeff left, and Steve and Randy rebuilt the corner of the kitchen that was totally rotted, while I washed tons of mildew off the kitchen walls.

Randy was amazing in getting so much done, Steve is a master builder and sheet rocker, and I do all the rest—"gofer" mainly and washing walls with Clorox. Feel great about what we are doing. The house is going to be wonderful.

I made a sale today—it'll just take them 3 months to pay!

I'm going to concentrate on my body early a.m., sales all day, and my house at night! Lisa's coming to help unpack! Yeah!!

The first time we went into what became my bedroom, and pulled at the draping yellow and black wallpaper, a huge sheet of it fell off at my feet, and attached were foot-wide sheets of black, sticky mildew stretching out as sheets of plastic wrap as the wallpaper fell away. Awful. The smell alone would have made me sick, but knowing that the mildew was behind *all* the wallpaper in the house made me even sicker. I had a vision of the house done, and that gave me the energy to go back to it every night. In the end, Steve had to re-sheetrock all the walls in the entire house.

This was 1990, I was coming up on my 52nd birthday, and yet I seemed to have the energy of a 20-year old.

Randy and I always end up together, still working. We painted the windows and doors in the kitchen oil-based gloss enamel—looks great! While I went in to work awhile, a friend, Jay, took a tree down outside the house that was diseased. Then Jeff, Steve and Randy moved the old shed, Jeff and Randy roto-tilled the yard, and I wallpapered. Got whole kitchen primed.

Went over at 4 a.m. and had lovely time getting to know the house.

Now I must concentrate on sales all week!

It had been David's hope that I could just move in the house and live in it as it was for a while, until CBR could recover financially. He had made a commitment early on in our relationship that I would have my own house. He had delivered. He needed me to now make sales and not spend money, and I was doing just the opposite! Mom had always lived on the edge, financially, and I was so used to it. David's fears didn't bother me very much.

As happened so often these days, a sale would always come in, eventually.

Lenoir Hospital called and they're buying— I'm so happy. Too long since a sale. House coming along; I'll move the 21st.

David would never sit me down and make me make calls, but I could tell he was getting more anxious each day.

Wallpaper in kitchen turned out great. 10 ft ceilings the toughest I ever did, particularly alone. Randy working hard. Updated Duke today. Texas is going to go. We're on a roll. Can't wait to be in my fresh home.

The fact that the Texas project was heating up helped me feel okay about having no sales. Young business people like me have a habit of thinking that a big organization's support can make sales. They do, but it takes a very long time and is very hard work. I didn't know that. I was sure that once the Texas Hospital Association started sending out announcements, the sales would roll in. They didn't. Somehow I managed to live a busy, happy life anyway.

Great, busy day. Swam 54 lengths, then went to Raleigh and had lunch with Pam, then book party for Jane P. for her Herbal Medicine book that I helped her with for months. I got a signed copy! Then off to see therapist for a teary hour, and then to see Lewis Gizzard—a very funny man, who does a standalone comedy. Laughing hard was just what I needed. Home to sleep early.

As we moved into spring, the house was beginning to mean something to me.

Easter Sunday. Great day. Painted wall rack for kitchen wall, rolled my bedroom for wallpaper, painted back porch and fed everyone steak and shrimp on the grill with fresh broccoli. Eating on front porch was fun. Lovely sun. Lisa and Gary called. Nice day. In evening visited Sunrise, played two games of pool (won both) and then ate dinner. The house is turning out lovely. I feel so confident and secure.

My times of feeling this confident and secure were few and far between. There was still hard work ahead.

Everyone was in transition. The office was looking good and getting organized. David had said it would cost us sales, and it had. My move to my first home was taking a toll, and yet it was the most exciting thing to happen to me personally in my life. A home of my own. I couldn't say it often enough.

The Texas Hospital Association and Healthshare, the Association's for-profit group, had decided to sponsor our software and were putting together a program. It would require me to travel to Texas often, doing a circuit from Austin to Dallas to Houston and then back to Dallas again, but I didn't mind, as long as it meant sales. The Association would get a royalty from each sale, and that pleased them.

On April 20th I moved into my house. It was in disarray, but I was happy. My daughter was coming to visit and help me settle in, and even though I knew this would further alter my focus, there was no way I would say no to her coming. I needed her with me. Each day was full, but still no sales. I felt desperate, even though I knew I was doing the best I could with all that was going on.

"Forgot" to pay my $2,800 in US and State taxes! Spent the money on the move instead. Sold some packages, but not nearly enough. Tired of phone work.

My daughter's visit helped me forget that we were financially sinking...again. She stayed for ten wonderful days and within the first few hours told me, "Mom, put everything you have, all your stuff, in the dining room, and then you have to get rid of half of it." She had learned this lesson from David. It was a job, but I did as she said and was glad I did. The house looked less cluttered, you could see the tops of tables, and all in all I looked settled in by the time she left.

We shared an awful disaster during her visit. One night she and I were lying in bed just talking, while a big rain was lashing at the house. To our horror, we both saw, at the same time, a wet stain begin in one corner of my bedroom ceiling and quickly spread. I was devastated. A bad roof was not in the plan. The inspector had said the roof was in good condition. Then why was it leaking? Lisa lost all faith in the house right then and there. But the house saga just got more complicated

In April we only had two sales, but May brought four, so our work was paying off. David was spending a lot of time with me on strategic planning and new strategies to help sales. The house had given me an incentive to earn more money, and David used the house as a means of teaching me how to earn that money.

Returned from Austin/San Antonio—9 days on the road was too long. Good for business, bad for me. Did large presentation to Texas Hospital Association members in Austin two different days and then drove to San Antonio to attend healthcare conference. Went in to dinner and "no place at the Inn for Cleo"(all the tables appeared full and I didn't know anyone), so I walked out, got drunk, and cried for hours. Called everyone I knew, and finally Hazel got me to calm down and go to sleep.

David didn't understand my stress. He told me to just treat the trips as vacations. I told him, angrily, not to call my trips "vacations."

This turned out to be the longest trip I had ever taken, and all my insecurities loomed large in my mind. Being alone a lot, not being sure I was accepted, wishing I had someone to talk with…it all added up to a big depression for me. Thank God for Hazel. In the end she got me to calm down, and I talked to her every day for the rest of the trip, and finally I came home and I thanked her immensely. David just couldn't understand my ups and downs.

Everyone has up and down days. I would like to make mine a little more even. Too much scared/ecstatic/scared.

When I step back a little, I can see that what happens, happens. I can really relax and enjoy the show. It's just that I seldom allow myself to step back. I'm always busy "doing." Just like when I was a kid and I spent every day "doing" because I felt better busy than home alone.

Owning a home is an accomplishment I never expected. Now what? What is my next goal? Reach 138 pounds. Become well known in field. Financially secure. Feeling better. I want to learn how to come home from work and say, "Cleo, you've done enough for the day, rest…" and know where to begin tomorrow.

Balance was not something I grew up with. Our home had no balance whatsoever as far as I could tell. So creating it in my life was very difficult. The other area I had problems with was setting limits. "Okay," I'd say to myself. "I'll work ten hours today, then rest for the evening." Seemed reasonable, but when the day was done, I had worked twelve or more hours, and gone dancing in the evening. When was my body to rest?

My personal life was feeling more complicated. Sunrise was dying. She had been my mentor. I believe cancer is rage turned against oneself, so was she angry with me for going away from her? Was I responsible for her death?

Sunrise flies to New York to live with her daughter, Holly, for a while. I don't expect to ever see her again. Sad, sad, sad.

The house bounced up and down in importance, depending on whether I was home in the Alabama house, or at work in the Broad street offices of CBR, ten blocks away. But no matter where I was, my mind was never far from business.

Business in transition. David in consulting role more and more and spending less and less time in the office each day. He's working as a turnaround specialist for all five divisions of Leggett-Meyers here in Durham. I still want a partner, someone who will dig in and have energy. I love my home. I want to get my office comfortable.

Interviewed a young man named Chris today to help me with sales. He seems to have the drive. Does he have the skill?

I was desperate to have someone work with me daily to relieve my stress. David agreed to let me try, even though I knew he didn't think it would help.

On June 22nd, Lisa turned 30 and we got our 75th sale! Big day and I celebrated by going dancing and playing pool.

On July 5th, Sunrise passed away at her daughter's home in New York City. She had taught me a lot, caused me pain, and then became a friend again. Now she was gone, and I really missed her. She had been a regular stop for me on my walking tours around Durham, and for months after, when I would walk by her street, I would want to turn and go sit under her tree, and sip a cup of tea and talk.

Cleo B. Robertson

Sunrise's service was by a small river at a friend's house. Everyone told stories about her, and we all learned she had done more than even we knew. Sage was burned, feathers shared, tears exchanged. We all knew someone very important had just left our lives.

Sunrise had made, collected, bartered and traded Native American Indian jewelry and artifacts for years. Her family asked me to put on a silent auction to raise money for her granddaughter. Though things were priced to sell, most of her friends didn't have the money to buy. I ended up bidding on many of the treasures myself and giving away special things to people who had been special in Sunrise's life. I knew that's what she would have wanted me to do. Everyone seemed happy with the deal, and I've enjoyed her great gifts for many years since. Her memory stayed charged with emotion for me for a long time.

Now Hazel was once again my main confidant and supporter. Between the two of them, I had learned many lessons. Here are some of their sayings:

Sunrise: "I have what I need."
"I will be given what I need."
"You will reach your goal, because you can see your goal."
"Sometimes, leave Cleo at home."

Hazel: "It's a long lane that doesn't ever turn."
"You have to have faith in yourself."
"God gives us a chance; it's up to us what we do about it."
"It can't shine all the time; if it shines all

the time, what do you get? A desert!"

My relationship with Jeff was on again, off again most of the time, but when things were good, they were very very good.

Went bike riding with Jeff under a full moon on Hillandale golf course—wonderful! We even saw beavers slapping their tails on the pond, loudly.

Great Sunday at Jeff's dad's farm—I even ran the tractor.

I am hiring Chris as Sales Associate. Big, forward step. David not so sure.

I weigh 148 and feeling great! Bought 5 dresses for $167!

Neck and hips difficult. Lots of pain.

Lisa fine. Dan is having a baby girl! He's happy.

Put in a good day on the phone. Can't wait for new salesman, Chris, to join me—we can do sooo much more!

I'm burned out. I think that will change.

Learning to live with my new, thin body was fun and scary. Small-sized clothes I had kept for years now fit. Heads turned when I walked into restaurants, pool halls, etc. It was exciting *and* it brought back feelings of being beach meat. Somehow the adult in me couldn't say, "Cleo, you're grown up now and in control. Relax and enjoy being thin." Nope. I still reacted as a 15-year old.

At CBR, Jeanne decided she did not like working with my erratic management style (she missed David's evenness, and challenging discussions). I was devastated, and begged her to stay. She agreed. I could see that she was only staying because I felt we needed her so, not because she wanted to. Chris, the sales associate, was trying hard, but he knew nothing—about selling, about hospitals, or about software. It was going slowly.

In mid-August, we hired Elisa as secretary and front desk person. I took her for her interview at a nearby restaurant, and within minutes I saw her vivacious and gregarious disposition, heard that she loved computers and said, "Well, why don't you join us then?" She accepted immediately, and we gave her $3,000 more than she was presently making. Everyone at the office, especially Randy, was somewhat taken aback. They had thought they would have some input into the decision. I just felt Elisa was so right, I made the decision alone, and it's one none of us lived to regret. Elisa brought a voice and attitude that were invaluable—her voice on the phone said, "We're glad you called, and we'll take care of you," while her attitude was, "I can do anything. Just try me."

Towards the end of August, Lisa and Andy came to visit. It was perfect timing. I needed a break, and they were great to be with. Randy joined us for a trip to the North Carolina coast, and we had a great time. I had rented a condo, and we swam, ate, swam, played games, and ate some more.

The only unpleasant thing to happen on this trip was a Portuguese man-of-war jellyfish stung me. I had been body surfing, and all of a sudden felt intense stinging across my chest and down my belly. I didn't know what had happened, and I didn't want to ruin Lisa, Randy and Andy's fun, so I went up to the condo and tried ice on the long, red welts that marred my chest, breasts and belly. It didn't help much.

When everyone came up from the beach, I didn't say much, because the pain was intense. No one noticed, though. That afternoon we went off to a park, and when I saw a Park Ranger, I asked about the stinging and showed him a little of my marks. He immediately said that the tendrils of this type jellyfish can grow to 80' long, and they often break off in storms (with the poison still in them). The tendrils have very sharp rasps that actually cut the skin, so the poison goes right inside the skin. He told me to put meat tenderizer on it, which did help, but the cuts stung, off and on, for over three weeks.

When I got back to the office, I was very disappointed in Chris's progress. He was spending all his time trying to change the product to suit the customer, and that was not what we needed. I went to lunch with David one day and told him I didn't think Chris was working out, but I'd give him to the end of the month.

His response was immediate, "Fire him today." It wasn't in my nature to do such a thing, but David said if it isn't working now, then it won't work at all, and why should we pay for something that's not working?

When I got in the office, I called Chris in and told him that our needs were different from what he could give us, and he should look for another job. I was startled when he said, "Wow, I didn't think you would do it so soon. I was planning on having time to look for a job while I was still working for you."

I laughed, said "No way Jose" and he packed up that minute and was gone.

One day David was coming by to pick me up for a luncheon discussion. I had on a light, cotton dress with tight waist and modest top, and I knew I looked like a knockout in it. When I walked out of the CBR offices and down the steps, David was just walking up.

The moment I heard David's admiration of my figure, I freaked. He said casually, "Wow, you're really looking great," and that was the last day I was thin, to the present time. My weight started to creep up, and ten years later it was still around 180. I started listening to the woman on the weight loss tape again religiously, but it didn't work this time. Old perceptions die hard, if they ever die.

Sitting in my wonderful new office one day, I came up with the idea to approach HBO, a supplier of mainframe patient and accounting software out of

WHIM OF IRON

Atlanta. I wanted to know if they could use the CBR quality management software with their financial management software they offered to hospitals. My primary exposure to HBO was through a local hospital, where everyone raved about the quality of their services and products. In my mind, a large company had more sales presence, and therefore aligning ourselves with them would benefit us. David, again, was not so sure. But one thing about David was he always let me try out my ideas. Sometimes I wished he'd just said no.

HBO turned out to be a very long-term relationship and very beneficial. In the short run, it almost took all the energy I had trying to work with them. Most of it was my own fault, because I didn't understand how big organizations worked. Physical problems were also exasperating me.

Going through menopause, bleeding heavily, clotting, stomach bloated. Lots of pressure to sell. Neck and hip in a lot of pain. Swimming a mile two to three times a week at the spa, but little relief.

The Texas Healthcare project was going fairly well. I was flying to Dallas, Austin, and Houston often to meet with hospitals and do presentations. Their strategy was to get up to 50 hospitals together at a time, let me present, then have us work each one. Or should I say, I worked each one. They kept thinking the sales would just flow in. David had taught me enough to know that wouldn't happen, even for the big guys. It was tough work. Hospitals in Texas were trying to just stay alive in many cases; others didn't know they were already dead. Or they were so big, they felt no pressure. I had one experience that will sum up our challenge at that time.

One large hospital in Texas had over 1,500 physicians on staff. The medical staff coordinator, who worked long and hard, knew she could not manage records on 1,500 doctors manually. She called me and said she had talked with her boss, and he had talked to the Medical Director and they were willing to meet with me. This was all at CBR cost, of course, so when I said yes, I was committing CBR to spending money speculatively. Again, my immaturity in sales got in my way. I thought it was great that *we would be allowed to meet with them*. Therefore, I didn't qualify them properly. I was sure if they saw what our software could do, they would jump at the chance.

When I arrived at the large and impressive hospital, the coordinator met me and seemed quite nervous. She said the medical director had been pretty testy with her that morning about meeting with me. I brushed it off, confident I could talk reason to anyone. When I walked into the room where we were meeting, there was the director sitting front and center with eleven other physicians seated behind him. I felt like I was in front of a firing squad.

The director, who looked at least 70 years old, took charge immediately. "So, young lady," he began, "you think you can be of service to us?"

I immediately told him I knew I could and said, "You have over 1,500 physicians, who must be credentialed every year. You are doing that manually. That means 30 letters per physician times 1,500. This is about 45,000 letters Cindy has to send out yearly, manually. Plus, she has to enter the data from those that are returned, and follow up on those that aren't. It simply cannot be done manually."

I continued, confident I was wowing him with my knowledge of his hospital. "With CBR software, this process is done automatically. Letters are generated by dates in the physician's file. The system tracks if their responses are back or not and allows easy entry so a complete profile is available at any moment. Just as importantly, from a productivity viewpoint, is the fact that CBR software comes loaded with *all the Boards and their addresses*, so Cindy doesn't even have to try to keep those up to date. The system then tells you which physicians are not meeting the standards *your hospital* has set for them in terms of credentialing."

I paused to see what he had to say to that, and his response was, "Our physicians do everything they're supposed to do to stay current."

"How do you know?" I asked incredulously.

He turned to Cindy and said, "Cindy, you're up to date, aren't you?"

Cindy, who needed her job, said, "For the most part, yes sir. But it sure would help when we have new applications. Verifying over 1,000 applicants per year manually is real time consuming."

The director straightened himself in his chair and said, "Miss Robertson, this hospital adheres to only the highest of standards. I don't really feel your software can be of any help to us."

I was shocked, as were many of the physicians in the room. They knew that JCAHO was looking carefully at physician's records to see when they were last verified. It had become important, for instance, for every hospital to know *every procedure* that a physician was qualified to perform. With so many on staff, these doctors knew that the hospital didn't know who was qualified to perform what. Only one young doctor stood up and said that he thought automation would be helpful to the staff.

The director put his hand up, closed the book that was in front of him, and said in a very condescending voice, "My dear lady, we have no need to check on our physicians. We only hire the best, and I have no doubt that they only do what is right. Thank you very much for your time, but we don't need to spend any more time on this subject."

Not all hospitals agreed with the man.

Did a presentation at Richmond Memorial Hospital and sold them PRIVplus.

Obviously I was learning just enough to have big ideas, but hadn't learned enough to know how hard it was to do. The Richmond sale in Washington, D.C. made me feel like a big deal. CBR was becoming something, I thought. Oh, so much to learn yet, with many humbling experiences waiting just ahead of me.

Whether I was sitting on my porch or waiting in my car for a light to change, I was continuously inventing.

I think we should offer a one-day quality management assessment to hospitals to help them know where they are. Software would be just one component. Major piece would be a two-page assessment and plan for fixing problems identified in the assessment.

May need more consulting to help organize hospitals' quality management program along with software. Provide after-installation system integration and enhancement.

The HBO deal was heating up. I flew to Atlanta for a big meeting and was most impressed with their lavish headquarters and meeting room. About ten people showed up, but it was their president, who was the most important person there, so I thought. It turned out, however, that others were more important, because the president fell asleep during my presentation, and they still agreed to take us on as a partner. It was agreed that we would be part of their dog and pony show when they went to a hospital to do a presentation. I was so used to the way I did these presentations, it never occurred to me how differently they would do them. Or what it would cost me to do them, physically and financially.

I managed to bring in five sales for October. I was dragging my butt. I was so tired. David wanted a total of 50 hospitals for the year and I was doing what I could, but my stomach told me it would be close. I always tried to reach or exceed his goals.

At Halloween I got a great break from the sales routine. My niece, Karen, and her husband, Jeff, showed up for a visit, and we had a blast. A friend was having a party, so Karen very patiently braided my whole head in tight braids, I put black paint on my face and arms, and Jay stuck a feather in my hair. After she got me dolled up, I had to run to the grocery store. I forgot all about my hairdo and makeup as I went to pay for my purchases. At the checkout, a man behind me said, "So I give up. What are you?" I realized what I looked like to him and answered, "I'm an Afro-American, female Indian." That broke up everyone who was within listening distance, and I walked out still enjoying a good laugh.

At this time, I voiced my desire to offer a Client's Conference to our clients so that we could give them extended training in the use of the power of each software program. Besides, we could learn from them what worked and didn't work. We booked a local hotel, sent out invitations and prayed they would come.

In mid-November, David flew me to New York City to have an interview with INC Magazine. They had heard that I had been nominated as "Woman Entrepreneur of the Year for North Carolina." It was a bogus title. I figured that they didn't feel women could compete with the men running businesses, so just like in sports, we had to have our own title. Nevertheless, it was an honor, and we took it seriously. They interviewed us, learned about our philosophy, our sales history, our goals, and put everything into a file. We didn't expect to see anything come of it.

All was not paradise, however. The pressure I was putting on myself was showing in pain and problems. Menopause continued to plague me with profuse bleeding. I had refused to go on estrogen… my belief was that if God intended for women to stop producing estrogen after 50, who was I to alter His plan? Self-doubt was again my frequent visitor.

I'm going through change, dramatically, and my body is falling apart. I am worth something. I do know something. I am worth something. I do know something. I am not just a girl from Pass-a-Grille without an education. God gave me some gifts, and I'm making use of them. To His honor. Aren't I???

On one trip to Dallas I was staying in a very nice Embassy Suites, my favorite hotel of all. One morning I woke up, picked up the phone from my bed, and said to Housekeeping, "Could you please send a couple of older women up here…NOW?"

They let themselves into the room, and as they saw me lying in bed, the older one said, "What's the matter, honey? You going through menopause?" I cried I was so glad to see her. I had awoken in a pool of blood, and couldn't get out of bed without making a *real* mess all over the floor. They cleaned me up, and we all went on our way.

My relationship with Jeff was entering its death throes, again. I spent a lot of time thinking about him, too, and that didn't help my energy level. By mid-December, I realized we had made five sales in October, three in November, and six in December for a total of 55 (five more than our goal). I felt wonderful.

I feel strong. My new tulip tree is planted and doing well, my house is in order and life is full of promise. We have exceeded our sales goal, so everyone can have a very merry Christmas.

Having met our sales goal, I flew off to Boston to be with my daughter, her husband and his family. I had a wonderful time, except for the menopause. It would send me off into crying episodes, which no one understood or wanted to deal with, so I just walked the woods and cried and cried. Perhaps menopause is when we empty the tears from the first half of our life, so we can begin fresh for the next half?

When I got back from Boston, I did a presentation to the four North Carolina psychiatric hospitals, and it went very well. They all bought, eventually. We also heard from HBO that they wanted a deal with us. When I heard this, it gave me a great sense of relief.

David and I had spent a good deal of time talking about our payroll and bonus system. Now that we were making a profit, it seemed natural to both of us to share it with the others. When Randy came over one night to help me take down my Christmas tree, I gave him a bonus check for $3,000. He was very happy, and I was very proud of him for being so good at what he loved.

David gave me a $22,000 bonus, which would cover my taxes for the year and pay off Visa. What a relief! He took very little for himself, and it still seemed strange to me that he was so patient. I asked him once why he didn't take more money out of the company when we had plenty, and he said, "I'll take mine when we've met all the financial goals you and I have set for your retirement." He was good to his word.

New Year's Eve was spent quietly with friends. Diane, Steve, Jeff, David...people stopped by, we drank a toast to all that had passed and prayed for all that was to come.

All in all, 1990 had been a great CBR year. In 1988, I had brought in $45,920 gross. In 1989, the first year David was with us, we grossed $270,865. And now, in 1990, we had grossed $424,119, and had a total of 101 hospitals. David's strategies were working!

1991 — Walking the Walk

The new year started out slowly. My mind had been busy inventing a new kind of window treatment that would allow me to change any wall I wanted, simply by changing what was hanging from the special hooks I designed. I drew sketches and designed wall hangings (with insulation, if needed). My mind would go off onto tangents like this, when the pressure of selling would get to me.

David and I met for a full day to lay out a plan for the year and to tighten our business plan. He told me his goals: to pay off all debt (seemed like an impossible dream to me), to pay off my home (even more impossible), and to start putting money in the bank. He explained that it was his commitment to see that I had enough money safely in investments so that I could live off the interest and never have to touch the principal. It sounded good to me, but pretty far-fetched. I didn't convey my doubt to David, however, because so far he had met every commitment he had made. I saw no reason to doubt him yet. I prayed he was right.

Cleo B. Robertson

The HBO agreement was looking good in terms of potential sales and as usual, I started making my phone calls and there was lots of interest. David kept trying to keep me focused, but I still thought if they expressed interest, surely they'd want to buy. How he kept his patience with me, I don't know.

By mid-January I had set up a travel schedule so I could appear at HBO demonstrations to show the quality management part that we were supplying. I went to Atlanta, Austin, Houston, Dallas, Chicago—there was no time to be bored and lots of selling opportunities. Randy had helped me redo my slides, and my presentation was going fairly smoothly. Still, I was overselling and losing people's interest.

The evening of a big trip. Computer acted up, but Randy fixed it. Off to Atlanta to present to Hamilton Hospital, on to HBO in Atlanta for three days to educate the salesmen about our software, then home 9 pm Friday night.

Sat 11am off to Dallas/Austin, train coordinators for two days, then I'll do presentation to 20 hospitals, next to Houston (21 hospitals), and finally Dallas (27 hospitals).

HBO had set up group presentations in Austin because the hospital people were used to going there for meetings. By the time my road trip was over, I had presented to 74 hospitals. HBO was very optimistic that we could make 50 sales within a year. Because they were big players in a big market, I thought they knew what they were talking about. They did in lots of areas, but not in the newly emerging personal computer (PC) world. It would take us years to reach 50 HBO installations.

Business was heating up. David was busy with his consulting work with Leggett Meyers, but he gave me a clearly defined game plan. He and I met every week at a restaurant or for a walk in Duke Forest. He would carefully take me through defining our goal, how we were to reach it, and what my specific duties and responsibilities were. These review meetings were as exhilarating as they were exhausting. We would talk until there was nothing left to say. I always went away charged up and ready to *selllll*.

HBO was my baby, my project. I had contacted the president. I had gotten CBR chosen as their quality management system. I had taught their sales and technical people the CBR software. And, I had done the traveling to cities to present to hospital personnel. In one of these years I flew to 90 cities. In the next, I flew to 50. It never occurred to me that the reason David said so little about all that I was doing, was because he wouldn't have given HBO the time of day. To his credit, he let me carry the ball (which became quite heavy with time) and I did. The cost was enormous.

From David's point of view, he always wanted to know, "What is it going to buy me?" "Will an association with HBO cost me too much? In time? In energy? In sales?" While I was spending all that time on the road, presenting to potential HBO financial systems customers, I could have been in the office making calls, which was a *proven* way to make money. I was taking a risk. I figured if a big firm like HBO wanted little ole me, then I would give them everything I had, to *prove* to them that I had the best quality management system around. What I didn't know was that HBO's sales cycle for their large in-house system was quite different from CBR's. CBR's sales could be consummated and installed in a day if need be, for $12,000 per module. An HBO system sale could take many years and end up costing a hospital in the millions of dollars.

David could see a cash flow problem brewing. If HBO only made three such sales a year, then CBR would stand to only make 12,000 x 9 (3 packages each hospital) or $108,000. For me to sell 24 packages by phone would cost us nothing. To sell with HBO cost us all my expenses plus time that I could have been selling. With an HBO sale, we didn't know when we'd get paid. With a CBR sale, it was cash up front, so we always knew where we stood. As long as I kept my quota of three sales per month up, we did fine. In other words, we could not put all our eggs in HBO's basket. I made sure that when I was traveling, I continued selling through phone calls.

During one trip to my hometown in Florida, while I was visiting with my niece and her husband, it occurred to me that she would be a perfect software trainer. Karen is a 5' blond bombshell, who can think and chew at the same time. I thought she would be great at training our clients. I convinced her to come up and give it a try. I knew that she either would or would not get into computers. She was my vision of the perfect trainer—patient, kind, encouraging, clear and willing to help. Luckily, she had enough sense to check out her interest before going to Durham and she decided, quite rightly, that she was a people person, but not a computer person.

Back from eight days in Florida. Lisa joined me for three days, and we had no sun for three days. Not good. She was pissed, and I couldn't relax so I got sick. Ugh. David went through my house and said I should fix it up, and then sell it in two years. We hope to pay it off this year.

David's comment about the house turned out to be a real laugh. I had never thought to own a home, and now it had never occurred to me to fix it up more than we had—some new wood, wallpaper, and some paint. David planted a seed in my mind, and I grew it... big. The house was soon to become an obsession to me. What David didn't understand when he bought my first home, was that the house immediately became something for me to focus on and take care of. It needed me. The challenge of making the house look good again distracted me from sales. It was more fun to decide how to design the kitchen than to make 100 calls on any day. *Anything* was more fun than making 100 calls a day.

$90,000 in money market and $17,000 in cash! Wow! And that's not even counting the $96,000 from HBO. Then why am I sick? And muscle spasms? House lovely. Randy terrific. Life good. I ask too many questions. Just be, Cleo.

There is truth in the saying, "Money isn't everything." In fact, I was wondering if it was doing me any good. Or, was trying to make it costing *me* too much? My personal life was minimal. I would leave on Monday and often not get home for a week or so. I was very good at stringing my trips together so I could get the most out of an airplane ticket and hotel. In retrospect, I think I was a little in awe of the act of traveling. I thought the more I did it, the more I could accomplish. I came to learn the opposite is the truth.

When the dust settled, I decided to "fix it up" as David had said. He wasn't around much, and I didn't think I needed him to help me make decisions about my house. After many negotiations, I finally contracted with Tom O'Dwyer, an upfront, honest-to-the-bone builder. It was exciting to start making plans. We were adding 400 square feet to the house and opening it up to the great outdoors. My absorption in the house came with a high price.

Sales way off, went to Des Moines and it was a waste of time. Got very depressed. Off to Washington for conference. House in process of being repaired. Glad we're under way. Money such an issue. Sent Hazel $300 so she could catch up.

I worried about money even as I made commitments to spend even more!

Architect coming today to advise me on house addition. Very exciting. Have to make a lot of sales so I can do it! Jeff and Jay for dinner. They are my good friends. I'm putting $300 in on a motorcycle with Jay! We will ride again this summer.

Throat still hurts. I have something "caught in my throat."

I think the phrase my throat would not express was, "Focus, Cleo. Focus on sales."

David was constantly routing self-help books to me, and they gave me a lot of insight. There was no *one* right answer, but each added to my understanding of me. Weight was my constant concern, but it just kept on creeping up slowly. Even today I believe I did it to keep me from being too feminine…removing feminine traits while doing business with men seemed essential. A choice, I think, to succeed in business. Obviously, I didn't think I could succeed in both *at the same time.*

David had opened my head to the idea of renovating the house through his casual remark about fixing it up. And oh, what a wonderful, expensive project I made out of it! It gave me focus, made me feel needed. When I returned to an empty house after a long trip, seeing the changes kept my mind content. Otherwise coming home to an empty house didn't feel any better at 50 than it had at 10. That was the other benefit of the renovations—there were always workmen around to talk with and make me feel like I had "family," even if a paid one. The fact was I did hire people to be around. Steve did carpentry, sheet rocking, spackling, yard maintenance, general repairs and anything else I needed. I hired him to help me, and he turned into a good and loyal friend. We both benefited from our association.

I bribed some friends with gifts from my travels. They would come to meet me on the nights I got home, and I would have fun distributing gifts, sometimes large, usually small. It never bothered me to hire people or bribe them, because my focus was on selling, and I'd do *anything* to keep me stable enough to continue to sell. It was not easy.

It was Jay who had introduced me to Tom who was a Chapel Hill builder of some reputation for doing daring, well-built designs for people. At the time I contracted him, he was light on work, so he decided to do the renovations I wanted. He thought he'd be in and out before he needed his men on another job. Boy, was he wrong on that one.

Tom came up with a design that corrected everything I didn't like about the house (too boxed, too small, no open spaces), and the price was good. He said he would calculate time and materials, and then let me know when he could begin. I was anxious to begin the project both because it distracted me from feeling alone and lonely, and because when I was in town, I could do something other than work. I knew I was working too hard.

When Jay suggested we buy a motorcycle together, I jumped at the chance. I had owned a Honda 350 dirt bike, which I had bought from Randy back in the '70s. Since then, I had ridden a lot of motorcycles, but never a street bike. Jay had taken me for many rides the summer before, and I knew I could trust him. In fact, it always felt as though we were one, when we'd go through the countryside in the evening, listening to birds when we stopped and admiring the farms and woods as we rode. Jay was an important friend I did not have to buy. He was in the throes of a divorce, had two small children he adored, and needed a friend like me, just as I needed him. Jeff was now out of my life completely, so Jay filled in, thankfully, just as a friend. No messiness.

During one of our monthly business review meetings, David brought up the subject of the money I still owed: the North Carolina State loan, the Small Business Administration loan, the Mitch Leon loan, the bank loan co-signed by the Hospital Association, and the money I owed to the North Carolina Hospital Association on sales we made through them. He had a plan to pay them all off by the end of the year. How he could do that was way beyond me, but it was clear that he could only do so if I sold the 40 packages we had targeted. He seemed confident, which helped, but inside I felt very scared. That night I drew up my first real "plan" for making sales the following week.

On April 29th, Hazel, my friend and listening board, had a heart attack. I was shocked, scared and frantic, but after a phone call and assurances from her son she was doing okay, I could do little else. I was at a workshop in Ocean City and wanted to finish as a team member. Besides, there was nothing to do for Hazel at this point.

The incident, however, brought back memories of when my mother died when I was living in Cleveland. She died 17 days after my third child, Randy, was born, and I had a urinary infection, so I truly could not go to her funeral. Besides, three children under three kept me pretty busy, and there was no way I could take them with me. So I had lots of excuses, but I never forgave myself for not being there in the end, when she really needed me. I vowed I would be there for Hazel, and I prayed her time was not now.

Missing my mom's funeral has *always* been a regret of mine. Since she died, I have learned what an important part of the grieving process the funeral is. I don't care if it's formal or at the beach; being part of a ceremony, crying together, sharing one's grief, helps one let go of the loved one. I never did that with my mom nor my dad, who was dead and buried before I knew anything about it. Now with Hazel, I also think I made excuses and stayed away because I didn't want the thought that she could die to come into my consciousness.

David had done some hard negotiating with HBO, through me. What he wanted was cash. So he offered them a deal they couldn't refuse. If they'd make an upfront payment of $96,000, we'd give them 20 percent of each $12,000 sale. After 40 sales, they would give us another lump sum. His reasoning was that he didn't want to wait for commissions, and we needed cash now. His strategy worked.

HBO contract signed, $96,000 check cashed; now we'll see where that takes us.

David was very happy to get the large check, and we deposited it immediately. The money bought HBO the right to get interfaces developed by CBR to their databases on their mainframe. The interface would avoid having the hospital staff enter the patient data twice. Randy did a great job in this project, and HBO was most happy. Now, when a patient was admitted at one of their facilities that had CBR quality management software, every incident regarding that patient could be collected, tracked, reported on, and analyzed to avoid future errors. A win-win for everyone.

For me, the check represented my first really solid, large sales call that I made on my own, and I closed on my own (with David's coaching, of course). But it wasn't the only sales accomplishment I needed for the year. By the end of April, I had brought in 17 sales, with an overall goal for the year of 40. I knew I had to keep the steam on, or I would never make it.

While I was busy selling, Randy was busy with the software. The software he wrote his code in had come out with a new version, and all our software had to be updated. His major commitment was to rewrite all the code in each of our three modules in the new version of our development software, *and* to make each of them multi-user, so more than one person could be in the system at one time. These tasks were not easy, by any means.

In the midst of all the pressure on him to get the new versions out, his new 486 PC shorted out the motherboard twice due to the lack of a 5-cent spacer. He also lost a hard drive, video card, network card, parallel/serial card, and a modem. To say that he was "smoking" the machines was an understatement. It got so that the rest of us walked in quietly each morning, and waited to hear if Randy's voice was calm or upset. After a few days, however, things settled down, and he was soon clicking away as usual. We all gained a new respect for his talent and patience.

Early in May, I began to worry about sales again. The work on the house was moving along, but my calls had suffered. By the end of the month I had only one sale, and that gave me the kick in the butt I needed.

At our weekly meeting, David told me that he had decided to pay off my house mortgage. His feeling was that as long as I owed the bank five cents, they could take it away from me.

Today I sent a check for $46,950.40 to First Federal and bought my home at 1110 Alabama. One year and one week after closing on it, just as David had promised. Not bad. Jay took me for motorcycle ride, and then Steve and Diane came over to celebrate. I always enjoy company, and I always enjoy the quiet. Buying the house was David's idea. Paying it off was David's idea. Bright man. Hazel still in hospital—heart not good—but she's doing fairly well. We talk often.

By mid-May, HBO's sales efforts were generating a lot of calls, and each caller wanted information on all three modules. David decided we needed another trainer, so I recommended he hire Brenda Cook. Brenda was from the VA Hospital in Durham, where I first met her. I had talked to her several times and was very impressed with her grasp of credentialing physicians, and financial and marketing theories. Julie, who we had hired to replace Jenny, was new at CBR and very good at the training, but with so many new hospitals coming onboard, David wanted two trainers overlapping each other. He constantly stressed the importance of cross training in a small business. Brenda bit the bullet, quit the VA, and came to work for us. She never looked back.

For every call I got from an HBO hospital, I followed up in the same way I did with any sale: I talked to the administrator, medical staff coordinator, quality assurance coordinator, risk manager, and medical staff director as well as the head of nursing, if she had an interest. Each would get to know my name both through the phone calls and through the mailings. They would each get three letters from CBR spaced over several weeks. Each letter addressed a different aspect of the software that the individual may not have been aware of.

We could have made this an automatic function, but I decided to take on the responsibility of writing the first letter to each contact at each hospital. I had a standard letter that I would edit for a particular person, adding in personal comments and information to help them identify with us. On any given day, I might send out ten to fifty of these letters, and it was Elisa, our new secretary, who saw to it that they went out on the right dates. Eventually she took over the whole process, after I had made the initial calls, and this helped me a tremendous amount. David's emphasis on cross training, and having everyone pitch in where they were needed, was working well.

As the HBO project evolved, it turned into a mess. They wanted me at every sales presentation, even though no one cared one iota what I had to say. If management decided they wanted HBO, then it was a no-brainer that their quality management people would buy CBR. To add to the confusion, we had trained HBO sales staff in how our software worked, but they could only do a very superficial presentation—quality management was a complicated subject. Because they couldn't really answer questions fully, I was being asked to follow up on their calls, which really added to my load. I began to see that working with a large corporation cost a small business a lot—something David already knew, of course.

I finished May with only one sale and panicked. I cancelled all travel for a few weeks, and started frantically making phone calls.

Early in June, we heard that <u>INC Magazine</u> had chosen me for Entrepreneur of the Year from North Carolina for Women-Owned businesses. I was happy to get the recognition. I had worked hard for CED, but they never pointed to our success and said "good job," so I was happy <u>INC</u> did.

The big celebration was in Charleston, North Carolina. Randy and I got all dressed up for a black tie dinner and drove to Charleston for the banquet. I was thrilled, not only because I had won, but because I hoped my son would see the recognition others were giving me and give me some credit himself. At this time in our lives, we were having a hard time. He had come to think that his programming was all that mattered, and that without him, CBR was nothing. He seldom had anything good to say about the sales, all my travel, or early mornings writing tons of letters.

This began a period when we worked together, but I had to swallow my pride, time and time again, because of something he would say. Perhaps I should not have tolerated his attitude, but I, too, thought CBR would die without him, so I swallowed hard and kept on "truckin." For his part, he was working as hard as anyone could work. He didn't know product is not important if there are no sales.

A good deal of my time during June and July went into the yard of my house. Steve was laying slate for the front walk and the whole back patio, so I helped him out a lot. It was more rewarding than calls, although I was happy to see five sales in June. By July I was feeling tired again and ended up with only two sales.

I decided to go visit Hazel in Princeton. I missed her, and I hadn't seen her since her heart attack. I made my plans and went. Princeton had been my home for twenty years—I had raised and educated my children in Princeton, and I had gotten divorced, married and divorced there. I had started my business there. I had lots of memories.

Wonderful trip to Princeton. Flew into Philly, rented a car and drove to Peacock Inn in Princeton, New Jersey. Put things away and walked around the town. Not so many changes. Ate on campus in front of Nassau Hall. Lots of memories. Some good times. Good place. So much bigger than Durham. I love Durham more all the time.

Went in afternoon to visit Hazel. She looks like she never had a heart attack. We had fun. I talked to Bobby, her nephew, who has taken care of her, so she could stay home. Cooked scallops and asparagus and taught Bobby a lot about cooking for Hazel, using the microwave.

That evening, walked around town. Bill the bartender still at the Annex Bar and Restaurant, an old Princeton tradition, and he remembered my name. Went shopping and bought Hazel a $500 recliner for $300! She's been sitting in an old broken chair too long. Got hibiscus and tomatoes planted in her small, front yard, and recorded more of her life on tape.

By the time I got back to Durham, I was stressed. My weight was shooting up, and I didn't seem to be able to stop it. All the good I had done was gone. David sent me to see my therapist again, and he helped me see that when I'm thin, I feel very vulnerable to men, seductive, too; so I feel safer fat. How awful. Knowing I didn't have to be vulnerable anymore didn't solve anything.

David had felt for some time that we didn't have enough expertise in quality assurance, so in July he began a search for a certified quality assurance coordinator.

> *Woke up fretting over losing Miami Baptist Hospital sale to Healthline. Then went on to think about new person we're thinking of hiring. JoAnn is an R.N., who knows computers, credentialing, quality assurance, risk management—she appears to be the person we need in our business right now. Flying her out here from Rockford, Illinois, next week. Got up and did the first organizational chart for CBR that makes sense. We are each going to have a lot to do—and we can.*
>
> *I am very happy—been making sales calls from home, and that works well. Also just plain feeling good. Sent out 818 announcements and thank you notes about <u>INC</u> award, and people have been very happy and supportive.*

JoAnn was one of many people we interviewed over eight months. What we wanted was not an easy position to fill, because QA is such a specialty area. David had also decided that I would be less disruptive to the office staff if I made calls from home, which worked for me. I had been getting more and more depressed because I wasn't making any sales and August wasn't too good either; three sales. What I actually started to do was go out to Jay's new house in the woods, and make calls. Not only did I get my calls done, but also I managed to stretch and rest a little.

One day when I was in the office, I had a call from a man named Harry. Harry had heard about our software when he was out selling a competitor's software. He had an interest in selling for CBR, and he couldn't have said anything better. David was supportive, but warned me that salesmen cost money, big money, and we would be splitting our income with him. I didn't care. I was tired of selling, and having someone to work with was all I wanted. Actually my dream was that he could take over sales and leave me to start some new software development.

David was still trying to get me to be less disruptive. I was always trying to get Randy to add something to the programs, take care of one more request, or add one more report. It's known in the business world that people who start businesses are often not the ones who can run them, once they start to grow. Entrepreneurs just don't have the management skills—we're inventors, and getting us to change our style usually fails.

The frustrating thing was that I *was* making my calls, and I believed the sales would come. David and I had gone over my presentation carefully. A new overhead image projector was now available from Sirtage, and that would give me the ability to put up quality slides and to show our software in living color. We spent the $5000, and I spent a good deal of time learning how to use it effectively. Now with the prospect of selling with Harry, I was even more excited about the overhead projector.

On September 22nd I turned 53, and I celebrated by throwing a party at a friend's gazebo in the woods outside of town. It was great. I hired a man I'd seen playing guitar outside a bar one night. He and his girlfriend sang songs together. Everyone enjoyed themselves. Even Randy came, which pleased me a great deal. He gave me a lovely Chinese vase on a wooden stand. The food was outstanding with shrimp gumbo and other goodies, including steaks prepared on the barbeque grills my friend had set up in the woods. I felt great, so I guessed that's what 53 was like, feeling great!

At the end of September, I received a request from Jay. His wife was trying to get the court to take Jay's right to visit his children away from him, and using me as the reason. She felt that Jay and I were having an affair, because I had given him an old car I didn't want and we had dinner together a lot. It sounded too silly to be true, but when I rushed to the court straight from a plane trip, sure enough, there was his wife telling the Judge how Jay's relationship with me was the reason she wanted a divorce. I almost couldn't wait for my turn to speak.

When the female Judge called me, the first question Jay's lawyer asked me was what my profession was. I took less than 20 seconds to say software development, sales, hospitals and quality management. I then had to tell about Jay and our relationship, which was easy. I told about our friendship—how he helped me when I was down, and I helped him when he was down. But I very calmly and emphatically added, "Any thought that Jay and I are having an affair is silly. I gave him the car because I didn't need it and he did. It was worth about $200. If anyone wants to ask our friends, they will tell the court that Jay and I are just friends, and nothing more."

The Judge asked me a few professional questions about my travel schedule, how I felt about Jay's wife, and then asked why I didn't invite both of them to my house for dinner. I told her, "She has been to my house, but she gossips and I simply have nothing in common to talk with her about." I was dismissed, and Jay was allowed to continue to see his children while the divorce was being settled. Our friendship grew even tighter.

My last trip of the month in September was to Chicago for an HBO demonstration. I visited with my friend, Bill, who had left the North Carolina Hospital Association and was now working with JCAHO (Joint Commission on the Accreditation of Hospitals). He was sure we would succeed wonderfully, and I hoped he was right.

As it turned out, again, the hospitals I presented to were just looking at other systems because they had to, but their minds were already made up to buy a competitor's product. It was frustrating to have to go through another meaningless presentation with no one listening. HBO didn't know how to qualify either, particularly for CBR.

An upside to this visit, however, was that I stayed at the Knickerbocker Hotel in downtown Chicago. It was a lovely, gracious place to stay. Jay had a woman friend he'd known for years, so I looked her up and she took me out on the town. What a time we had. She knew everyone, so we danced, drank and laughed till my sides were sore. It was a much-needed break.

Flew to South Carolina and met with Kelly from HBO. In a.m., did 2½-hour quality management presentation and was very well received. The $5,000 image projector was worth every penny. When I got back to Durham, I went to dinner with Jack and Pete —we had a great night talking business.

Jack and Peter continued to be my good friends. For reasons I never understood, none of my friends seemed to warm up to David. As I watched, I saw it was because David kept a very narrow focus on goals and worked to reach them, while most people wanted to think bigger.

Jay and I went to see Sting in concert. I had thought I was going to a play called "The Sting!" When I learned it was a band, I realized how out of it I am. Ruth here to see about selling for us. I like her a lot. Signed HBO agreement for them to add Quality Assurance and Risk Management to what we sell to their hospitals! No sales, and they are coming!

October started out with a lot of traveling. I flew to Washington, D.C. to meet with Harry and do a presentation together, which went fairly well. He was trying to learn what our software did, but as most new salespeople do, he tried to redesign the software so there would be no question that it did *everything* the client wanted. Even though I didn't have real good vibes about Harry's sales ability, I kept hoping he could work out. I needed the help.

I then flew to Boston for an HBO presentation, which went well, but again the people listening simply had no interest. I was beginning to fear that all the money we were spending on trips was a waste. My final leg of the trip was to San Diego, where I presented at a large conference on health care. Over twenty presenters were all "on" at the same time, so the eight people who came to see me was a pretty good turn out. In the sense of "was it worth it?" the answer was clearly no. I still was not qualifying clients well enough, and with the HBO contract, it was almost impossible to do.

When I came back, I was exhausted and David could see it on my face. He suggested that I take up scuba diving. As was his usual style, he had started with a friend, gotten good at it, and was now a certified instructor taking people out on trips. He offered to train me, and I accepted. I loved being taught by David because he always took his time and let me learn at my own pace.

The first time we got in his pool, David took a good deal of time to teach me how to clear the mask underwater. The next session, he told me he was going to pull my mask off, I was to retrieve it, and put it back on and clear it, all while still under the water. Within minutes we were in the water, I felt my mask leave my face, I saw it and got it quickly, but I could not clear it! In a moment of panic, I went to the top of the water, got my breath, and then held onto the side of the pool, while I recovered.

David came up, waited until I was breathing normally again, and then said, "You get to do that one time. You just did. If you do that again, I will fail you."

He wasn't kidding. I didn't do it again, and eventually I got certified. What patience the man had with me.

On October 11th, my new neighbor across the street, Sara, brought her mother, Anna, over to meet me. They were from Sweden and we had a wonderful time! What a literate, interesting woman! Sara and I had become friends over the months since she and her husband, Stefan, had moved into the little house that looked directly at my house. They were both graduate students at Duke, so they were very interesting. Meeting her mom would turn out to be a very important event in my life.

Hazel is 83 today. They took her toe off because of her diabetes, but she is feeling better than she has in months. Great day yesterday. Worked with my therapist on my feeling of disappointment when I was a kid and there was no food in the refrigerator. God wanted me to know how it feels to be hungry, lonely and scared. My path will allow me to see that in others, and give them comfort.

Came home and got Boude then went back to work till 10:30 p.m. and really got caught up. Went to visit Black feather, a Native American Indian. I bought a wonderful deer skull, throwing arrows and dream catchers as Christmas presents.

Hazel's toe had given her a fit for years, so losing it was actually a good thing. She continued to be a constant source of comfort to me, particularly as I traveled. I knew I could call her at any time, and I did. She never failed to lift my spirits.

The Texas Hospital Association and I planned a big trip in order to get the word out to more hospitals. I went to Dallas and presented to 40 hospitals there, and the response was very encouraging. I stayed at one of the oldest hotels in Dallas, the name of which escapes me, but I remember that it was elegant and beautiful. My bed was big and comfortable, with three pillows made of down. One of the pillows I particularly loved, and at the end of my visit, I called the Hotel Manager and asked if I could buy the pillow. He asked me to hold on, and then came back to the phone and said, "I'm sorry Mrs. Robertson, but we don't have any pillows left to sell."

I said, "You don't understand. There is *one pillow in particular* that I want to buy, because it is perfect for me."

He was quiet a second, then he said, "Well, we can't sell you a used one, but I can *give* it to you, so please accept the pillow as our gift."

I did and I still have it, and I still love it. As the saying goes, "Ask and ye shall receive."

October ended with five sales, which gave me breathing space again. David and I had spent a lot of time in October talking about growth (to grow or not to grow), and he agreed I could look for more help. Harry, Ruth, and others, were tried, but I learned something about sales people. If they couldn't sell the product, they wanted to *change* the product. It was assumed that it was the product that was failing, not them. I got back on my calling schedule, but kept trying to get the others to sell, too. The HBO project was going very slowly.

By November, I was just barely keeping up. I booked a trip to Des Moines, Iowa, to present to a group of hospitals that wanted to share their credentialing process among three hospitals. We didn't feel that hospitals could share the process, because each had its own requirements, timing pressures and needs, but they seemed determined to try it in order to lower costs. I went away feeling discouraged.

Every time I spoke to someone about centralized credentialing, I could see in my mind's eye the changes and enhancements such a system would need. The cost of building a centralized credentialing system was not worth what we'd get as a return—sales would be difficult because no one thought it would work, outside of administration. The reasons were simple. Hospitals are each personally accountable for every health care worker under their roof. For every physician, nurse, technician, etc., they employ, they must verify that all of them really went to school where they said they did, interned and did residency as they said they did, and so forth. In a centralized system, Hospital A might want someone credentialed immediately, because they needed the person on staff, and the central credentialer may be backlogged. The general consensus I heard was that the hospitals would rather do it themselves, manually.

My next trip took me to Pittsburgh, then on to Dallas, Austin and San Antonio. I gave my presentations, they listened, but there was little interest in buying. Even the Hospital Association people were surprised at the apathy among hospitals to ensure the quality of care they deliver to the public.

San Antonio was a great place to visit...for two days. After that, the smell of the fumes from boats on the River Walk really got to me, and sitting by the water to eat was impossible. On a whim, I decided to drive to Corpus Christi to check it out. On the outskirts of town, a gas station attendant suggested I drive out to Padre Island for some fun, and I did.

As I drove out a desolate road to the island, I suddenly saw a bar stuck back off the road, surrounded by shrubbery. I stopped and played some pool and asked where I might find some dinner. A woman suggested Port Aransas. As I arrived in this laid-back town, the smell of barbecue grilling beckoned. I was directed to a nearby shack with the instruction, "Go see Yankee."

WHIM OF IRON

I approached the shack and knocked on the window. As it slid open, a large head covered with white, wild hair peered down at me, and a very gruff voice said, "What do you want?"

I said back, just as gruffly, "I want a barbecue sandwich."

He paused a moment, then smiled and said, "Well, come back in an hour and you can have one."

I went over to a bar, had a beer, and watched boats. After an hour, I started walking back. When I got close to the shack, the side door to the shack flew open and a Chinese man said to me, "Yankee says you're to come in."

The shack was just that—a small room, 15 by 20' at the most, with a large table dominating the center of the room. Around that table, Yankee was busy cutting beef, arranging the table, checking on the potatoes—he obviously knew what he was doing and seemed to be enjoying himself. The Chinese man introduced himself and a black man, who was sitting on top of a large cooler. The black man asked me what I wanted to drink.

I ordered a vodka and orange juice and was soon treated to the crazy stories from all three of these men. Within a short time Yankee said, "Okay, come eat." There, on one end of the long table was a place setting for one. I sat down, and Yankee put a raw onion in one of my hands, a pickle in the other, and a large slab of the best smelling barbecue I had ever had the pleasure of experiencing, right on the table in front of me, on brown butcher paper. I dug in. One bite of onion, one bite of beef, one bite of pickle and... munch. Oh my, it was good. All in all, I spent four hours, most of them laughing, with these good people, and had a most memorable day. When it started to get late, I asked them what I owed. They said $5.

I was shocked and said, "But what about the drinks?"

"Oh," they said, "we can't charge you for the drinks...we don't have a liquor license."

I immediately understood the situation, gave the two men a $20 tip, and thanked them profusely. I had experienced another wonderful day of Texas hospitality.

One day when I was overwhelmed with travel, I asked Brenda if she would take some hospital people over to Duke to see the software work. Brenda gave the appearance of a Southern Belle but underneath, she was tough as nails. She had told David she wanted to try her hand at sales, so I figured this would give her some experience. I heard later that she did a great job and obviously enjoyed herself. I didn't know it then, but it was the beginning of the end for me.

After one very long trip, I returned to the office to find everyone very busy getting ready for our client's conference. Funny skits were planned so they would laugh. Workshops were designed to answer all their questions and show new things they could do that they didn't know about. All in all, 77 coordinators flew in from all over the US, and it was a great success. Brenda turned out to be quite the organizer and was beginning to show her managerial skills as well. She could not have thrilled me more.

Right after the conference, we interviewed Kathy, who was a coordinator at a nearby hospital. Randy loved her; Brenda, too. And I could see she was very well qualified, so we offered her a position, which she accepted. That felt like a big load off my mind in terms of work, but of course, there was more pressure to make payroll.

Thanksgiving came, and we celebrated royally at my house. Plants had been put in, the yard was cleaned up, and the inside was clean and ready. Lisa, Andy, Andy's brother Joel and my first husband, Carl, came into Durham, and we celebrated together. Between being very tired and hurting in my bones and hips a lot, I was barely there. My mind was also on sales. We closed November with five, which left me still two short of my goal of 40 for the year.

By December, I realized that if I stayed on the phone, I could sell. David's reservations about working with HBO had come true—sales were slow, required a lot from us, and it would not get any easier with time.

My body is 195#'s and I'm working on an exercise program. Have tendonitis of the heels, but getting better. Stretch program working— would be even better if I wasn't so tired.

Cleo B. Robertson

The weight was adding to my tiredness, yet when I traveled it was food that gave me comfort. The tendonitis came from a one-mile walk down and up a mountain I had made earlier in the year, in moccasins. The pain improved with stretching, but often I fell into bed, too tired to stretch. I was on a downward spiral.

Mid-December I went on some sales calls in the Boston area, with Harry. Watching him do a presentation was painful. He was hesitant, awkward about the nomenclature, and unsure of the product. I flew home with little hope he could make any sales. We were paying him advances on future sales and spending lots of energy training him, but it just wasn't going to work.

By the time the CBR staff convened at the exclusive University Tower between Chapel Hill and Durham for a grand dinner and Christmas celebration, I had brought in six sales for the month! That gave me a total of 44 and meant that we could reach all our goals.

After some tough negotiations, David paid off the State TDA loan that was at 50 percent yearly interest. We finally settled for $83,000 on a two-year $50,000 loan.

Next, he called SBA and got a payoff amount, which he sent immediately. And as if that wasn't enough, he also paid the North Carolina Hospital Association what we owed them for sales and the loan from the bank they had co-signed. Everyone was happy. Actually, I was dazed by all our successes.

WHIM OF IRON

In the beginning of the year, David had told me to focus on sales. I did. He focused on everything else, and it had worked. We ended the year debt free and with $40,000 safely tucked away in investments. We ended up with $160,000 in sales per employee, up from $105,000 in 1990. I had sold $540,000 worth of software during the year, which was mind-blowing to me. I kept saying to myself, "Over half a million dollars worth!" again and again.

David and I went off for a day to talk about the year and how to distribute the extra money. As was his custom, he designed the day, but only told me what to wear—shorts for the woods, slacks for the plane, dress for a resort, etc. He knew I was overwhelmed with selling, selling, selling. He knew he was asking a lot of me, and we both knew I was doing my best, so we were both happy with where we were. He never failed to try to give me a treat to show how much he appreciated my efforts.

On this particular day, we started with breakfast at the Washington-Duke Inn, the on-campus, up-scale dining facility on Duke University's campus in Durham. We had a particular window he had picked out on our first of many visits over the years, so he had us seated there again. He ordered for me—poached eggs with spinach, English muffin without butter, and decaf coffee. He knew what I liked; I was glad not to have to look at a menu. All I had to do was sit back and look out at the lovely golf course.

"We've come a long way," I heard him saying.

Cleo B. Robertson

I looked at him. David has a very strong, clear, open face with eyes that convey more than his words. He had grown up on a farm outside Little Rock, Arkansas, with his mother, father and two brothers. He didn't talk about family much, and I just came to assume that he would like to keep it that way. He hadn't gone to college because he didn't want to. Instead, he went to work for NCR and eventually attained the position of North East marketing and sales manager. At some point he struck out on his own. After a stab at the restaurant business, he finally settled on turnaround management, which he had learned on-the-job as he had worked through the years.

His philosophy was simple:

- Make more than you spend.
- Never, ever have any debt.
- Focus on quality and client services.
- Stay focused.
- Use your business plan.
- When you need more people, have current employees make a list of their responsibilities, and cut it in half (it always works).
- If you need more space, throw out half of what you have (this works too).
- Don't get greedy.
- Honor God.
- Honor yourself.

- Share what you have, but not all of it.
- Smile and have fun.

Now, as I heard him saying how well we had done, I turned to him and said, "Yes, David, we have. And I have you to thank for that."

He smiled his special smile that says, "aw shucks," and said, "Yes, and I have *you* to thank."

We laughed, toasted each other with our orange juice, and sat quietly for a few minutes.

When he spoke, I recognized his mode—all business with important decisions that needed to be made. He said in one sentence, "I want to review with you what we accomplished in 1991, what our plans are for 1992, how I think we should distribute our profits from the year, what I think our strengths and weaknesses are, and what we should do about them."

He shuffled through some papers, and then continued. "We have $160,000+ left over after all the bills and debts have been paid, the taxes are deposited, and we owe no money to anyone." He paused to let me digest his words.

It took me awhile to respond. $160K *left over!* That was *after* I had been fully paid in commissions and all our debts were paid. I finally said, "That's a lot of money, David. Tell me what you think we should do with it."

He smiled and said, "Okay, but let me review first." He proceeded to go over the highlights of the year—HBO contract, salespeople, 44 sales, paid off all debts, paid off my house, Brenda Cook and Kathy Howard joined us, updating of all software...in short, a lot of accomplishments.

"For 1992, I think we can stay comfortable with 40 sales as the goal again," he said with a smile at me. I could see he was enjoying himself because we had all come so far.

He continued, "I want us to focus on bug-free software and updated training manuals, and to continue a high level of client contact and support."

Each time he paused, I took a deep breath.

"With 145 clients, each paying $1,500 per year for support and enhancements, we're guaranteed a little over $200,000 from that source of income alone. Our operating expenses are about $250,000, so if we just make 4 sales, we're even. Of course, we want to be more than even, which is why we're going to set the goal for 40 new clients."

He stopped and waited for my reply. My mind was overwhelmed. I had never had a conversation of this type before in my life. Yes, 1989 and 1990 were big years, but we had debt, lots of it, I didn't own a home, and I wasn't making the kind of money I was now. I wondered for a moment about a God so generous to me that He would send a David. I was blessed.

WHIM OF IRON

I smiled directly at him and said, "David, you've done a terrific job, training each of us to do what we do best. I think we should give everyone a big bonus. Let's not go by any 'rules,' but give what we feel each person deserves."

David's smile told me he agreed. "First, I'm putting a chunk into investments for your retirement. That's our first goal we have to achieve. I estimate that we'll need $1 million in investments in order for you to live off the principal." He waited as I assimilated what he had just said and reminded myself that he was talking about *my* investments. $1 million. Me. Cleo. WOW!

He continued, "Then I suggest we give bonuses to each employee—Randy $10,000, Elisa and Kathy $1,000, and Brenda $2,000."

My mind went back to my days of secretarial work at the hospital consulting firm, and how my confidence and loyalty went up each year when they gave me $2,000 and $3,000 bonuses.

I said firmly, "I agree with Randy's, but I think Elisa and Kathy should get $1,500 each, and Brenda, $3,000."

Immediately, he said, "Done." He then added, "I am recommending I get a $5,000 bonus."

We had been down this path the year before. David never asked enough for himself. At this time, his salary was $40,000, just like mine, but he never submitted his expenses for all the times we used the plane, or all the breakfasts and lunches he bought me.

"No, David, double it," I said, happy to have the power to make such a decision.

"Thank you. It is much appreciated," was all he said on that subject.

He added in summary, "The rest goes to you. $35,000 has to go into a savings account, and $10,000 you can do with as you want."

I was delighted, for many reasons. I needed to give Tom $7,000 in two weeks to begin remodeling my house. I was also delighted that for the first time in my life, I would have money in a savings account.

I said with joy in my voice, "Well, I couldn't be happier. But David, even $50,000 for the year is very little for you, and all you are doing. Are you sure you don't want more?"

David smiled and said, "No, I'm doing okay. I'll get mine when all your retirement has been funded, we are still debt free, and the company has enough in the bank to reinvent itself for a year, if the market were to change and we needed a new product."

He had said once that he always planned in three-year clumps. Within that time period, the government could mandate credentialing and do it through their organization. Or the JCAHO could take it over. No matter what happened, he always had investments, which we could use if we needed to, in order to develop a new product or market. That was David, always thinking about the future, about CBR's success, and about my personal comfort.

For the first time in my life, I prepared presents for Christmas without a sick feeling about money. I made picture albums for each of my children, which they thoroughly enjoyed.

My visit to my daughter and son-in-law in Westford, Massachusetts, for Christmas this year was a mixed bag of emotions. On the one hand, I was delighted to be with my whole family. Gary and Randy had flown in, and I was overwhelmed with a sense of belonging, but not for long. Menopause was causing such huge mood swings, even more than the year before, and I often would burst into tears for no reason at all. It never occurred to me that everyone would get mad at me (they didn't know anything about menopause either)! Again, I spent many hours walking in the woods, just crying and crying with no earthly idea why. To my children, I was just being difficult. To me, I was in double pain—crying for no reason, and my family was upset with me. I was glad to fly back home where I could go through my mood swings in private.

Towards the new year I signed a contract with Tom for $40,000 to put a new kitchen and sunroom on the back of my house. Life could not get better, I thought.

But it did. At the end of December, I was awarded the First Flight Award from the North Carolina Technological Development Authority for paying off my loan. For the first time in my professional life, I felt professional. Debts paid, money in the bank, and a business plan that was working.

Our financial report for the year confirmed it. We had sold 44 units and brought in $573,810; up $152,000 from 1990. We now had a total of 145 sites, and our name was becoming well known in the quality management field for health care. I ended the year happy about CBR, but unhappy about my body and personal life. I wouldn't let me have it all!

1992 — More Changes are a 'Comin!

The year started out with a bang. Harry sold credentialing to Baltimore Regional Hospital, and three HBO sales came in within the first few weeks. Even though we wouldn't get our money for a month, we were excited. To add to the excitement, David had found more cash than he had thought we had, so he put $22,000 in a pension fund for me, and $9,000 in Randy's. To me, these were huge signs of success.

David had implemented daily review meetings right from the beginning, but now that we were under pressure, he stepped up their importance. David had designed these meetings to be usually less than half an hour, *every day,* with the entire staff and me. We met every morning at 8 a.m. so we could review what we were supposed to do that day, by what time, and what it would take to reach our goal. If someone needed help, it was at these meetings that others would volunteer to help. Everyone was being cross-trained.

The purpose of these meetings was multi-fold, but a strong focus was to not spend people power on things that didn't matter. Another focus was to see that everyone had the help they needed when they needed it to reach a goal everyone had agreed on.

One morning at a daily review, Elisa reported that a hospital in Austin felt the coordinator needed an extra day of training and wanted to know if we would charge them. Yes, we charged $500 for an extra day of training. We knew, however, from experience, that people just couldn't absorb more than two days of intensive training. Allowing the hospital to spend that kind of money when we knew there would be little return on their investment was not acceptable.

At the morning meeting, everyone immediately wanted to know, "Why does this hospital need an extra day of training?" At these meetings, the question "Why" was continuously being asked. The answer was that they didn't need an extra day. Our two-day training provided everything a person could absorb in such a short time. Another day would be overwhelming. Perhaps in six months or so, additional training would be beneficial to the hospital, but not initially.

Elisa didn't know how to tell them that. We had to teach her. David saw to it she got the training and support she needed, until her confidence was such she could make decisions confidently on her own. Occasionally, all of us used poor judgment or didn't have enough information before we made a decision that might cost CBR time and money. But David had created a culture that said, "That's okay this time. Just learn from what you did." He felt the more freedom we had as members of the CBR team, the more responsible we would be in our decisions. He was so right.

Elisa got the training she needed in managing people, and she became the best front-door-representative of CBR anyone could have ever asked for. Her voice was happy and immediately said, "Don't worry. Someone is here who can fix your problem." I loved hearing her voice every time I called unexpectedly. I was always gratified to hear that she knew what her job was, and of what great value she was to CBR, *because we had told her many times.* The large financial bonuses said thanks, too, particularly to a single mom. When Elisa finally moved on to something else years later, it took quite a few tries before another perfect front door representative of CBR was found. And they did find her.

During another one of these meetings, I learned how much David called a spade a spade. One day at lunch a few weeks prior, I had confidently said that I would get another Texas hospital in by the end of the month. I had already met my monthly goal, so I didn't need the sale in that month, but I was challenging myself. I said I would do it.

At a review meeting, some weeks later, I presented the fact that I had met my goal of three sales for the month.

When I was done, I heard David say quietly, "So you failed."

"Failed?" I asked blankly. I thought I had done pretty well. I had already flown to ten or more cities since the beginning of the year, I had started a group sales initiative that was going very well, and I had tested the last version of our software.

"Yes, you failed," he said to me again.

I waited but he didn't say anything more. I finally realized he was using me as an example, and he was being quiet so everyone could understand that he was going to do with me what he would at times do with them. He wanted them to "see" what a professional interchange looked like.

"David," I said exasperated, "What do you mean, I failed?"

Once I realized this was a lesson for me, but also for the staff, I really got into it. David had never been wrong when he taught us a truism in business. I knew in my heart that whatever I had "failed" at, would soon be clear to me, and I would know how not to fail again.

"Didn't you tell us a week or so ago that you would have another hospital from Texas in by the end of the month?" he asked calmly.

The room was silent. A drama was being enacted, and everyone *wanted* to know how it would turn out.

"Yes," I said straightforwardly.

WHIM OF IRON

"Well, you didn't, that's all. You said you would and you didn't. You failed." The finality in his voice was unsettling. I immediately started feeling like a 3-year old, but then he went on quickly.

"It's okay to fail," he added encouragingly, "but you need to admit that you set a goal and you failed. Only when you admit you failed, will you be open to see how *not* to fail again. If you don't admit you failed, then I can't help you. But if you admit you did, then we will explore why, and we'll design a way to ensure you don't fail again." There was complete silence into which he inserted the comment, "Of course we'll all fail in many *other* ways."

We came out understanding something we hadn't before. It's okay to fail. Just learn from your failure and move on. Try not to fail in that way again. We got it.

David continued the lesson, "What did you do to make sure you got this sale?"

I spent a few minutes reviewing the process I had gone through to get the sale. When I was done, he quickly went for my throat.

"So the administrator said he would send in a check," David asked abruptly. "Did he say when? Did you ask him when you could expect it? Did you get him to make a commitment?"

Everyone's eyes were on me. I kept watching David, unafraid to admit that no, I did not get a commitment. His point was well taken. In fact, he was plain, outright, right. I had done nothing to tie the administrator down as to when we'd get the check.

I said clearly to David, "Yes, you are right, I did fail. I thought it sounded so crass to say, 'Yes, I'm delighted you purchased CBR. Now when will we get our money?' But now I can see that if I don't ask, I won't know."

David was pleased I got it and then proceeded to review my handling of the account. He asked me questions about who had purchasing control over the software, who made the decision to purchase CBR, and who would write the check. Had I called the cashier to see if a check was on the way?

His point was that I had to make sure I marketed to *everyone* and then followed up with everyone, in order to ensure CBR got a check. This example was perfect for the CBR team, because it was clear where I had failed during the sales process. I had been timid and didn't ask when we'd get their check. That oversight could have cost me a sale. Closing the sale meant you knew when you would get your money. I didn't know. I hadn't closed. It all seemed so simple when David explained it to us.

David taught us many principles during these meetings. He was putting together a team, and he wanted us all to understand the rules. It was new for Randy and me to follow rules, but I think it was hardest on Randy. He had worked without rules for quite a few years, and having to follow David's didn't always sit well.

Here are a few of his rules that saved CBR:

- It's important for each member of the team to state goals and discuss problems with the rest of the team in group meetings. We learn from each other.

- Everyone has the right to have their say about anything.

- Focus every day. Focus every hour. Focus every minute. Focus.

- Ask why we are doing something, and question whether it needs to be done or not.

- Offer help where it is needed. Don't wait to be asked.

- Sometimes we give our products away for free, because the public relations payoff is beneficial; but we never give less service, because we gave it away.

- We have to bring in more money than we spend.

- It takes three times for people to hear a company's name before they will think of it on their own.

- We are a team. Pitch in. Everyone.

David said that name recognition was immensely important. He gave the following example:

"What credentialing software are you going to buy?" an administrator is asked unexpectedly at a hospital conference. "CBR," he answers confidently, having read three letters from CBR in the past six weeks, each one of them less than one paragraph. Each one educating him as to why CBR cares about him more than others do.

Focusing on name recognition for CBR was a brilliant strategy David instituted, and it worked flawlessly.

My personal life was about to get very complicated. Tom, my contractor, had drawn up plans and was ready to start on my house. Everything had to be moved into the front half of the house—furniture, everything. I was excited, but what a mess! My furniture consisted of a lot of eclectic pieces of antiques that I had collected over the years. A big, comfortable 1940s overstuffed chair, an ornate dining room hutch, old dining table with six chairs, and many, many other pieces. I made a decision on a whim. Steve helped me pack up every antique I had into a rental truck, and he drove it up to Lisa in Massachusetts. She was so surprised when he knocked on her door. (I had just warned her I was sending a surprise, and to make sure she would be home.) Meanwhile, I too was happy. There was room to move around, I had a bed on the floor, and I was just fine. I'd think about furniture when the house was done.

HBO asked me to fly to Atlanta and do a presentation at their beginning-of-year salesmen's conference, and I agreed, skeptically. We all knew the HBO salesmen didn't want to learn CBR software—they had bigger fish to catch—but I hadn't learned to say "No" yet. It would take a long time before I learned that saying "No" was often the easiest and cleanest way out of something. In hindsight, I think the child in me was so excited to be *asked*, that I *couldn't* say no. Their request for my presence made me feel important.

Because I would be in Atlanta anyway, I set up meetings, without qualifying them fully, with other people involved with hospitals in Atlanta, who had expressed interest in CBR software. The HBO conference went as expected—very little interest, and of course, I didn't make any sales, because neither of the hospitals I visited were serious buyers. Would I never learn? Qualify, qualify, qualify.

Lots going on, and I'm very happy with who I am and what I'm doing. Only body deserts me. Started period again, and all my aching and stiffness right back. Damn.

I was on a roller coaster, both because of sales and menopause. Up one day because someone called and wanted the software; down the next, because no money came in. I had come to think that hot flashes were as close to sexual arousal I would ever get again, so I decided to enjoy them.

One day a University of North Carolina professor called. He taught MBA students and brought in local business people to tell their stories. I agreed to present, because I loved to present, and the students loved the story. There was a little awkwardness over the fact that I didn't have any degrees. I laughed it off and encouraged them to get all they could (even though I didn't personally buy all that degree stuff if you are going to be an entrepreneur). When they asked about Randy's computer background, and I answered he was "self taught," a small murmur could be heard in the room. We were not the kind of business people they were used to listening to, but they were warm to our story.

My car was dying, my house was being torn apart and reborn, sales were slow, and when I almost fell into the street as I got out of my car one night, I knew I was pushing the limit of my energy. Only one check came in for January, and I knew immediately it was because I was spending so much time on the house, car, and my personal life. I needed to refocus. But first I had to get menopause under control.

One day I called a North Carolina herbalist, whom I had known for a few years. He was trained by Native Americans, grew his own medicinal plants, and knew a lot about healing. I told him about my menopause blues and my unwillingness to take estrogen, and asked him if he could help. He asked me a few questions about what I was already taking, how I was feeling and my moods, after which he said he'd get back to me. About a week later a package arrived in the mail, and it had four bottles of tinctures made specifically for me to help with menopause! I started taking the tincture immediately.

Within a week my whole body started to settle down. Fewer hot flashes. Less irritability and crying. I felt I was definitely on the road out of menopause and grateful for the help.

The true saga of my house began in earnest during February. We expected some damage, but nothing like what they found when the workers tore off the back of the house—all rotten wood; not even the weight-bearing beams were solid. In fact, one day an inspector reached his hand into the corner beam of the house and pulled out a handful of dust!

Tom upped the repair costs by $30,000, and David and I decided to go ahead. We were between a rock and a hard place. If we didn't save the house, I couldn't live in it. If we tore it down, we would get about $15,000 for the lot. And if we tore it down and rebuilt, we would be governed by new building codes and the already small house, would have to be four feet narrower. We were both nervous about money, but you also can't stop in the middle of something. We proceeded with trepidation.

David was having me re-negotiate our contract with the Texas Hospital Association because I was doing all the selling, instead of their sales people. We also wanted to lower their commission. I was not very comfortable negotiating, because I always felt I should do more than my fair share. This time however, I could see David was right, and I stuck to my guns. They finally agreed, and that helped us a great deal financially.

On February 27th, Tom lowered the boom on me again, though it was not his fault. Termites had eaten the entire house, and it was clear that the building inspector who passed the house had either never seen the house or lied. Tom's new price for the addition, renovations, repairs to the existing structure (they'd have to lift the house and redo the entire basement), recoating the whole house in stucco, and replacing the front porch, came to $90,000. It was one of those moments when you just want to put your head down on your arms and cry.

Luckily, David rose to the occasion, and coached me on what to do. I was soon talking with the inspector, the termite company, the real estate broker, and finally, a lawyer. Here again, I learned a truth that is hard to swallow. You can sue people all you want, but if they have protected their money or simply don't have any, you end up with legal bills, and that's it. The inspector admitted he didn't inspect the house—the owners were friends of his—and we settled for $12,000. Oh well. There was no point in suing for more. The renovations continued, but we knew it was not a profitable situation.

The Texas Hospital Association asked me to come do some more presentations, so I flew off to Austin and then Ft. Worth. There was lots of interest by the Texas hospitals, but they were so slow in making decisions and/or allocating money. I knew I had to do these trips, but I came to dread them more and more.

After one five-day trip, I came home to find the City Building Inspector wanted to condemn my house. When he looked at it, he said he'd never seen such damage. I got him to agree that I would get a quote on the repairs. Of course I already had it, but I wanted to be further along when he found out we were going to save the old Spanish house.

My involvement with CED was waning. The February meeting was on "Effective Sales Strategies." By now I knew that unless they applied the information directly to hospitals, I didn't know how to use the tools they wanted to give me. That's why David was having success in teaching me sales strategies. He would teach me the psychology behind marketing and selling, buying and not buying, *as it directly related to hospital administrators*. He spent a lot of time teaching me the pressures that are on CEOs and administrators of hospitals.

After he explained the hospital reimbursement system, for instance, I better understood why they couldn't pay their bills. To give you a brief summary, hospitals supply all the people power, tools, equipment, facilities, etc., to run a hospital, and pray that the bills they submit to insurance companies for work they have done get paid. Often they don't. Hospitals can have a difficult time controlling their cash flow.

Only a very few, select times did I agree to install a system at a hospital on payments. Randy came up with a brilliant idea to build a "bug" in the software that would go off ten days after their payment check was due in our office. When the check didn't arrive on time, the notice in the system appeared and told them to call CBR (they could not use the program until they did). They called, they paid, and soon they were running smoothly again. We only did this a few times, but it was very successful.

The North Carolina Hospital Association held its yearly Winter Meeting in the Research Triangle Park, so David and I went for a short time. He was not one to schmooze for very long, so we seldom stayed longer than an hour. We both would eat our fill and would have said hello to those we wanted to acknowledge. David "worked" a group and then left. Often he would then take me some nice place for dinner and talk more business. We never tired of talking business.

After Dallas, I went on to Houston, again on HBO business, but I didn't feel any sales would be forthcoming. I was beginning to panic. I planned a trip to Princeton to distract me.

Went to Princeton, NJ. Met with Hospital Association about sponsoring our software, and I did well, but no cigar. Also presented to Princeton Medical Center. Their system is very internalized, very self-protective. Worried about sales. Worry is what I do most.

The visit was good for me. I spent a lot of time with Hazel. Some Trenton hospitals had said they were interested on the phone, but when I called for an actual appointment, I found out they had no money. I was learning that qualifying a buyer saved me time and energy.

The president of the New Jersey Hospital Association had been one of my bosses when I worked at the health planning company back in the '70s. I had been his secretary. While he was pleasant and listened, he didn't want to hear "manage doctors."

My entry at this time shows how much was going on:

Cash is down to $65,000. David worried; me too, somewhat. I'll get the cash up again. Off to Florida to recharge for two days. Washington conference good. Personally feeling terrific. I think I'm on the tail end of menopause! Yeah!! House being ripped up but feel good. The house and my body, we are a' changing. Jay, Diane, Steve, and Sara—they keep my world sane, while I go on the road. I am blessed with good friends.

It was difficult for David to see us get so close to the edge, financially. I had lived that way most of my life, so I worried, but expected no more. David expected more, and we had some lengthy meetings about motivating me to sell. He knew I was making calls. He also knew I was very involved in my house where workers were taking off walls, jacking up the house and rebuilding the whole thing.

By the end of March we had six sales in…that was not enough to keep us going.

Des Moines was still trying to do a multi-hospital credentialing system, and they were finding out all the reasons why such a system doesn't work. They asked me to meet with them. I did and I let them tell me what they needed, and then I told them why it wouldn't work. They didn't believe me. We decided to build the software interface they wanted, because if it did work, we could have a new market—multi-hospital corporations. It didn't work in the end, for all the reasons we knew it wouldn't.

At the end of March I flew to Washington, D.C. for a health care conference. These visits always meant I could visit with my brother and his wife. They pointed out how tired I looked, and I told them how scared I was, and we all agreed there was nothing to do but go forward.

The Florida Hospital Association asked me to present to their annual meeting, so I flew off to Orlando.

Back from presenting to Florida Hospital Association. Everyone said quality assurance is important, but no one wanted to do anything about it. Home to less than $15,000 in cash! Living on the edge. My fault. Too much travel and not enough phone time. I have no focus, I'm detached from things. Something in me is shut off. I don't care.

Of course it was my tired mind shutting down from all the travel. I finally decided to stay home and make calls, and I did for the next seven days. It helped. Two sales came in within a week, and another towards the end of the month. The fact that I spent many sleepless nights added to my stress. As researchers have since learned, if you are sleep deprived, your body will fall asleep during the day to get the sleep, even when you're driving. I felt like I wanted to lie down and take a nap all the time.

Every morning I woke feeling I was letting the company down. The house was a diversion from my fear of failing at CBR. There were nice people at the house who were always glad to see me, which was not true at work. My inventive spirit was wearing on everyone, so I rationalized that staying home was good for everyone.

Mid-April, I flew to San Antonio to do a presentation to the Texas Branch of the National Association of Medical Staff Services (NAMSS). My subject was how software could move data on patients from the financial billing system, which usually resided on a mainframe (big computer), to our quality management system on a PC. Attendance at the conference was light, and the subject was too heavy. At some point, we finally stopped sending me to these kinds of meetings, because they never produced any sales.

$42,000 and counting. We have 1½ months of cash left. And yet I feel we are on the verge of some great sales. Testing Randy's update to physician privileges. He did a lot as usual. Stopped to see Jane E. She is having a blast learning to polish and grind rocks—mostly opals and turquoises. The back of my house came off today. So much light. It will be worth the wait, the mess and the cost.

While the house was coming along, CBR was not. Sleep eluded me, so I began to take Unisom, which helped if I didn't take a whole pill. I knew I was the only one who could sell, and that I needed to do more, but all the phone calls in the world didn't seem to make a difference.

David says if no sales within 30 days, cut staff. Oh God, help! I'm not going to let that happen. We flew to Pearson Co. in David's plane and sat in lawn chairs and talked about how to rearrange the business so not so bumpy financially. Cutting all expenses. Biggest thing is I have only $12,000 more to pay for my house renovations, and then they will have to seal it up, unfinished!

My diversions and fears were impacting business, but we were also beginning to hear that hospitals were not spending money at this time, since they didn't know what was going to happen to the reimbursement system. The federal government was brewing lots of reimbursement changes that could very negatively affect hospitals' income base. Hospitals were scared and holding on.

For some time, David continued to feel that more calls would solve the problem. To be careful, however, he made the decision to cut all salaries by 20 percent, including his and mine. We met with the staff, presented our bills and income, and they agreed to go along with the cut. Within a few days the results of all my calls paid off—$36,500 came in for software,

WHIM OF IRON

and we could all breath again. The roller coaster was at least still rolling.

AMI, a hospital chain like HCA, showed an interest in our software. In my talks with them, I had extolled the virtues of management being able to look at physician patterns *across hospitals and disciplines*, and they were interested. After a long Miami meeting, they decided to let each hospital buy one at a time, instead of mandating one system that could provide overall management support.

I wondered if they didn't really want to know how they were doing in terms of quality. If they didn't, they weren't alone. Not one of the chain hospitals I met with saw the advantage of having standardization, and overall accountability by health care workers (doctors, nurses, technicians, etc.), versus fragmentation and lack of information. One administrator said he didn't know what he would do with the information, if he had it. Discipline his doctors? Require continuing education classes? No way!

Towards the end of May, I gave a presentation to the State Chapter of NAMSS. My subject was, "Enhancing your professional status in the hospital community." My presentation took some standard patient data (age, sex, type of illness, type of surgical procedure, etc.) and showed them how to present it as information to the administrator, medical staff, public relations, marketing, physician recruitment, etc.

The medical staff credentialing people loved the show, but, as they told me, they couldn't sell *information* to their management people even for free. Everyone was afraid to *manage* the medical staff. They didn't see we were trying to help the medical staff avoid legal suits. We were trying to reduce errors, so patients didn't have to suffer more than they do. We were trying to reduce costs.

Ah, but there was the rub. As one small-hospital administrator told me, "If a physician screws up and leaves a cotton swab inside a patient, the resulting surgery to remove the swab is billed to insurance. If we stop screwing up, we stop billing. No way." He was right, but that didn't make it right.

Sometimes there are those moments in life when something unusual happens and there is little you can do but keep a straight face and hope everyone else will, too.

As I was presenting to North Carolina NAMSS in Wrightsville Beach last week, I farted. In front of 50 women all looking at me, I FARTED. It happens more frequently these days. And I can't hold them in. I don't even know they're coming. I just looked at everyone in the room and went right on teaching. We were all women, and they knew I couldn't help it. Probably all the garlic I've been eating to ward off colds!

By the end of May, four sales had come in, but they were old ones I had been working, not new ones. I kept telling David something was happening, and he kept telling me to make more calls. I tried, but in my gut, I didn't feel good. Finally in June, when only one sale came in, David came and got me, and we went off for a real soul-searching talk.

When David had first joined CBR and put together a business plan, he said that some day we might want to drop the price so low that it wouldn't be an issue to an administrator. Now, as we walked through the woods discussing sales, I remembered his words.

"Well, David," I finally said, "maybe it's time to lower the price."

David smiled, stopped walking and said, "Maybe you're right. How about $2,900 instead of $12,000?"

I had been thinking about $5,000, but I could see his point. At $2,900, *any* hospital could buy without a big deal being made over it. In the long run, we were much more interested in the $1,500 the hospitals paid us *every year afterward,* for our continuing support and updating of the software they licensed from us.

The next day, David swung into action. He had thousands of announcements printed and mailed out over the next few weeks. He had me start calling every hospital that was on the edge and give them the news. He had me call the Texas Hospital Association and listen as they swore at me (they only got a percent of the sales price, and they weren't happy we were lowering it). He also had me call every hospital I ever talked to who *hadn't* bought.

The response to all this activity was interesting. Our competitors called, assuming we were about to go out of business, and asked if we were for sale. My response was standard. "No, hospitals are having a tough time with reimbursement right now. We developed the software under a grant, so we don't need to make any money back, and we're not greedy. That's why we dropped the price."

They didn't believe us, and they tried to use it against us, but to no avail. We were on a roll getting ready for a big rush of sales. Brenda and Randy had made the installation process seamless and bug-less. Training was down to a science. David had a big smile on his face, and so did I.

There was an energy being created by the medical staff coordinators who were so appreciative of the price drop. Now they could make the decision and buy. We all felt good about what we were doing, and everyone was working hard and well, as a good team should. David had done a terrific job in getting us ready. All we needed was sales.

No bleeding since February, and all I'm doing is taking Will's herbs. Had complete GYN checkup and all good. Weight 189. Worked 8 hours on Sat and got so much done—48 letters, and filled out an application for Small Business Person of the Year for Durham Chamber of Commerce (I told David that at 189 pounds, I couldn't be small business person of the year…he just laughed).

I developed an idea for a newsletter for health care called HEALTHprobe and a new system of health care that I felt certain could work. David was always so good at letting me know with some very polite words that the ideas wouldn't work. He knew I always wanted to improve the world, and he also knew that most people wanted the world to stay just as it was.

Right now, I fear for my house, which is at least getting fixed, and for my business, which needs cash, and my body, which needs love and tenderness from me. I am going to weather all this. God never gives us more than we can handle.

My house, if it could speak, may have wanted to question the final statement. It had been jacked up and down three times, walls ripped off, pipes torn in half, the roof redone, and they were working on finishing the kitchen. I never knew where I'd find my cot each night, but wherever it was, it would be neat and folded and ready for me.

The first week in July, things began to happen. Six orders came in, with checks, and all our preparation began to pay off. While Brenda, Randy, Elisa and Kathy took care of installing and training, I continued with sales...we needed cash, and we needed it fast. In my anxiousness, I continually failed to qualify prospects, primarily because I was *desperate* to make a sale.

Amherst Associates, a large hospital consulting firm, called and wanted to see what we had. I was thrilled, because I knew of their organization and respected what they did. We paid for the trip, but we could have saved our money. They were really just looking for ideas; I went home very disappointed and a little bit more tired.

A physician group contacted us regarding using our credentialing software for their large practice. When I went to meet with them, I was most impressed with the level of statistical knowledge the staff had. It was very nice to have the software used seriously and extensively. While we thought this was a new market, it turned out few had the same desire to know how they were doing.

Ruth, in Florida, was getting some interest, so I flew down to Miami to help her out. She had a nice presence, but didn't know how to close. I tried to teach her, but I left feeling like she had other things on her mind.

While at the office, the wheels were oiled for all the new sales from the reduced price. At home I was still moving around room to room as my house got renovated.

Started practicing my speech for 16 hospitals in Florida. Randy helped me; then we had lunch, and he helped me empty out my kitchen and bedroom—the back wall should come down this week! Steve came and moved my stuff out of my bedroom and kitchen so they can finish the wall.

WHIM OF IRON

David and I were still nervous. Six sales wouldn't do it. We needed hundreds. We kept our fingers crossed, and I kept picking up the phone.

Trip to North Carolina Hospital Association wonderful. Met with seven people who all agreed we can do something. I told them my vision of a Health Meeting Center. Ed excited. We'll see. Went to NJVP/NJHA on Thursday and again had great reception to our products. Down to $21,000 cash. I'm trying.

It had occurred to me that a Health Meeting Center would be good for all the hospitals in the State. Under this Center, hospitals could have help understanding the new information computers were giving them, learn what questions to ask in quality and risk management, and share knowledge among administrators. I don't remember why the idea never got very far, but it was one more of my "save the world" visions that led nowhere.

David helped me sort out priorities as we go into $2,900 environment, which is very different for us. On the phone all day—still not easy to sell $2,900 package. Hope it gets better.

By the end of July, the dam had broken. A total of 31 new sales came in, with checks, and you couldn't get the smiles off anyone's face. We knew we had to keep it up, but confidence just oozed from everyone. The phones were ringing off the wall!

At this point, I worked on starting a consulting division that would go out and help hospitals understand what their data was saying and what actions they could take to improve their quality. I hoped it would be well accepted. Wishful thinking on my part. Toward the end of July, I went off on a tour of Texas. I stopped in Abilene to speak at the Northwest Texas Hospital Association's annual meeting. My subject was "Managing Quality." I got lots of compliments on my speech, but no interest in doing it.

Lots happening. 68 orders were placed within six weeks. Lots of changes, and many of them are uncomfortable for everyone.

By mid-August it was clear we would make a lot of sales, so I decided to go off for a short vacation in Florida. Jay had time on his hands so he decided to join me, and we had a great time. All my family liked Jay a lot and as always, we had a good time together. Since there was no intimacy between us, we both felt free to do what we wanted when we wanted, and we didn't always have to be together. On our way back to Durham, my stomach started to tighten up. I think I knew that big changes were ahead for CBR and me.

David was in more often now because we all needed help dealing with a new structure in the business. We didn't need any more development. We needed Randy to help with training, installations, and most particularly, management.

I wasn't around much, and David needed someone to step in and manage the day-to-day operations. Brenda was starting to sell, which was a big help, but Elisa was doing as much as she could, and

Kathy was not a management person any more than I was. It was a struggle. Randy didn't like to manage and just couldn't get interested in the subject. David was insisting that Randy be part of the team, and to my sadness, I could see that Randy was thinking about whether he wanted to work in this new environment. He had lots of other options.

In the first week of September, I passed my scuba test. I was excited to go off to Florida for my open water dive. It was a great accomplishment for me, and David had done a good job. There was a lot to be happy about.

David Beyer continues to blow my mind. Not only has his four-year strategy worked (we have $240,000 in the bank), but he is also helping me see personally that I am a very bright, pretty, energetic, articulate visionary (I LOVE the man!). I have every right to let the world see me whole (without extra weight).

House going slowly, but well. Waiting for electrical inspection. Talked to Lisa. I'm going up there the 16th and then going to Maine, fishing with Del. Life is good. David is helping me do less at CBR—he knows I'm tired so he's encouraging me to step back from the management and let the others create a team and run it themselves with David as overseer.

$240,000, over ¼ million, in less than three months. Oh, if we can keep the momentum up!

Cleo B. Robertson

Good dreams about me really flying on my own. Very tired. To bed. Change is <u>very</u> stressful. Head hurts.

There is no free lunch. Money was pouring in, but there was lots of chaos. Just handling all the travel arrangements for all these new coordinators to fly in to Durham for training took a lot of time. Elisa did a fantastic job, but it was overwhelming sometimes. In addition, we were still offering to move data on physicians from existing systems into CBR systems, and that was taking a lot of Randy and Kathy's time. Brenda was working feverishly on sales, follow up, training and just about anything else that came across her desk. In short, we were all pulling our own weight.

David and I setting scene for me to get out of CBR software division and into CBR consulting.

David seemed to think the consulting was a go, but actually, I think he just wanted me out of everyone's hair. I was the president, the entrepreneur, and I was just too disruptive. I tried to stay focused, but it wasn't in me. Seldom is with entrepreneurs, I've learned. That's why I could start the business and why, eventually, I would have to leave it.

Jane says I need a month off to rest and a month to travel. Sounds divine, but David less than enthusiastic at this moment.

A hospital corporation with 34 hospitals endorsed us. Looks good. 31 sales in for September. Randy working hard on software design competition being held in Durham soon. Lisa started new job at Bank of Boston, and she's doing very well. I sent her two bouquets of flowers and everyone knew she had arrived!

Just completed an incredible trip. Flew in to Ft. Meyers, rented Buick Park Avenue and drove through Homestead (week after Hurricane Andrew). Cried for an hour as I passed mutilated buildings. At one point I drove past a huge condo, and the whole side was ripped off—on every floor I could see people's clothes hanging in their closets that didn't have doors on them. I could even see unmade beds and clothes lying over chairs!

Went to motel in Tavernier, where I was going to stay, but the room was too small and right next to the highway, so drove south 2.5 miles, over bridge, and there was the Sandbar Restaurant and Hotel. They gave me a 6th floor suite with two bedrooms and a balcony for $75/night. Sea breeze rushing through. God wanted me to have a good rest.

Went scuba diving in 3-5' swells and 20-knot winds. Not enough weights, which was difficult (I am very buoyant) and a diving buddy who couldn't have cared less about me. Did very well anyway. I learned I was technically competent. Saw Moray eel, lobster, etc. No other boats went out for the day. I learned I was on what is called a "cattle boat," which sends you in, prepared or not.

The trip did me good, even though the water was rough. I met a lot of fun people and partied for four days, before coming home to dig in again.

When I got home, Randy greeted me with good news—he had come in second place for the 1992 Developer's Conference, and I was as proud of him as I could be. The competition had been tough. Programmers came from all over the U.S. to compete in this very prestigious event. They all got to set up their own computers in a room full of other computers, and without any advance notice, they were given an assignment to build an application. Randy's task was to build a database and reporting program for cataloging primates at the Duke University Primate Center. Everyone was given a specific amount of time, and then left to work their magic. Randy's application was excellent, and the prize was well deserved.

One delightful story comes to mind involving Brenda. David and I had discussed with her how difficult it was to install and support software with larger hospitals. Brenda was not a technical person, so as we talked about mainframe interfaces and downloading data, she heartily agreed we didn't need to do work with those types. It was particularly not worth doing at $2,900. One day, I overheard Brenda on the phone, speaking to someone in her most southern drawl:

"Well, sure CBR's software can download data, but you know, HealthCare really is a larger company and better suited to taking care of you than we are. Would you like their number?"

WHIM OF IRON

When I asked her about the call, she said with a straight face, "They had 1,000 beds and I *know* they'll need an interface to something, so I sent them elsewhere." It turned out to be a good move. Since CBR was a service and software business, it was much better to be able to sell to hospitals where we could talk to the people we were servicing, instead of going through data processing and spending a day to solve one problem. David and I began to concentrate on smaller hospitals (under 250 beds), and even discouraged larger hospitals from buying CBR.

People ask what I'll do when the house is done. How about nothing?

The house was really getting near to completion. Furniture was ordered, new appliances in, and I now had 1,400 square feet to roam in, versus the original 900, with an open view to a huge magnolia tree directly in back of the new addition.

Can one have too much fun? As tired as I am, seeing what I envisioned coming true is extraordinary!

I'm sitting on my couch looking out at a windy, clear day. Clouds rushing across the sky. No birds to the feeder I put up yet. They're mad at me for ignoring them this year. The yard is looking magical. Tony from the Garden Shed is turning a small piece of land into a landscaping wonder. There's even a pond! I am happy. I get scared I'm so happy. Randy scares me because he might move on. Just finished organizing all my slides—have to put show together before next Monday. My home will keep me warm and happy for the rest of my life. The sun is up—time to go swim at the spa.

The house was tangible proof of I had accomplished, both in redesigning it, and by the fact I could afford to do it. Each day I awoke, I was thankful that God had been so good to me. When I went to the office, however, it was another story.

The pressure was on Randy and me to stop being entrepreneurs and start being managers. CBR needed managers to get the software bug-free and running smoothly. I had admitted freely that I didn't *want* to manage, and David had therefore put me into the sales arena, because that was what CBR needed at that time.

David tried to get Randy to understand that, in order for CBR to succeed, we had to concentrate on managing the software, and the sales, and installations. Randy didn't want to handle support calls unless they were very technical. That left only Elisa and Kathy to handle all the others, but with the amount of bugs in the programs, because Randy and I kept changing them, they couldn't do it all—they needed him to help.

Randy's focus was programming. That's what he knew best, and that's what he liked to do. It gave him pleasure to please people by having the software do everything they wanted it to do. We just simply could not afford to have him doing that *at this time*. Support was killing us with so many orders coming in

WHIM OF IRON

at a time. It was one of those things that happens to all businesses when you have to do what is needed, not what you want, in order for it to survive. I could see a collision course ahead, but didn't know what to do about it. Randy was a top-notch programmer, who just was not willing to do phone support, testing, etc. The thought struck fear into my heart.

David said to me one day, "We don't need a programmer at this time. We need phone support, testing and documentation. We need the programs themselves to be documented. What would happen if something, God forbid, happened to Randy? How would we fix bugs then?"

I had no answer. David felt we needed to take Randy to lunch and get him to understand what CBR needed from him now. I wasn't sure how Randy would react, but I agreed we had to try.

We took him to a very good restaurant, ordered a great lunch and then started to talk. David very directly told Randy that CBR needed management from him now, not programming. Randy disagreed, of course, and David, in exasperation, said, "You are a replaceable employee, you know." The look on Randy's face told me everything he was thinking. Replaceable employee? Hadn't he worked long hours, showed his faithfulness and commitment and created one hell of a set of programs? I cringed inside as I saw how angry he was.

David tried to explain that we are all replaceable. That if what a company needs, for instance, is software support, then someone has to do it, regardless of whether it's what they want to do or not. All David was asking Randy to do was what CBR needed him to do, now. We left the restaurant with nothing resolved. Randy was angry. David was upset. I was scared of the outcome.

With great effort, I pushed the luncheon out of my mind and prayed that everything would be all right. My house renovation was finally finished and I reveled in the joy of living in my "new" home—a place where I could find much needed rest and recuperation after my long trips. To help me celebrate, Lisa and Andy were flying in, as was my niece, Kathy, whom I adored. I had decided to have a party to honor all those who made the house happen—I invited 37 people including the plumbers and carpenters, stucco experts (one was 70, the other 65, and they had been doing it for 50 years!) and everyone else who helped. A friend put out a wonderful spread. I gave out 14 funny T-shirts, each one with the person's name on the front, and something funny about his or her role. Great fun was had by all, and everyone was glad to see the house and yard done. It had been a long eleven months.

While I had spent a lot of time on my house, I had never let my guard down about sales. AMI was a big hospital corporation, and I was intent on getting them on board as we had HBO and HCA. Between meeting with their people and training those that did buy, we slowly started to win over their corporate team. I had begun training again simply because we needed more hands. Training others was definitely something

Randy would not do, even though I thought he would have been very good at it.

The end of the year was coming, and it was bonus time again.

I ordered bonus checks and got them yesterday. What a proud feeling. I gave Randy a $5000 raise (to $45,000) plus a $9000 bonus. Brenda $8000 bonus, Kathy $6000 and Elisa, $5000. I don't know what I can take yet, but David is taking nothing. We had raised his salary to $42,000 and he said he felt that was enough. I didn't, but he seemed to be okay, so I let it be.

As was his custom, David wanted to review the year and go over what worked, what didn't work, and what we needed to do to ensure success in the coming year.

David and I took everyone in the office to Farrington Inn for a review of the year. It was great. David did the show well. We reviewed our goals: be the best, give the best, and lead in state-of-the-art software, installation and support.

It was a good overview, and David, as always, taught us a lot about team playing.

All this was happening as the holidays closed in on us. Lisa was happy with her new home, Gary was pursuing a Ph.D., and Randy and I were dealing with a lot of changes. It was clear Randy didn't like the new restrictions on his inventiveness.

On December 22nd, David and I asked Randy to meet with us in my office. David told him that he was valuable, that we did not want to lose him, that we would increase his salary to $80,000 (Randy said that was the going rate in the Research Triangle Park for someone with his responsibilities, and we agreed), and we would send him for management training, so he could be groomed to be vice president.

After David had presented all this to Randy, Randy very calmly handed me a letter in an envelope. My stomach lurched as I outwardly, very calmly, opened it and read what he had to say.

Randy quit CBR today. He wants more freedom to invent, not less. He also wants to create, and the route we are going will not allow that for a long time.

My fears have come true. Amidst my tears, I wish him well. It is best for CBR—it's just the transitions that are hell. David is very upset, feels responsible, and knows it is best for CBR. We will miss bright Randy.

Randy talked a little about having others interested in his work. We said very little and finally he stood up. We all shook hands and wished him the best. It was a sad moment for me to watch my son as he walked out the door of CBR for the last time. David held me a brief moment as I cried, but we soon sat down to talk about the realities of what Randy's resignation really meant to us. We were both quite shaken.

I spent Christmas in Boston with Lisa, Andy, and his family, but Randy didn't come up. I felt sad, but I knew this was a difficult time for him, too.

After he gave us his resignation, Randy thought that was it. David, however, was devastated with what had happened. He felt he was responsible, and that he had failed. It was his job to create a team, and he had not handled one of the team members correctly, and therefore Randy had quit. David had failed. As we all soon learned, no one was ever harder on himself than David.

He took me on a long walk along the Eno River and told me how unhappy he was. It was true that Randy had not been the team player we needed *at that time*. He wanted to program. We wanted him to spend his time on support. Our program was overdeveloped as it was, as David had pointed out to me within the first month I knew him. We had programmed in tasks that no one had even thought of doing, He reasoned that 90 percent of our clients used 10 percent of any one of our programs as it was. To build in hundreds of other capabilities for the 10 percent that might use them, didn't make sense. Every programmatic change required documentation, testing, beta testing, and then release through a new version. David wanted all this to stop for a while so we could bring in sales to ensure our financial future and viability as a business. You can have the best product in the world, but if you don't have any money, you will fail. Randy was right in wanting the very best for our clients. He just didn't see that we couldn't afford to do it *at this time*. The cost of testing was taking valuable time away from servicing our new clients.

By the end of the walk, David had formulated a plan. He would offer Randy $100,000 for six months time to train a new person we'd hire. The challenge David had designed for the new person was that he or she clean up the software, document the code, and get rid of all bugs. Randy's training of a new person would be invaluable, and his significant input regarding documentation would be invaluable, too, in this process. We would continue to look for a new programmer.

New Year's was quite subdued. 1992 had been an emotional roller coaster for me. Our annual report, which came out in February of 1993, was a masterpiece of "telling it like it is." Even as I reread it for this book, I was impressed with the straightforward way David told of our year and of each of us. David wrote it, with contributions from staff. But as I reread it, I could hear his voice in my ear.

Writing our Annual Report became just one more end-of-year task, and a great tool in keeping us focused. What did you say you were going to do? What did you do? Who did what? What was the overall summary of what you did? What it did for the staff was to make them feel appreciated. What it did for David and me was to help us measure what we had really accomplished. What it did for the team was to keep things moving towards our defined goal.

Because of the dramatic drop in price, we had brought in 116 sales and a total of $745,181 in income for the year. Our 261 clients were giving us good feedback. All in all, we managed to be viewed as a service organization instead of just a software company, and that was our most important goal for the year. Pride was on all our faces.

Randy was not around for the holidays. I spent New Year's Eve alone in my new house. I felt mad, glad, sad and scared all at once. Life, I believe, is lived in "eras," and one of the most important eras of my life had just ended…working with my son. But, as an older woman told me once, all things pass, the bad *and* the good!

1993 — The Handwriting on the Wall

The first week of the new year, Randy, David and I ironed out an agreement that Randy seemed happy with. He told us he didn't want to work for us anymore (I could hear that in his head, he had already moved on).

He did, however, agree to help us transition to a new person. We agreed to pay him $45 an hour for three days a week in January, and then two days a week to the end of May, plus a $15,000 bonus in six months. David wanted Randy to be happy with his transitional period so he would train our new person and feel good about leaving. He seemed excited to be moving on, and several companies were interested in him. To his credit, he was looking around, taking his time, and figuring out what would be best for his future.

Over the month of January, Randy was very cooperative, documenting programming code and helping out all he could. We all still felt very attached to him. It was hard to see him slowly disengage himself from the day-to-day work, yet we all knew that was what he needed to do.

It dawned on me that I, too, was disengaging myself from the business. Ever since the drop in price back in July, Brenda had been handling all sales at the new price. I continued the HBO and Texas Hospital Association sales efforts, but I began to see slowly that Brenda could take over my job without a problem. I had become a replaceable employee myself.

Brenda was a unique bird. With a lot of training from David, this southern belle had turned into a tough sales cookie, something I could never be. The other advantage we had in Brenda was that she had worked in the Veterans Administration (VA) Hospital system for many years, so she was well connected. It was her decision to go after all the VA hospitals (she got all of them to buy CBR, eventually), and she did a remarkable job.

Between enjoying my house and travel, I hardly noticed that everyone was giving all sales leads to Brenda. I was being left out of the loop, more and more. When it started to dawn on me, I felt hurt. *And* I knew it was essential. I had outlived my usefulness to CBR. I needed to move on. But where? All my life, I had justified my right to live by doing good things for others and working hard. *My work was my worth.* Now, as I thought about life without CBR, my baby, all I saw was a blank. A very lonely blank.

WHIM OF IRON

When I wasn't on the road, I was interviewing to fill Randy's position. We felt our greatest need was for technical support, and finding such a person was not an easy task. Young people usually want to be in larger organizations, so they have more exposure to people. CBR's four women didn't appear as much of a challenge.

David had been thinking about farming the programming out to a company in California that had written applications for American Express and Visa. There would be no payroll expenses incurred, and the company had a team, so they could get a lot more done at one time. But it would be very costly. We finally decided to try to hire two people—a technical support person to deal with clients on the phone when their systems wouldn't work, and a programmer to document and clean up all the code. David wanted it bug-free. Period.

I was working on transferring all the manuals and documentation into a word processor that was geared towards publishing. The hours flew by when I did this kind of work, and I was most thankful. It was a strange feeling to see everyone busy, making decisions, answering phones, and no one asking me any questions.

To keep myself stable, I started to invent a new software product in my mind. I wanted to develop an application that would integrate Emergency Room treatment with any other treatment given to a patient at any time. It had always seemed to me that the ER had more computers than anywhere, so it should have lots of information on patients that could be shared with the in-house system.

It turned out not to be true. Most of the computers were used for billing and were not communicating with the in-house system at all. The reality was that a patient could show up at the ER, get treatment, have a problem, get admitted to the hospital *and a full accounting of all that had happened to the patient so far would <u>not</u> be available online*! My goal was to have a quality management report on any patient at any time, regardless of what services were being used in the hospital.

While David understood that I was bored and had no challenge, he also did not want a new product confusing the issue at the moment. Even though it might have been a good idea, neither of us wanted to hire more people. Until David's financial investment goals for CBR and me were met, he didn't want to divert energy or focus from straight sales. I understood. I just didn't know what to do with my time.

February 2nd I was opening the mail, and amongst all the bills was a resume that got my attention. It was from a woman who worked on a support desk for a large corporation and supported 500 employees. Now, that was the kind of person we wanted. I called her place of business up north, learned she was moving to Raleigh, and sent a registered letter inviting her for an interview. She came in at 4 p.m. on Monday, we talked, and I offered her the position by 5. She called that evening and accepted, and we haven't been sorry since. Sharon worked well with Randy and within no time, was handling support like she'd been with us for years. That took care of the technical support person.

Sleeplessness was stalking me again, something I battled with off and on. My mind was restless and had no focus. I decided to give a humdinger of a dinner party, which was prepared by George, a great chef, who was a friend of mine. A local art gallery brought in art and put it around the house, and each couple paid $100 for a smashing dinner. George and his crew, each in a tux, served us champagne, scallops and shrimp, poached salmon and rack of lamb! Wow! The eight guests had a wonderful evening, but no art sold. The point, however, had been to show off my house and have a lovely evening. From that point of view, it was a great success!

Sharon, our new technical support person, began work on February 15th, and it was my responsibility to teach her what CBR was all about. She proved to be a very quick learner, and within a very short time, was taking phone calls and solving problems. Everyone sighed with relief.

By the end of February, the office was in organized turmoil. Seventeen sales had come in, Sharon was handling more and more each day, and Elisa and Kathy and Brenda were doing all they could to keep up with installations, training, downloads and support. The atmosphere was one of relief,. We had a team and David had come up with a brilliant strategy to keep that team in tact. He asked Brenda, Kathy and Sharon to go out and research how much they would be making in salary five years from now, assuming they were at the top of their field.

A week later, David called a meeting and asked them what they had learned. He got from $35,000 to $42,000 as answers. He immediately told all three that from that day forward they would make $50,000 each. He explained that he would never raise their salaries, but that this way his payroll costs were fixed. They would, of course, still receive bonuses based on performance.

David's goal was to put golden handcuffs on each of them. We couldn't afford spending our time looking for new people. We had a team. We would all benefit, if we kept it together. Ten years later, it still was.

We got a call about this time from HBO, saying that they were ready to let clients buy directly from us. That was terrific, because it would shorten the sales cycle. David had been pushing for that from the very beginning, but it took all this time for HBO to realize it was far more efficient with us selling directly.

Back at the office, Randy was training people and doing quite well. Mid-March, I interviewed and hired a man named Andy, for our programming position. Andy had done a lot of programming, seemed easy to work with, and we needed to get someone moving on the software. I got the monthly newsletter out to our clients and started to teach Andy about CBR and our business.

WHIM OF IRON

I felt left out and pushed out of the happenings of the office. I could see, however, that the office was doing better without me. It was a hard pill to swallow.

One evening I got a phone call that really put me over the top. My friend Jay had committed suicide. For the next two weeks I was totally out of the office, and stricken with immense grief.

Back in February I had called Anna, the Swedish mother of my neighbor, Sara, and asked if I could go visit her in Sweden. She had invited me the first time we met, but until it was clear I was out of CBR, I hadn't given it a serious thought. I was also so upset about Jay's death, I felt getting away would be good for me.

I had never traveled much outside the U.S. and wasn't sure what it would be like, being in a country where I couldn't speak the language. Nevertheless, we decided I should go in June for three weeks. It was a very exciting prospect and the planning helped take my mind off all the changes in my life.

The office was buzzing along very well, which I viewed with mixed feelings. We had decided to give Brenda signatory power, so if a check had to be signed while I was in Sweden, she could do it. I knew, however, that the reason was far more extensive than that. David was grooming Brenda to run CBR, money and all. His instincts about people were never wrong, so I had no doubt she would be great.

I left for Sweden early in June, learning somewhere over Chicago, from my seat partner, that Anna, the woman I was going to visit, was a famous author in her country! That surprised and delighted me, and from the very first, Anna and I got along like a house-on-fire! At the end of the first week she planned a luncheon with eight of the top women in arts, music and government in Sweden—eight women who could not stop talking and having a great time.

From that luncheon, I managed to string out four months of travel and fun. One of the women had a mother in Spain, whom I went to visit. Then I went to the Greek Islands for a while to get away from the summer rains in Sweden. When I returned, Anna let me use her guest apartment in the southern part of Stockholm. I had a most wonderful time with these sweet, good people, all of whom are educated and speak English better than most Americans.

I had been formulating a book manuscript that really lit my imagination. I named it <u>Death in Disguise.</u> I started laying out the murder mystery based on true stories I had heard in hospitals, without ever identifying a hospital. While I was in Sweden over the end of the summer, I started writing. Brenda shipped my portable computer over immediately. My mind needed something to do, and writing became my focus.

By the time I returned to Durham at the end of September, I had two-thirds of the manuscript done and I was feeling a lot better. My house was perfect, the gardens lovely, and CBR was doing very well.

WHIM OF IRON

On October 1st, I went to meet David for lunch. He took time to update me and to listen to my exciting stories. At some point, he very gently suggested that I should consider retiring from CBR. The team was in place and working well, we were in good financial condition, and the years ahead were ones of cleaning and solidifying what Randy and I had worked so hard to create. The "team" had added 67 units in 1993 for a total of 328 clients across the United States.

I knew the day was coming when I would really have to leave CBR. Hearing David say it out loud, however, made it real. What I knew was that CBR was running better without me. It didn't need a mama anymore. In many ways, I even felt a little ready for life without CBR.

When we were done with our review, David drove me back to the office. I immediately went into my office and packed up all my personal belongings and went home, before the tears came.

I was glad I was finally out of the way, and I was sad I had left my passion. My biggest consolation was that CBR was growing up and doing just fine. It's a sad contradiction in life that the very babies we love and help grow, are the ones that have to turn and leave us in order for them to mature. As I looked back over the years, I just marveled that we made it at all!

What started out as a whim, grew to be as strong as iron. My greatest feat was recognizing that I didn't know enough and having David join us. My next greatest feat was in doing "everything he told me to do, whether my gut felt good about it or not."

CBR has a whim of iron of its own now, and it's doing quite well. In 2002 a survey rated CBR as the leading quality management software company in the United States. Not bad, eh?

Epilogue

There's a saying that if life gives you lemons, make lemonade. That's exactly what I did with CBR. It took a few years, a lot of work and great inventiveness, but we achieved a level of success. But it was not until David Beyer joined us and we started following his simple rules, that we became a successful company.

The messages David brought to me, and to CBR, were ones that would help *any* business succeed. The messages are simple, hard to follow, and seldom do entrepreneurs listen to them. I present them for those who would like a crash course. Heed their message, and you have a good chance of winning, too.

Rules for a successful business:

- Start with a Business Plan, and keep checking it to stay focused.
- Bring in more money than you spend.

- More money seldom saves a company. Instead of bringing in more money, reduce expenses.
- No debt allowed. Pay off what you owe; don't incur any more.
- Cash is king.
- Focus. Ask yourself again and again, "Is this what I said I'd do in the Business Plan?"
- Identify who is a buyer (Who is the person who can write a check or cause a check to be written?), before setting up an appointment.
- People don't buy products, they buy solutions.
- Don't focus on selling product; focus instead on what they need to know to say Yes. The only thing holding up a sale may be that someone needs a reference to call.
- Keep your answers simple. Most buyers don't want too much information. They just want to know they are doing the right thing in buying *your* solutions.
- People don't want to know what reports they are going to get or how fast the machines will go. They want to know how you will solve their problem.
- If buyers perceive a need, they will buy.
- Listen for when a client has bought, and then stop selling. Clients have bought when they ask a question like, "So if I get your software, what hardware do I need?"
- Keeping a team together takes focus and commitment.

- Identify individual talents and then build on them through education and training.
- Cross train, cross train, cross train.
- Be a team, think as a team, and honor everyone on the team.

As David said to me when we first started working together, running a business is really about sticking to Marketing 101. From my experience, I have applied all the rules to my personal life, too, and find they work there just as well. Success in anything takes discipline and a few simple rules.

I am now 65 years old. I've been retired and living well in my hometown in Florida for ten years. I had come for a visit, and David decided to join me. While I was busy swimming, he was busy finding me the perfect house, which he bought for me in one day. On August 1, 1994, I became the proud owner of a wonderful house on the water. David had finally managed to get me "out of Durham," so to speak. CBR was in good hands, and I knew they didn't need my hands anymore.

I still miss the passion I had for CBR. I miss the passion of inventing and designing. I miss the passion of making people happy.

I do not, however, miss the day-to-day work, and as CBR enters its 24th year, I am glad that the company is in good hands, but not *my* hands. They are still following the simple rules that keep them successful. They now have over 600 clients all over the United States, and two internationally. David is still overseeing all the operations, while Brenda is now the Chief Operating Officer.

In November of 1999, I entered a kayak race that I thought was three miles long. It turned out to be six, and as I dug in with my paddle, I kept saying to myself, "Why did I enter this race? I could be home, sitting in my hot tub or swimming. Why did I have to compete? I'm 61, it's time to rest, not race!"

In the end, I kayaked the whole six miles, and as I looked from the beach where we ended the race, out at the long route we had just taken, I wondered again how I had kept on going, kept putting my paddle in the water, and pulling. I had ended in the penultimate position, second from last. But I did it. I finished.

That's how I feel about CBR Associates, Inc. There were many times I wondered how I kept paying bills, kept living with insecurity, kept selling. One day the answer came to me. I had done it just like I did the kayaking—the water's there, the paddle's in your hand, just a few more strokes…ah, the sweetness of success!

About the Author

Cleo Robertson tells how she succeeded in starting a software business even though she had no degrees, no credentials, no money and no marketing or sales experience. Five years as a secretary at a hospital consulting firm in Princeton, New Jersey was all the education she needed. After producing fifteen long-range plans for hospitals, she knew how they worked. When unemployment, poverty and debt, stranded her in a black neighborhood in Princeton in 1980, she turned her misfortune into a fortune. This is the story of how she did it.

Printed in the United States
202046BV00001B/1-51/A